THE HEALER'S CODE

A PRACTICAL GUIDE TO IDENTIFYING INNER BLOCKS AND
FULLY LIVING YOUR CALLING

JOY KAHN

MATT KAHN

DIVINE TIMING BOOKS

CONTENTS

WHY THE HEALER'S CODE MATTERS NOW

We are living in a time of accelerated awakening.

Conversations about consciousness, trauma healing, nervous system regulation, embodiment, intuitive intelligence, and energetic mastery have moved from the fringe into the mainstream. More people than ever are doing the inner work. They are unpacking conditioning, questioning inherited belief systems, and stepping into greater self-awareness.

As that shift unfolds, a new generation of healers, coaches, and conscious leaders are stepping forward to hold space for an emerging new world. If you are reading this book, you are one of them.

You may not have always called yourself a healer. Perhaps you desired being seen and valued for your love of service, passion, and growth but have assumed you needed to reach some elusive level of perfection before having the right to support others. But at some point, your journey stops being about fixing yourself and becomes centered around helping others navigate a more evolved way of being.

This is the beginning of an exciting chapter in your journey and where a new challenge appears.

Because once you begin serving others, you will quickly sense how generally-framed growth principles and generic modalities are no longer enough. You need a reliable way to access precision – for yourself as well as others.

Most modern healing and coaching models are built on a series of static principles: Reframe your thoughts. Heal childhood wounds. Shift your beliefs. Align your habits. Build better strategies.

All of these are valuable. But they are not specific. They assume that transformation follows the same sequence for everyone. Yet if you have worked with enough clients — or if you have observed your own growth closely — you know that this isn't true. Some people thrive when given structure. Others shut down under it. Some heal through emotional processing. Others through action. Some lead from vision. Others from stability.

Some expand through risk. Others through refinement.

The deeper you go into healing work, the more obvious it becomes:

There is no 'one-size-fits-all' path to purpose. And yet, most systems still operate as if there is. This is where the Healer's Code becomes essential.

The Healer's Code is not another modality.

It is not a belief system.

It is not a personality label.

It is a structural framework derived from the Book of Life — a system that maps human development through a precise, mathematical architecture tied to your birth.

At its core, this system recognizes four domains of wisdom that every human being develops in a unique sequence and intensity:

Emotional wisdom — how you relate, connect, and regulate.

Mental wisdom — how you think, process, and perceive.

Physical wisdom — how you build, sustain, and manifest in tangible form.

Spiritual wisdom — how you integrate awareness and higher perspective.

Each of these domains is symbolized within a 52-card system that functions as a living map of human consciousness.

When you calculate your chart, five core archetypal cards emerge. These five form your Healer's Code.

Those five cards reveal:

- Your primary operating frequency and growth edge
- The type of responsibility you are designed to carry
- The environments that amplify you
- The patterns that will repeat until integrated
- The medicine you naturally embody for others

This is not abstract philosophy.

It is pattern recognition in its most precise expression.

If you have ever wondered:

Why do certain themes keep repeating in my life?

Why do I feel called to serve in a particular way?

Why do I excel in some roles but feel drained in others?

Why does my leadership style look different from my peers?

The Healer's Code answers those questions with clarity.

It reframes your life not as a series of problems to fix, but as a sequence of evolutionary milestones aligned with your design.

One of the most practical shifts this framewok offers is this:

Purpose dissolves the illusion of "problem."

Many high-level healers and leaders unconsciously carry the belief that if they could just resolve the final layer of trauma, insecurity, or self-doubt, they would finally feel ready. But readiness does not exist in the absence of challenge. It occurs through the integration of it.

When you understand your Healer's Code, you begin to see that your challenges are not inherited defects. They are pressure points designed to refine specific aspects of your capacity. In essence, you stop trying to eliminate them because you begin learning how to leverage them. This is where everything can be seen as a part of your purpose, instead of an enemy to defeat or a problem you must solve.

The Four Kingdoms of Wisdom

The historical roots of this system trace back to ancient teachings that described humanity as evolving through four kingdoms of wisdom. These were symbolized by the Heart, the Club, the Diamond, and the Spade — corresponding to emotional, mental, physical, and spiritual mastery. Across cultures and generations, this system has demonstrated a consistent ability to map individual temperament, recurring life themes, and leadership patterns with surprising accuracy.

For a healer, coach, or leader, that level of clarity is invaluable. Because when you understand your own architecture, you stop copying other people's strategies. You stop overextending in misaligned roles. You stop trying to serve in ways that contradict your design. Instead, you step to the forefront of your journey by understanding your purpose and all the nuances and complexities that make you -- so uniquely you.

The Healer's Code matters now because the world does not just need more healers. It needs aligned ones. It needs leaders who understand their nervous system, their growth edge, their natural authority style, and their energetic bandwidth. It needs coaches who can differentiate between what is universally true and what is individually designed. And it needs individuals who are no longer chasing identity — but embodying the architecture of their soul's archetype.

Throughout the following pages, this book will walk you through:

• The four domains of wisdom

• The structure of the Book of Life

• The five cards that form your Healer's Code

• How to interpret those cards

• How to apply them to your healing, leadership, and impact

Because the next evolution of your work will not come from doing more.

It will come from becoming precise.

How This System Found Us

Systems like the Book of Life are never encountered by chance. It occurs through divine appointment. Joy's introduction to this system did not begin in a classroom. It began in meditation.

During a period of deep contemplation, she began receiving symbolic imagery. A deck of cards appeared. Each card represented a person. Each person embodied a pattern. Each pattern revealed a developmental curriculum.

The understanding was immediate and precise: human beings are not moving randomly through life. Each person is born into a specific sequence of refinement — emotional, psychological, relational, material, and spiritual.

The cards represented those sequences.

They were not meant to define people as identities. They were assignments their soul incarnated to complete.

She perceived that when an individual consciously integrates the curriculum encoded within the archetypes of their pattern, something shifts fundamentally. Perception clarifies. Reactivity softens. Life becomes less adversarial and more miraculous and participatory. The relationship with reality evolves from survival to co-creation.

There was another layer to the vision.

She understood that this structure had been hidden. Preserved in plain sight within the 52-card deck.

The message was direct: This is the curriculum for human awakening.

As profound as this revelation felt, Joy did not accept this blindly. At the time, she was deeply engaged in academic study. Her background included psychology, human development theory, coaching methodology, and the mechanics of learning and behavioral change. She was on a path toward becoming a licensed therapist – exactly one month away from receiving her Master's Degree. She understood attachment theory. She understood trauma integration. She understood cognitive frameworks, emotional regulation models, developmental stages, and the neuroscience of pattern formation.

She knew how the mind can create meaning. She knew the difference between projection and pattern recognition. So instead of proclaiming the revelation, she tested it.

She began looking for historical anchors. She was led to the writings of Olney H. Richmond, founder of the Mystic Brotherhood in the late 19th century. Richmond taught that the common 52-card deck was originally part of a calendrical and archetypal system — what was referred t as the Book of Life. Fifty-two cards. Fifty-two weeks of the solar year. Four suits corresponding to four domains of human development.

Richmond described these four suits as representing emotional, mental, physical, and spiritual evolution. He referred philosophically to a tradition called the "Kingdom of the Four Rivers" — associating the system's symbolic roots with ancient Atlantis and later Egyptian transmission.

The structural system described by Richmond is philosophically consistent and mathematically precise. Each birth date corresponds to a fixed position within the 52-card annual cycle. That placement generates a Birth Card. From that card, additional fixed placements produce what are often referred to as planetary influences — forming a layered developmental map.

Joy studied the mechanics. She worked with mentors. She ran charts. She compared placements to psychological models. She correlated her findings to patterns observed in people.

What she found was repeatable. The placements mapped temperament. They highlighted recurring relational themes. They exposed responsibility patterns. They revealed refinement points.

As her research deepened, she made a pivotal decision. Instead of pursuing traditional therapy alone — which often addresses healing through pathology — she chose to integrate this archetypal architecture into her work as a guide.

Meanwhile, Matt's path was unfolding through a different doorway.

Through years of deep meditation and spontaneous awakening experiences, he was guided inward — not toward symbol, but toward the quantum field.

In his contemplative practice, he began accessing what many spiritual traditions refer to as the Akashic Records.

For readers unfamiliar with the term, the Akashic Records is described across mystical lineages as a field of informational consciousness. It is understood as a dimension of awareness containing the energetic imprint of all human experience across time — patterns, probabilities, soul-level trajectories.

One could describe it psychologically as access to archetypal pattern recognition at a non-local level. In practical terms, accessing this field allows for the perception of underlying developmental architecture beneath the surface of personal circumstances.

Matt began working with individuals around the world — guiding them through healing, awakening, and integration. He became known not simply for emotional reassurance, but for articulating and revealing the deeper structure beneath the floorboards of human suffering. He could perceive not only what someone was experiencing — but why and how that particular theme was refining them.

While Joy was decoding structural timing, Matt was perceiving energetic pattern. Two very different paths. One shared realization: Growth is not random.

When Joy and Matt met, their work merged and matured through observation and application. Joy brought structural mapping — grounded in both historical transmission and academic understanding. Matt brought direct field awareness — refined through thousands of real-world sessions.

They began comparing charts with intuitive readings, archetypal placements with observed life themes, and timing structures with energetic perception. The convergence was striking. The Book of Life did not contradict intuitive awareness. It mapped it. It provided structural coordinates for what Matt had been perceiving through direct field access.

And over time, they saw the same patterns emerge again and again. When someone understood their structural placement, confusion decreased. When someone understood their refinement points, resistance softened. When someone understood their leadership

Just as the Kingdom of the Four Rivers describes, human development unfolds in four directions. All growth originates from one source. All wisdom begins in awareness and completes in integration. But just like each river demonstrates, not all rivers flow in the same direction.

This is why you are here – uncovering all that the Healer's Code is ready to reveal. As gifts of grace for the evolution of your personal journey and the unique contributions you were born to express.

Welcome to the Healer's Code.

Matt & Joy Kahn — *Life Chart*

		K♠	8♦	10♣			
A♠	3♦	5♣	10♠	Q♣	A♣	3♥	☿
2♥	9♠	9♣	J♥	5♠	7♦	7♥	♀
8♣	J♠	2♦	4♣	6♥	K♦	K♥	♂
A♦	A♥	8♣	10♦	10♥	4♠	6♦	♃
5♦	7♣	9♥	3♠	3♣	5♥	Q♦	♄
J♦	K♣	2♣	7♠	9♦	J♣	Q♣	♅
Q♥	6♠	6♣	8♥	2♣	4♦	4♥	♆
♆	♅	♄	♃	♂	♀	☿	

THE QUANTUM FIELD –
A COSMIC DANCEFLOOR

Before you had a name, before you had a body, before anyone spoke your existence into language, you emerged from a field of intelligence.

Modern physics calls it the Quantum Field — a non-local field of potential in which possibility exists prior to form. Mystical traditions have described it as source consciousness, unified awareness, or the great intelligence from which all life arises. Whatever terminology you prefer, the premise is remarkably consistent: form emerges from a field of infinite potential.

Birth is not merely a biological event, it is movement from non-local awareness into individualized perspective. And when you entered this world, you did not just emerge out of emptiness, you stepped into position.

Imagine life as a vast dance floor — not inherently chaotic, but structured. A floor mapped with precise coordinates. A floor that repeats in cycles. A floor where every position carries a different vantage point, a different angle of perception and a different sequence of movements.

The Book of Life maps that floor.

The 52-card structure that makes up a single book of cards corresponds to the 52-week solar cycle. It is calendrical, not arbitrary. Time itself becomes the stage. Each birth date corresponds to a fixed position within that repeating annual structure. When you are born, you do not simply arrive — you take your place on the cosmic dancefloor. That place determines your angle of view.

Two dancers standing in different positions on the same floor do not see life the same way. Their orientation determines what, throughout life, feels easy and what seems difficult. What feels stable and what appears risky. What feels natural and what requires effort.

Similarly, your placement within the 52-card system establishes your primary vantage point on reality. From one position, relational intensity may define growth. From another, responsibility may shape development. From another -- discernment, vision, refinement, or stabilization may become central themes. This is not a system describing personality, it is the underlying perspective that informs your personality and shapes the movement of your experience.

Each position on the dance floor is marked by a card, representing the core curriculum assigned at birth. We see this as a choreography that helps you dance with life with more ease and flow. It's not a fixed destiny, but it does reveal a unique understanding of life and your place in it.

In dance, choreography is not meant to limit expression. It's the opposite. It is meant to provide a structure for each dancer to move through the dance -- synchronized by time. It creates a rhythm of tension and release. It determines when you step forward, when you pivot, when you extend, and when you pause. It gives each dancer a sequence through which mastery becomes possible.

Your Birth Card functions in a similar way.

It describes the themes that will consistently refine you. It reflects the relational dynamics that will stretch your emotional intelligence. It reveals the types of responsibility that will shape your maturity. It highlights the developmental pressures that will polish your capacity.

When you resist your position, the dance feels chaotic. When you attempt to replicate someone else's placement -- you collide. When you compare your rhythm to another's, you lose timing.

But when you understand where you are standing — and why — something settles. Life's movement begins to make sense. What once felt like recurring problems begin to reveal themselves as refinements of a greater purpose. What once felt like misfortune begins to look like precision in motion. The goal of the dance is not to escape your position or the dance floor of this world. It is to master your movement within it so fully that you can move with awareness rather than reaction.

In the original philosophical transmission of the Book of Life — including references to the "Kingdom of the Four Rivers" and the Atlantean lineage preserved in later esoteric schools — human development was described as unfolding across four domains: emotional, mental, physical, and spiritual. These domains correspond to the four suits in a deck of playing cards, which represent the four directions in which consciousness matures.

And when enough dancers become conscious of their placement and movement, the collective dance changes. The confusion dissolves, the rhythm expands, and the field becomes co-creative rather than reactive.

In the next section, we will show you how to consciously enter the dance by finding your position on the floor.

You will identify your Birth Card — the central marker of your curriculum. From there, you will begin to see how additional placements form your Healer's Code: the five-card structure revealing your dominant frequency, your refinement points, and the architecture of your leadership.

Understanding the Chart

As a way of familiarizing yourself with how the chart is read, it begins in the first position with the 3 of Hearts in the upper right of the second row. From there, the pattern moves horizontally across seven positions to the left, making up the top row. The rows continue down the page, one row at a time for seven rows, before we return to the top of the chart, with three cards on top and 1 card (the Joker) set to the side.

Please Note: you do not need to understand or memorize the structure in order to access and internalize your Healer's Code. It is offered for general reference and to help you remember: The Chart is precise and everything carries a deeper sacred meaning.

Along the chart, the symbols to the far right and bottom represent planetary influences — additional layers that shape how each archetype expresses itself over time. For greater reference, a full chart of each planetary symbol and their meaning is on the next page.

Symbol	Planetary Label	Keywords
☿	Mercury	Awareness, Thought, Logic, Sudden Impacts, Nervous System, Planning, Foreshadowing
♀	Venus	Acceptance, Forgiveness, Relationships, Beauty, Fame, Creativity, Sensuality, Feminine
♂	Mars	Self-Responsibility, Courage, Passion, Anger, Determination, Divorce, Contracts, Masculine
♃	Jupiter	Activation, Opportunities, Luck, Pleasure, Play, Theology, Spirituality, Travel, Ethiscs, Morals
♄	Saturn	Acceleration, Discipline, Outer Responsibility, Control Patterns, Consequences, Authority, Rules, Accountability, Delays, Limitations
♅	Uranus	Transmutation, Change, Tension, Interruption, Social Connections, Science, Space, Extra-Sensory, Extra-Terrestrial, Independence
♆	Neptune	Integration, Dreams, Fantasy, Vision, Theatre, Mysticism, Theosophy, Imagination, Attachment

BEGINNING YOUR HEALER'S CODE JOURNEY

Your birthday corresponds to a single card in the Book of Life. It is known as your Birth Card.

To find your Birth Card, please reference the chart on the following page. Locate your month across the top row of the table. Then find your day of birth along the left column. Where those two coordinates meet, you will find your card.

For example, using the chart on the following page: March 10 aligns with the King of Diamonds.

The position of your birthcard determines the larger architecture of your birth chart — and from that architecture your Healer's Code emerges.

DAY	JAN	FEB	MAR	APR	MAY	JUN	JUL	AUG	SEPT	OCT	NOV	DEC
	MONTH OF BIRTH											
1	K♠	J♠	9♠	7♠	5♠	3♠	A♠	Q♦	10♦	8♦	6♦	4♦
2	Q♠	10♠	8♠	6♠	4♠	2♠	K♦	J♦	9♦	7♦	5♦	3♦
3	J♠	9♠	7♠	5♠	3♠	A♠	Q♦	10♦	8♦	6♦	4♦	2♦
4	10♠	8♠	6♠	4♠	2♠	K♦	J♦	9♦	7♦	5♦	3♦	A♦
5	9♠	7♠	5♠	3♠	A♠	Q♦	10♦	8♦	6♦	4♦	2♦	K♣
6	8♠	6♠	4♠	2♠	K♦	J♦	9♦	7♦	5♦	3♦	A♦	Q♣
7	7♠	5♠	3♠	A♠	Q♦	10♦	8♦	6♦	4♦	2♦	K♣	J♣
8	6♠	4♠	2♠	K♦	J♦	9♦	7♦	5♦	3♦	A♦	Q♣	10♣
9	5♠	3♠	A♠	Q♦	10♦	8♦	6♦	4♦	2♦	K♣	J♣	9♣
10	4♠	2♠	K♦	J♦	9♦	7♦	5♦	3♦	A♦	Q♣	10♣	8♣
11	3♠	A♠	Q♦	10♦	8♦	6♦	4♦	2♦	K♣	J♣	9♣	7♣
12	2♠	K♦	J♦	9♦	7♦	5♦	3♦	A♦	Q♣	10♣	8♣	6♣
13	A♠	Q♦	10♦	8♦	6♦	4♦	2♦	K♣	J♣	9♣	7♣	5♣
14	K♦	J♦	9♦	7♦	5♦	3♦	A♦	Q♣	10♣	8♣	6♣	4♣
15	Q♦	10♦	8♦	6♦	4♦	2♦	K♣	J♣	9♣	7♣	5♣	3♣
16	J♦	9♦	7♦	5♦	3♦	A♦	Q♣	10♣	8♣	6♣	4♣	2♣
17	10♦	8♦	6♦	4♦	2♦	K♣	J♣	9♣	7♣	5♣	3♣	A♣
18	9♦	7♦	5♦	3♦	A♦	Q♣	10♣	8♣	6♣	4♣	2♣	K♥
19	8♦	6♦	4♦	2♦	K♣	J♣	9♣	7♣	5♣	3♣	A♣	Q♥
20	7♦	5♦	3♦	A♦	Q♣	10♣	8♣	6♣	4♣	2♣	K♥	J♥
21	6♦	4♦	2♦	K♣	J♣	9♣	7♣	5♣	3♣	A♣	Q♥	10♥
22	5♦	3♦	A♦	Q♣	10♣	8♣	6♣	4♣	2♣	K♥	J♥	9♥
23	4♦	2♦	K♣	J♣	9♣	7♣	5♣	3♣	A♣	Q♥	10♥	8♥
24	3♦	A♦	Q♣	10♣	8♣	6♣	4♣	2♣	K♥	J♥	9♥	7♥
25	2♦	K♣	J♣	9♣	7♣	5♣	3♣	A♣	Q♥	10♥	8♥	6♥
26	A♦	Q♣	10♣	8♣	6♣	4♣	2♣	K♥	J♥	9♥	7♥	5♥
27	K♣	J♣	9♣	7♣	5♣	3♣	A♣	Q♥	10♥	8♥	6♥	4♥
28	Q♣	10♣	8♣	6♣	4♣	2♣	K♥	J♥	9♥	7♥	5♥	3♥
29	J♣	9♣	7♣	5♣	3♣	A♣	Q♥	10♥	8♥	6♥	4♥	2♥
30	10♣		6♣	4♣	2♣	K♥	J♥	9♥	7♥	5♥	3♥	A♥
31	9♣		5♣		A♣		10♥	8♥		4♥		Joker

The Meaning of the Numbers

Before you understand your suit, it is essential to understand your number. The suit tells you the *area of life* where your lessons unfold. The number tells you the *stage of development* within that area. From Ace through King, the cards represent progression. Each number carries a specific pattern of growth. They describe the energetic stage you are working through.

Ancient civilizations treated number as a sacred framework rather than simple counting. In Egyptian cosmology and later Hermetic philosophy, numbers described order, sequence, and development. Creation itself was understood as unfolding in stages. Zero exists before the cycle begins. One initiates. Two relates. Three creates. Four stabilizes. Five disrupts. Six restores. Seven tests. Eight amplifies. Nine completes. This book uses numbers in that same structural way.

Zero — The Origin

Zero represents potential before direction. It is the field before form. In this system, Zero corresponds to the Joker archetype — not as a personality, but as origin. Zero holds possibility. It does not express until it chooses a direction. Every cycle begins from potential. Every identity emerges from choice.

One (Ace) — Initiation

The Ace represents beginning. It is the first spark of energy in any realm. This number carries focus and intensity because it is concentrated at a single point. At its lowest expression, the Ace can feel isolated or overly self-reliant. At its refined expression, it becomes clear, catalytic, and decisive. The Ace does not follow. It innovates.

Two — Relationship

The Two introduces polarity. It represents awareness of "other." Tension, contrast, attraction, and choice all begin here. When unrefined, the Two can struggle with indecision or seek validation. When refined, it becomes balanced, relational, and capable of partnership without losing itself. The Two evolves through interaction.

Three — Expression

The Three releases tension through expression. It represents communication, creativity, and outward movement. When unrefined, the Three can scatter energy or overextend. When refined, it becomes expressive, engaging, and influential. The Three turns connection into a celebration of intimacy.

Four — Structure

The Four stabilizes energy. It builds systems. It creates order. When unrefined, the Four can become rigid or resistant to change. When refined, it becomes dependable, disciplined, and strong. The Four teaches that freedom requires structure.

Five — Disruption

The Five introduces movement. It challenges what has become stagnant. When unrefined, the Five can feel chaotic or restless. When refined, it becomes adaptive, transformative, and catalytic. The Five views any conflict asks 'what must change?'

Six — Responsibility

The Six restores balance after disruption. It represents responsibility within relationship. When unrefined, the Six may overcorrect or overgive. When refined, it becomes stabilizing, supportive, and generous without self-sacrifice. The Six is the builder f harmony.

Seven — Testing

The Seven turns inward. It questions, evaluates, and tests. When unrefined, the Seven can withdraw or doubt excessively. When refined, it becomes discerning and wise. The Seven searches for truth beneath surface appearances.

Eight — Power

The Eight amplifies energy. It represents strength, authority, and momentum. When unrefined, the Eight can overcontrol or misuse power. When refined, it becomes leadership through responsibility. The Eight is the force that inspires momentum.

Nine — Completion

The Nine concludes the cycle. It integrates lessons and prepares for renewal. When unrefined, the Nine may cling to what is ending. When refined, it releases with awareness and compassion. The Nine closes the chapter so the cycle can begin again.

Ten — Amplification

The Ten represents expansion of the original spark. It carries the energy of the One operating at a larger scale. At its lowest expression, the Ten can feel overwhelming. At its refined expression, it becomes stewardship of expanded capacity. The Ten invites continual expansion.

Jack (11) — Development

The Jack represents emerging identity. It carries heightened sensitivity and awareness.

This is where integrity is tested. Role is explored. Participation becomes conscious. At its lowest expression, the Jack may seek approval or confuse performance with connection. At its refined expression, it becomes relationally intelligent and ethically aware. The Jack is learning to be nourished by honesty instead of threatened by its outcome.

Queen (12) — Integration

The Queen represents internal mastery. It is the matured expression of creative intelligence. At its lowest expression, the Queen can overprocess or overanalyze. At its refined expression, it becomes perceptive, composed, and influential through humility. The Queen carries power without being performative.

King (13) — Stewardship

The King represents embodied responsibility. It is structure matured into leadership. At its lowest expression, the King can become rigid or controlling. At its refined expression, it becomes dependable, stable, and trustworthy. The King becomes the structure of leadership others rely on.

THE MEANING OF THE SUITS

If the the numbers describe development, then suits describe domain. Each suit represents a specific realm of personal experience.

Hearts

Hearts govern emotion and connection. This is the realm where we learn through attachment, vulnerability, love, and loss. When unrefined, Hearts energy can cling, idealize, or fear rejection. When refined, it becomes compassion, intimacy, and emotional courage.

Hearts represent the realm of relationships.

Clubs

Clubs govern thought, belief, communication, and perspective. When unrefined, Clubs energy can overthink, distort, or manipulate information. When refined, it becomes clarity, insight, and strategic intelligence.

Clubs represent the mental realm.

Diamonds

Diamonds govern physical life — resources, work, exchange, security, and worth. When unrefined, Diamonds energy can grasp, fear loss, or equate identity with status. When refined, it becomes stewardship, generosity, and grounded self-worth.

Diamonds represent the physical realm.

Spades

Spades govern transformation, discipline, authority, and maturation. When unrefined, Spades energy can become rigid or controlling. When refined, it becomes wise, steady, and transformative.

Spades represent the spiritual realm.

Bringing It Together

Four realms. Every conflict lives inside one of these. Every breakthrough does too. Your suit reveals where your lessons unfold. Your number reveals how you are developing within it. And together, they form an architecture -- your Personal Healer's Code

THE CARDS THAT MAKE
UP YOUR HEALER'S CODE

The following cards are highlighted on your chart:

Card #1 — Your Birth Card

Your Birth Card represents your core frequency — the archetype through which you entered this lifetime. It reveals your instinctive strengths and your primary growth edge. When expressed from alignment, your Birth Card becomes the stabilizing force in your Kingdom. When expressed from fear, it can magnify distortion. Understanding this distinction is the beginning of conscious influence.

Card #2 — Your Mars Card

This card reveals how you act, pursue, defend, and express drive. It governs how your passion is activated — and how it may misfire when misunderstood. Aligned, this card channels focused energy into purpose. Misaligned, it can turn into frustration, overextension, or suppressed anger. This placement teaches you how to move without force or overcompensation.

Card #3 — Your Neptune Card

This card governs intuition, fantasy, spiritual perception, and subconscious longing. It reveals how you relate to illusion and awakening. Aligned, it helps you build a higher vision for your life. Misaligned, it can blur boundaries or cause you to be lost in fantasy. This placement teaches you how to dream without escaping reality.

Card #4 — Your Pluto Card

This is your crucible. The placement that presses on your deepest pattern. It reveals where you are most tested — and where your greatest breakthrough lives. Aligned, it becomes the key to stepping forward. Misaligned, you are likely to remain stuck by repeating old patterns. This placement teaches you to transmute fear into power.

Card #5 — Your Cosmic Result Card

This card reveals the type of people you are here to stabilize, awaken, or challenge. Aligned, this placement becomes your key to magnetic attraction. Misaligned, it may feel like overexertion or misdirected effort. This placement reveals who your meant to help, how you're meant to help them and the blessings that enter your life as a result.

THE HEALER'S CODE ARCHETYPES

"Any book written in a language other than symbolic, must in the course of time become nearly non-understandable through changes of language and meaning of words, to say nothing of loss through translations, etc. But symbols are the same in all tongues and among all peoples." – Olney H. Richmond

THE HEARTS SUIT

The Hearts Suit governs the realm of love, belonging, and emotional intelligence, guiding us through the full maturation of the heart:

From the innocence of the Ace,
to the polarity of the Two,
to the expressive Three,
to the visionary Four,
to the freedom-seeking Five,
to the embodied Six,
to the discerning Seven,
to the devoted Eight,
to the responsible Nine,
to the fulfilled Ten,
and finally the Court —
where it transforms into
the Initiate as the Jack,
the Nurturer as the Queen,
and the Visionary Leader as the King.

If your Birth Card lives in the Hearts Suit, your life is shaped by relationship — not only with others, but with yourself and the Divine — and your journey is not simply to feel deeply, but to learn how to love without losing yourself, to give without depletion, and to embody devotion in a way that becomes strength rather than sacrifice.

On the following pages, you will find all cards contained within the suit of hearts. The hearts have been organized from Ace to King. Each card begins with a snapshot of its chart followed by a detailed description.

Matt & Joy Kahn

A♡

Life Chart

	K♠	8♢	10♣				
A♠	3♢	5♣	10♠	Q♣	A♣	3♡	☿
2♡	9♠	9♣	J♡	5♠	7♢	7♡	♀
8♣	J♠	2♢	4♣	6♡	K♢	K♡	♂
A♢ MERCURY	A♡ HEALER'S CODE BIRTHCARD	8♠ MOON	10♢	10♡	4♠	6♢	♃
5♢ HEALER'S CODE PLUTO	7♣ HEALER'S CODE NEPTUNE	9♡ URANUS	3♠ SATURN	3♣ JUPITER	5♡ HEALER'S CODE MARS	Q♢ VENUS	♄
J♢	K♣	2♣	7♠	9♢ TRANS-FORMED SELF	J♣ COSMIC LESSON	Q♠ HEALER'S CODE COSMIC RESULT	♅
Q♡	6♠	6♣	8♡	2♣	4♢	4♡	♆
♆	♅	♄	♃	♂	♀	☿	

Card #1: Your Birth Card A♥

To be the Ace of Hearts is to carry love at its source-point. Not love as romance, not love as performance, not love as something you earn or bargain for—but love as an original frequency. The kind that remembers what matters before the world teaches you what to chase. There is often something quietly luminous about you, even when you don't feel luminous at all. You can walk into a room and sense what is missing—not because you are judging it, but because your heart is tuned to wholeness.

And yet, this card can feel tender in a way few people understand. Because when you carry love as an ideal, the world can feel startlingly loud, blunt, or distracted. You may have felt unseen—like your sincerity didn't translate, like your devotion landed in places that couldn't hold it, like you were speaking a language of the heart that others only pretended to know. That can create a quiet hesitation: a reluctance to give yourself fully until you are sure it is safe, sure it is real, sure it is worth the offering.

The Ace of Hearts is not here to "learn how to love." You already know how. You are here to learn what love looks like when it becomes embodied—when it takes shape in choices, boundaries, follow-through, and actual lived devotion. That is where your power is. Not in withdrawing your heart to protect it, and not in pouring it into everything indiscriminately, but in becoming someone who can recognize what is worthy of your love and let your love become real through action.

As a healer, coach, or leader, this gives you an uncommon gift. You can feel the difference between true care and emotional theatre. You can sense when someone is trying to be "nice" versus when they are being honest. You can recognize when a space is aligned with love—and when it is simply decorated with spiritual language. Your chart is not asking you to lose your idealism. It is asking you to mature it, so it becomes guidance instead of longing.

Card #2: Your Mars Card 5♥

Mars reveals how your passion moves—and with the Five of Hearts, your passion moves through liberation. You are not designed to stay where your energy is drained, where your attention is siphoned, or where your heart is asked to overgive. Something in you knows when it is time to release. Not out of coldness, but out of devotion to something truer. Your fire is activated when you choose what nourishes you and let the rest fall away.

This is a beautiful, playful, life-giving Mars card. It wants laughter again. It wants breath again. It wants the kind of community that doesn't demand you prove your worth every time you show up. It reminds you that love is not only depth—it is also lightness. It is shared ease. It is being able to enjoy people without becoming responsible for their inner weather.

But the Five of Hearts also tests a deeper truth: can you let go without turning it into a story of failure? Can you move on without shaming yourself for "not making it work"? This card teaches you discernment in motion. Not the kind that hardens you, but the kind that says: *I honor my life force. I honor my calling. I honor what love requires in reality.*

When this Mars card is aligned, your desire becomes clean and clear—not clinical, not detached, but unburdened. You stop negotiating with what drains you. You stop trying to be lovable by staying too long. You begin choosing with dignity. And your passion returns, not as urgency, but as direction.

Card #3: Neptune Card 7♣

Neptune is the dream that pulls you forward—and the Seven of Clubs dreams of truth. Not surface-level truth, not borrowed truth, but the kind that you have tested, studied, lived, and earned through sincere inquiry. You are wired to learn deeply, to explore teachings with intensity, and to understand the hidden architecture beneath what people casually repeat.

This makes you a natural guide, mentor, or teacher—especially for people who are tired of fluff. You can translate complexity into clarity. You can help others name what they feel but cannot yet articulate. You can take a concept and bring it into the body, into language, into real life.

Yet this Neptune card has a very specific temptation: the belief that the "next layer" will finally be the layer that satisfies you. The Seven of Clubs can keep searching for the more refined teaching, the more advanced approach, the more accurate frame—until devotion becomes difficult. You may sense this in yourself as restlessness, as a subtle inability to settle, as an ever-present awareness that something could be improved.

Your chart is not shaming this. It is revealing it with compassion.

Because you are not here to chase truth forever. You are here to embody what you already know. The dream is not endless learning. The dream is becoming the kind of leader who can *stay*, who can commit, who can let wisdom ripen through repetition and lived experience. When you do that, your vision becomes trustworthy—not because you know more than others, but because your knowing is integrated.

Card #4: Pluto Card 5♦

Pluto is the crucible. It is where the parts of you that want to float above life are asked to meet the physical world as it actually is. With the Five of Diamonds, your deep work is to learn how to make decisions based on real feedback—especially physical feedback. Not just what you feel, not just what you sense spiritually, not just what you understand intellectually, but what reality is communicating through timing, results, energy levels, money flow, health signals, and the simple consequences of choices.

This can be confronting for the Ace of Hearts, because your heart can be so convinced by love, so moved by inspiration, so certain of what *should* be possible—while the physical world says, "Yes… and there are steps." Pluto teaches you not to interpret physical resistance as rejection, but as instruction. It teaches you to stop spiritualizing what is actually a practical adjustment. It teaches you that embodiment is not a compromise—it is the path through which love becomes real.

And this is where your refinement becomes sacred.

Because you truly do see how things could be more beautiful—relationships, environments, systems, expressions. You can walk into a space and instantly sense what would make it more harmonious, more elevated, more alive. But the Five of Diamonds asks you to refine with discernment, not compulsion. To change what matters, not everything. To honor the moment where "better" becomes avoidance of what is already good.

When Pluto is integrated, you become someone whose love can build. Someone whose intuition can lead *and* execute. Someone whose devotion doesn't dissolve when life gets real. This is the grit of your chart—not the harsh kind, but the grounded kind. The kind that can hold a vision long enough for it to become tangible.

Card #5: Cosmic Result Q♠

Your result is the Queen of Spades—wisdom with grace.

This is one of the most powerful culminations for an Ace of Hearts, because it answers the deepest longing of your birth card: not just to love, but to love in a way that is *true*. To become a conduit for divine intelligence without becoming ungrounded. To carry insight without losing warmth. To speak clearly without losing tenderness.

The Queen of Spades is not merely "smart." She is integrated. She holds the mind, the heart, the physical, and the unseen in the same conversation. She can sit with someone in their confusion without needing to fix them. She can name what is real without shaming what is tender. She can guide people back to themselves—not through force, but through presence.

If the Ace of Hearts is love as origin, the Queen of Spades is love as embodied wisdom.

This is what your life is shaping you into: a soft authority. A nurturing clarity. A leader who doesn't have to prove anything, because the steadiness of your integration speaks louder than your personality ever could.

Integration — Your Healer's Code in Motion

When we step back and take in your chart as a whole, a pattern emerges that is both tender and strong.

You begin with love as a high ideal. You move through liberation in love. You dream of truth and mastery. You are tested through physical reality and real-world consequence. And you arrive at integrated wisdom—wisdom that can guide others without leaving your own body behind.

In distortion, this chart can look like hesitation. Like waiting for the perfect love, the perfect teaching, the perfect path, the perfect moment when your devotion finally feels "safe." It can look like constant refinement that never ends. It can look like an ache that says, *I know what's possible… why can't I find it?*

In alignment, something shifts.

You stop asking life to meet your ideal before you participate. You begin participating as devotion. You let your discernment become loving instead of suspicious. You let the physical world teach you timing instead of disappointing you. You let your mind serve your heart instead of protecting it. And slowly, steadily, your path becomes clearer—not because everything is perfect, but because you are present.

So how do you know if you are living your chart?

Notice whether your love feels like a reaching, or a radiance. Notice whether your refinement feels like inspiration, or like restlessness. Notice whether your learning is helping you embody truth—or keeping you in a perpetual "next step." Notice whether you are honoring what reality is communicating through your body, your energy, your resources, and your results.

You are not here to find the perfect way to love.

You are here to become love that is trustworthy.

And when you do, you don't just inspire people. You stabilize them. You help them return to themselves. You remind them that wisdom can be gentle, and devotion can be grounded.

Affirmation of Alignment

I let love become real through my choices, my boundaries, and my presence. I trust the wisdom I embody, and I lead with grace that is grounded.

2♡

Matt & Joy Kahn — *Life Chart*

		K♠	8♦	10♣			
A♠	3♦	5♣	10♠	Q♣	A♣	3♡	☿
2♡ HEALER'S CODE BIRTHCARD	9♠ MOON	9♣	J♡	5♠	7♦	7♡	♀
8♣ HEALER'S CODE NEPTUNE	J♠ URANUS	2♦ SATURN	4♣ JUPITER	6♡ HEALER'S CODE MARS	K♦ VENUS	K♡ MERCURY	♂
A♦	A♡	8♠	10♦ TRANSFORMED SELF	10♡ COSMIC LESSON	4♠ HEALER'S CODE COSMIC RESULT	6♦ HEALER'S CODE PLUTO	♃
5♦	7♣	9♡	3♠	3♣	5♡	Q♦	♄
J♦	K♣	2♣	7♠	9♦	J♣	Q♠	⛢
Q♡	6♠	6♣	8♡	2♠	4♦	4♡	♆
♆	⛢	♄	♃	♂	♀	☿	

Card #1: Your Birth Card 2♥

To be the Two of Hearts is to be born with an instinct to *join*. Where the Ace of Hearts can feel like love rising from within the self, the Two of Hearts feels like love reaching outward, searching for the place it belongs. You are not here to live life at arm's length. You are wired for closeness, for partnership, for the sacred friction and tenderness of relationship—because through relationship, you discover who you are.

And under that longing to connect, there is an even deeper longing: to be seen. Not admired. Not "appreciated." Seen. Understood. Valued for who you actually are. The paradox is that the Two of Hearts often becomes an expert at seeing *everyone else*. You notice what people need. You remember what matters to them. You feel the subtle emotional weather in the room and instinctively try to make it gentler, safer, more harmonious. Over time, if you're not careful, you can become indispensable—and invisible at the very same time.

This is why the Two of Hearts can carry a quiet loneliness, even in a full life. People know how they feel when they're with you… but they may not know *you*. And you may have learned early —through loss, disappointment, or the simple experience of being "the dependable one"—that it's easier to care for others than to risk being fully met. Yet the truth of your card is not self-erasure. It's sacred reciprocity. Your heart is not designed to be the supportive background music of everyone else's story. It is meant to be heard, honored, and held.

As a healer, coach, or leader, this makes you profoundly relational. You don't just understand transformation—you sense it through the nervous system of connection. You can help others feel safe enough to open. But your mastery begins when you stop measuring love by how well you care for everyone, and begin recognizing that your needs are not an inconvenience. They are part of the design.

Card #2: Your Mars Card 6♥

Mars reveals how your passion moves, and with the Six of Hearts your passion moves through *harmony*. You want people to be okay. You want the room to soften. You want the edges to stop scraping. You can feel conflict before it speaks, and there is something in you that would rather repair the emotional field than win an argument. Your drive isn't fueled by competition—it's fueled by the desire for peace, belonging, and mutual well-being.

This is a beautiful Mars placement for a healer. You can bring people back into coherence simply by being present. You often become the one who remembers birthdays, remembers details, remembers the invisible threads that keep relationships alive. You can hold groups together. You can help families, teams, and communities feel like something more than a collection of individuals.

But here is the refinement: the Six of Hearts can confuse harmony with responsibility. You may feel that if someone is upset, you must fix it. If the space is tense, you must smooth it. If people are disappointed, you must compensate. And what starts as care can quietly become a life pattern where your own truth is postponed in the name of keeping everything "good."

Your Mars card is not asking you to become harder. It's asking you to become *truer*. Real harmony is not the absence of tension. It is the presence of honesty held with love. When your passion is aligned, you stop managing emotions and start modeling maturity. You learn that peace does not require self-abandonment. It requires self-respect.

Card #3: Your Neptune Card 8♣

Neptune represents vision—the dream that pulls you forward. With the Eight of Clubs, your dream is not small. This is the vision of the devoted mind: the part of you that wants to grow, build, refine, master, and make something meaningful out of your gifts. You are not only relational—you are *capable*. You can learn quickly, lead intelligently, and hold a bigger mission than people might assume when they only see your tenderness.

This Neptune can create a quiet intensity beneath your softness. You may feel called to develop your voice, your teachings, your craft, your message—something that requires discipline, structure, and courage. The Eight of Clubs doesn't want you to stay in the background. It wants you to claim authority in your own life and stop borrowing your direction from the needs of others.

And yet Neptune can also blur. It can turn your vision into pressure. It can make you feel like you must earn your place, prove your value, or "get it right" before you let yourself be fully known. The Two of Hearts already fears being misunderstood. The Eight of Clubs can add the belief that being seen requires being excellent.

Your chart offers another way.

Your vision is not asking you to become impressive. It is asking you to become *expressed*. To let your mind serve your heart, not override it. To let your competence become a bridge that carries your love into the world—without turning you into someone who is always performing.

Card #4: Your Pluto Card 6♦

Pluto is the crucible—the place where your patterns are purified through reality. With the Six of Diamonds, your deep work is learning how to create *true balance in the material world*. Not just money, but time. Energy. Commitments. The practical agreements that determine whether your life feels supportive… or whether you feel like you are carrying everyone.

This is where the Two of Hearts is tested.

Because your instinct is to give. To be generous. To be the one who makes sure everyone is okay. But Pluto asks a sharper question: *What happens to your life when your giving has no limits?* At first, it looks like love. Over time, it can become burden. And the Six of Diamonds is the card that says: love must become sustainable, or it slowly turns into resentment wearing a kind face.

This Pluto placement is not here to shame you for caring. It is here to teach you stewardship. To help you build a life where your resources are not constantly drained by unspoken expectations. To help you recognize that the people who truly love you will not require your self-erasure to keep the relationship alive. They will meet you in mutuality.

When Pluto in Six of Diamonds is integrated, your generosity becomes *wise*. You still support others—but you stop funding everyone else's comfort with your nervous system. You stop proving love through sacrifice. You begin receiving as a practice, not as an accident.

Card #5: Your Cosmic Result Card 4♠

Your result is the Four of Spades—the sanctuary.

This is the quiet gift your whole chart is guiding you toward: a life that feels stable inside your body. A rhythm you can trust. A foundation that holds you even when other people are disappointed, emotional, or messy. The Four of Spades is not a flashy outcome. It is a profound one. It is the experience of being able to rest without guilt. To say no without fear. To be devoted without disappearing.

The Four of Spades brings the medicine the Two of Hearts secretly needs: *a home within yourself.* Not a home you earn by being helpful, but a home you inhabit because you belong there. When you land in this result, you stop measuring your worth by your availability. You stop confusing love with obligation. And your relationships become cleaner—not clinical, not detached—just simpler, truer, more breathable.

This is the grounded leader archetype. The healer who is not leaking energy. The coach who can hold space without absorbing it. The heart that remains open because it is also anchored.

Integration — Your Healer's Code in Motion

When we look at your chart as a whole, we can feel the journey it's asking you to live.

You begin with a heart that longs for connection, not as dependency, but as a path to self-understanding. Your passion wants harmony, but must learn the difference between peace and self-silencing. Your vision wants mastery and meaningful expression, but must release the need to prove your worth. Your deep work is learning to balance the material world—time, money, energy—so your care becomes sustainable. And your result is a steady inner foundation: the ability to rest, to trust your structure, and to let love be reciprocal.

So how do you know if you are living your chart?

Notice whether you feel seen in your relationships—or whether you are only needed. Notice whether your "harmony" costs you your truth. Notice whether your vision is growing from devotion—or from pressure. Notice whether your generosity feels open and chosen—or heavy and expected. And notice whether your body can rest. Because the Four of Spades doesn't just want you to have love. It wants you to have a life that can hold love.

Your Healer's Code is not asking you to stop caring.

It is asking you to stop vanishing.

And when you do, you become what you have always been seeking: a sacred partnership with yourself—one that finally makes room for others to meet you there.

Affirmation of Alignment

I honor my need to be seen, not just needed. I build a life that supports my heart, and I let love become reciprocal, steady, and real.

3♥

Matt & Joy Kahn — *Life Chart*

	K♠	8◊	10♣
	MOON		

A♠	3◊	5♣	**HEALER'S CODE** 10♣	Q♣	A♣	**HEALER'S CODE** 3♥	☿
URANUS	SATURN	JUPITER	MARS	VENUS	MERCURY	BIRTHCARD	
2♥	9♠	9♣	J♥	**HEALER'S CODE** 5♠	**HEALER'S CODE** 7◊	**HEALER'S CODE** 7♥	♀
		TRANSFORMED SELF	COSMIC LESSON	COSMIC RESULT	PLUTO	NEPTUNE	
8♣	J♠	2◊	4♣	6♥	K◊	K♥	♂
A◊	A♥	8♠	10◊	10♥	4♠	6◊	♃
5◊	7♣	9♥	3♠	3♣	5♥	Q◊	♄
J◊	K♣	2♣	7♠	9◊	J♣	Q♠	♅
Q♥	6♠	6♣	8♥	2♣	4◊	4♥	♆
♆	♅	♄	♃	♂	♀	☿	

Card #1: Your Birth Card 3🖤

To be the Three of Hearts is to carry a heart that is *alive*—curious, expressive, socially radiant, and hungry for connection in motion. You are not here to love quietly in the corner. You are here to *share* love. To demonstrate it. To animate it. To walk into a space and make it more human, more playful, more bright—often without even trying. There is a natural magnetism to this card, as if your presence invites people to loosen their grip and remember that life is meant to be experienced, not merely managed.

HC 3 of hearts

And because you are wired to connect widely, you often want to meet everyone in the room, not just one person. Your heart learns through variety—through stories, personalities, laughter, and the surprise of new encounters. You may have always felt that love is something you can *give* in a thousand creative ways. The Three does not simply feel—it performs feeling. It puts warmth into words. It turns care into gestures. It can be beautifully verbose in its affection, as if the heart itself is an instrument and you're here to play it out loud.

HC 3 of hearts

But there is a refinement here that matters, especially for the healer, coach, and leader.

Because the same gift that makes you so engaging can also become a subtle defense. If you are always expressing, you don't have to pause long enough to listen. If you are always dazzling, you don't have to risk being ordinary. If you are always "on," you don't have to feel what's underneath the performance. The Three of Hearts can sometimes talk *at* life instead of letting life speak back. And when this happens, the heart begins to hunger—not for more attention, but for deeper satisfaction.

In distortion, this can show up as wanting to be liked by everyone while quietly disliking what feels unresponsive, unimpressed, or unavailable. Not because you are unkind, but because your nervous system equates attention with safety. If the applause fades, the Three can feel exposed. If the feedback doesn't come, you may judge the room, judge the audience, judge the people around you—because it's easier to critique than to admit you want to be seen.

Yet your deepest truth is not performance. It is celebration.

You are here to celebrate life. To remind people of joy without bypassing depth. To lead others back to their hearts through laughter, connection, and genuine presence. And when this card is aligned, you become someone people trust—not because you are entertaining, but because your warmth is real.

Card #2: Your Mars Card 10♠

Mars reveals how your passion moves—and for you, it moves through the Ten of Spades: the restructurer. The improver. The one who sees a system and instantly knows how to make it more meaningful, more efficient, more coherent. This is not a cold type of intelligence. It is purposeful. It is energetic. It is the drive to take what already exists and refine it until it actually serves people better.

This is why the Three of Hearts can be far more work-driven than people assume. You may appear playful, social, light—but underneath is a strong work ethic, and a deep desire to be excellent at what you do. You want to deliver. You want to lead. You want to be at the top of your game, not simply for status, but because something in you feels called to make an impact.

And this Mars card comes with a warning that is also a blessing: you can run yourself into the ground.

The Ten of Spades will keep restructuring and refining as long as you let it. It will keep optimizing until the nervous system forgets how to rest. You can overwork not because you don't love life, but because you love what's possible—and you can feel how close the next breakthrough might be. The Three's high energy becomes intense. The mind speeds up. The body tightens. Anxiety can rise—not as a flaw, but as a signal that your gift needs pacing.

When Mars is aligned, you become a masterful architect of transformation. You don't just inspire people—you reorganize the inner world in a way that makes healing sustainable. You help others simplify their chaos into something workable. You bring structure to what felt overwhelming. And you do it best when you remember: your work is meant to be powerful, not punishing.

Card #3: Your Neptune Card — 7♥

Neptune is the dream that pulls you forward, the longing you cannot shake. With the Seven of Hearts here, your dream is to take love to a higher octave. You are not satisfied with surface-level affection. You want love that grows. Love that evolves. Love that becomes more honest, more mature, more embodied. The Seven of Hearts does not settle for emotional performance— it longs for emotional integrity.

For the Three of Hearts, this is both fuel and friction.

Because your natural personality wants to be seen, liked, received. But your Neptune wants to be *recognized for the depth of your care*. You don't just want attention. You want acknowledgement of sincerity. You want your devotion to be felt. You want the world to understand that behind the brightness is a real heart—one that truly wants to help, truly wants to love well, truly wants to be better at love every day.

This is where your vision becomes sacred as a leader.

You are here to bring loving solutions into the world—solutions that feel practical, not just poetic. You are here to show that joy and depth can coexist, that celebration can be intelligent, that warmth can be wise. Yet the Seven of Hearts also places you at a threshold: love must become real. Love must take shape. Love must be embodied in the physical world—or it stays as longing.

And this is why the next card matters so much.

Card #4: Your Pluto Card 7 ♦

Pluto is the crucible. It is where life tests what you claim to value.

With the Seven of Diamonds, the test is the material world—money, worth, receiving, sustainability, and the uncomfortable truth that love does not erase the need for exchange. The Three of Hearts often decides, consciously or unconsciously, that everything should be done "for love." That purity matters more than payment. That caring should be free. That wanting money makes the heart less holy.

And at first, this may even feel noble.

But Pluto is honest.

Because when you give endlessly without receiving, you don't become more loving—you become depleted. When you refuse to value your work, you don't become more spiritual—you become more vulnerable to being taken from. And if you have experienced loss—loss of people, loss of opportunities, loss that taught your nervous system that wanting leads to disappointment —you may have made a quiet vow: *Better not to want anything. Better to give it away before it can be taken.*

This is the wound that the Seven of Diamonds exposes, not to punish you, but to free you.

Because your path forward depends on receiving.

This card asks you to let wealth be part of love, not separate from it. To let support be part of devotion, not a betrayal of it. To let your work be valued so it can endure. The Seven of Diamonds is not about greed. It is about *worthiness*. It is about allowing your life to hold what your heart is trying to give the world.

And of course, this integration requires discernment. If you've been taken advantage of, you may swing the other way—overprotecting, tightening, withholding, bracing for loss. Pluto teaches a middle path: boundaries that honor the heart. Receiving that doesn't collapse your integrity. Prosperity that doesn't harden you.

This is the alchemy that opens your result.

Card #5: Your Cosmic Result Card 5♠

Your result is the Five of Spades: the transformation agent.

This is a potent destiny. It means you are here not only to love people, but to help them change. To help them pivot. To help them shift the one or two key patterns that are keeping them trapped inside pain, confusion, betrayal, neglect, or a life that feels smaller than their spirit. The Five of Spades sees the doorway out. It knows where to apply pressure—and where to stop applying it.

And what's so beautiful is that this result doesn't demand that you abandon everything to transform. It teaches transformation through commitment. Through wise pivots. Through staying with the path that truly serves and adjusting what must be adjusted without burning your whole life down. In this way, the work you do for others becomes the continual transformation you were seeking for yourself.

When you embody the Seven of Diamonds—when you allow receiving, allow sustainability, allow your work to be valued—the Five of Spades becomes your gift in motion. Your care becomes powerful because it is resourced. Your insight becomes potent because it is grounded. Your joy becomes healing because it is not performative—it is resilient.

Integration — Your Healer's Code in Motion

Your chart carries a very specific rhythm.

You begin as a heart that wants to connect widely and express love boldly. Your passion wants to restructure what doesn't work and make it serve people more deeply. Your vision longs to evolve love itself—to bring love into maturity, to be seen for sincerity, to offer the world more intelligent devotion. Your deep work is learning to receive—learning that money, value, and support are not separate from love, but one of the ways love becomes sustainable. And your result is transformation: the ability to guide people through real change without losing your own center.

In distortion, this chart can feel like too much.

Too many people. Too many ideas. Too many obligations. Too much energy running through the system. You may find yourself chasing approval, overworking to deliver, giving away your gifts, and then wondering why the joy you offer so freely doesn't always return to you.

In alignment, something steadies.

You still shine—but you listen. You still lead—but you pace yourself. You still care—but you allow care to include you. You stop treating receiving as a compromise, and begin treating it as the very thing that makes your service trustworthy.

So how do you know if you are living your chart?

Notice whether your expression feels like authentic joy—or like you're auditioning. Notice whether your work ethic feels like devotion—or like anxiety. Notice whether your love stays in words—or becomes embodied through follow-through. Notice whether you are resourced enough to keep giving without resentment. And notice whether the changes you create are sustainable—whether for your clients, your community, or your own life.

The Three of Hearts is not here to become smaller.

It is here to become *truer*.

To let joy mature into wisdom.

To let love become embodied.

To let your gifts be valued so they can endure.

Affirmation of Alignment

I allow my love to be expressed with joy, listened into depth, and grounded through worthy receiving. I am a catalyst for change, and I let my gifts be supported as they transform lives.

4♥ — Life Chart

Matt & Joy Kahn

	HEALER'S CODE	HEALER'S CODE	HEALER'S CODE			
	K♠ COSMIC RESULT	8♦ PLUTO	10♣ NEPTUNE			

A♠	3♦	5♣	10♣	Q♣	A♣ TRANSFORMED SELF	3♥ COSMIC LESSON	☿
2♥	9♠	9♣	J♥	5♠	7♦	7♥	♀
8♣	J♠	2♦	4♣	6♥	K♦	K♥	♂
A♦	A♥	8♠	10♦	10♥	4♠	6♦	♃
5♦	7♣	9♥	3♠	3♣	5♥	Q♦	♄
J♦ MOON	K♣	2♣	7♠	9♦	J♣	Q♠	⛢
Q♥ URANUS	6♠ SATURN	6♣ JUPITER (HEALER'S CODE)	8♥ MARS (HEALER'S CODE)	2♠ VENUS	4♦ MERCURY	4♥ BIRTHCARD (HEALER'S CODE)	♆
♆	⛢	♄	♃	♂	♀	☿	

Card #1: Your Birth Card 4♥

To be the Four of Hearts is to be born with an inner blueprint of what *could* be. You don't just look at life and see what is. You look at life and feel what it is trying to become. You can sense the highest version of a relationship, the most beautiful version of a community, the most inspiring version of a business, a program, a movement, a family system. Your heart carries a kind of architectural hope. It doesn't only dream—it often sees the steps, the structure, the "how," the pathway that could bring something into form.

This is why you can feel both magnetic and misunderstood. People are drawn to you because your vision makes them feel hopeful again. Your presence can restore the part of someone that forgot what was possible. You are often likable in a way that seems effortless—because your belief in people is real, and your desire to bring out the best in them is sincere.

And yet, the Four of Hearts lives with a particular tension: you can blur the line between vision and illusion. Not because you are naïve, but because your heart is committed to the ideal. You can want every marriage to work. You can want every conversation to end in unity. You can want every group to come together and finally agree. You can feel a world where everyone remembers love—and then feel the ache when the current world doesn't match what you can see.

Your gift is not to lower your standards or dim your light. Your gift is to become a steady steward of your vision. To remember that your role is not to force the world to live in your ideal, but to create the *space* where people can grow toward it. When you hold that truth, you become a builder of possibility instead of a defender of fantasy.

Card #2: Your Mars Card 8♥

Mars reveals how your passion moves. With the Eight of Hearts here, your passion is relational. It moves through community, connection, shared purpose, and the creation of spaces where people feel seen, heard, valued, and included. You are not energized by hierarchy. You are energized by *belonging*. By the feeling that a group can become more than the sum of its parts.

This is one of the most natural "space-holders" in the deck. You can gather people. You can create buy-in. You can invite others into a shared yes. You can make a room feel like it has a heartbeat again. And when you are aligned, you don't lead by standing above others—you lead by standing *with* them, moving from inside the circle, helping everyone contribute their gifts.

The shadow is subtle, and it often arrives wearing good intentions. Because when you can see the ideal so clearly, you may start to unconsciously control the expression of others. You might become the one who decides what the group should be, how the conversation should go, what the "right" solution is. Not because you want power, but because you want the vision to succeed.

But the Eight of Hearts asks you to do something braver: to trust the collective. To allow other people's ideas to shape the outcome. To create a forum, not a funnel. When Mars is integrated, you become an extraordinary facilitator of transformation—someone who doesn't just host community, but *unlocks* it.

Card #3: Your Neptune Card 10♣

Neptune is the dream that pulls you forward. With the Ten of Clubs, your dream is devotion to a living idea. This is the vision of carrying something long enough for it to mature. It's not just inspiration—it's commitment. It's the willingness to stay with a message, a mission, a teaching, a structure, and let it deepen through time, feedback, refinement, and real human participation.

This is where the Four of Hearts becomes more than a dreamer. You are meant to become someone who can nurture an idea into a system—one that actually serves people, one that actually lasts, one that helps others step into their own purpose.

And yet, there is a tender edge here. This Neptune placement often brings a complicated relationship with leadership. You may be called into the role of "the leader" again and again, even when a part of you doesn't want the spotlight. You may not want to be idolized. You may not want to be put on a pedestal. You may feel pressure when people expect you to have every answer—because the truth is, your heart doesn't want superiority. It wants shared creation.

This is a sacred tension to work with, not avoid. The Ten of Clubs teaches you that leadership is not the same as being the authority. Leadership can simply mean: *I go first.* I take the first courageous step. I model what it looks like to move. I hold the thread. And then I invite others to weave with me.

When you stop resisting visibility and stop needing it to look a certain way, your vision clarifies. You become the kind of leader people trust—not because you pretend certainty, but because you embody devotion.

Card #4: Your Pluto Card 8♦

Pluto is the crucible—the part of the chart that tests your relationship with the material world and reveals what must be transformed. With the Eight of Diamonds, the lesson often centers around worth, work, health, money, support, and the belief that "the more I do, the more I matter."

This card can attract intensity. You may find yourself drawing in people who are driven, exhausted, high-achieving, stretched thin. People who have been pushing themselves to the brink. People who are trying to prove something, earn something, hold everything together through effort alone. And because you are a Four of Hearts, you can often see the *heart* beneath their overworking. You can see the goodness. You can see the person they are trying to become. You can help them remember that love and life are not meant to be earned through burnout.

But Pluto always turns the lesson inward.

Because somewhere in your own system, you may carry a version of the same pressure. The Four of Hearts wants to build the ideal. The Ten of Clubs wants devotion to the idea. The Eight of Hearts wants to hold the community. And the Eight of Diamonds can quietly whisper: *Work harder. Carry more. Do more. Prove it.*

This is where your chart asks you to transform your relationship with support.

The Eight of Diamonds wants you to receive. To allow prosperity. To let resources come toward you without guilt. To let people of means be drawn to you not as a threat, not as a transaction, but as a natural reflection of the value you offer. It also asks you to honor the body—because your vision cannot thrive if your nervous system is constantly braced.

When Pluto is integrated, you stop wearing exhaustion like a badge. You stop equating love with over-delivery. You begin building a life where your vision is funded by sustainable rhythms instead of personal depletion.

Card #5: Your Cosmic Result Card K♠

Your result is the King of Spades—the sovereign.

This is the outcome your whole chart is trying to mature you into: not just someone who can see the ideal, but someone who can hold the line of truth while the ideal becomes real. The King of Spades is deep wisdom. It's discernment without cynicism. It's clarity without cruelty. It's the ability to see what is actually happening beneath the surface—and respond from a place that is both compassionate and uncompromising.

This result matters for the Four of Hearts, because your tenderness can sometimes overextend toward hope. The King of Spades brings a different kind of love: the love that protects the sacred. The love that knows when to say no. The love that understands timing. The love that doesn't need everyone to agree in order to remain steady.

The King of Spades is not "cold." They are clear. They have learned the difference between empathy and entanglement. They have learned the difference between vision and projection. They can lead without performing. They can be seen without being owned. They can stand in authority without needing to be worshipped.

This is the leader who can build what you came here to build—because they are anchored in truth.

Integration — Your Healer's Code in Motion

When we step back and feel your chart as a whole, we can sense the arc.

You begin as a visionary heart, seeing the highest possibility in people and systems. Your passion wants to gather others into community and shared purpose. Your dream is devotion—to carry an idea long enough for it to become real. Your deep work is learning how to be supported in the material world, how to receive without guilt, how to honor the body, how to stop proving your worth through exhaustion. And the result is sovereignty: the grounded wisdom to lead with discernment and truth.

In distortion, this chart can feel like heartbreak disguised as hope. Like carrying an ideal that the world keeps failing. Like trying to hold a community together by sheer will. Like wanting to lead but resenting the pedestal. Like overgiving, overworking, overbuilding—until the body quietly asks you to stop.

In alignment, something changes.

You keep your vision, but you release the fantasy that everyone must be ready for it today. You create spaces where other people's gifts can shape the outcome. You step into leadership without becoming the authority figure you never wanted to be. You allow support to meet you— financially, relationally, practically—so your mission can breathe. And you become the King of Spades not by hardening, but by clarifying.

So how do you know if you are living your chart?

You can feel it in your body first. You are building without burning out. You are leading without craving approval. You are holding community without controlling it. You are devoted to the mission without needing to be idolized. You are receiving support without guilt. You are still dreaming—but your dream is now partnered with discernment, pacing, and truth.

This is the path of the Four of Hearts: to become the visionary who can actually *finish the build*. Not because the world finally becomes perfect, but because you become steady enough to guide others toward what you already know is possible.

Affirmation of Alignment

I honor my vision with discernment, devotion, and steady leadership. I allow support to meet me, and I lead from truth that strengthens love.

5♡

Matt & Joy Kahn — *Life Chart*

	K♣	8♦	10♣				
A♠	3♦	5♣	10♠	Q♣	A♣	3♡	☿
2♡	9♠	9♣	J♡	5♠	7♦	7♡	♀
8♣	J♠	2♦	4♣	6♡	K♦	K♡	♂
A♦	A♡	8♠	10♦	10♡	4♠	6♦	♃
5♦	7♣	9♡	3♠	3♣	5♡	Q♦	♄
		HEALER'S CODE			HEALER'S CODE		
SATURN	JUPITER	MARS	VENUS	MERCURY	BIRTHCARD	MOON	
J♦	K♣	2♣	7♠	9♦	J♣	Q♠	♅
	TRANS-FORMED SELF	HEALER'S CODE	HEALER'S CODE	HEALER'S CODE			
		COSMIC LESSON	COSMIC RESULT	PLUTO	NEPTUNE	URANUS	
Q♡	6♠	6♣	8♡	2♣	4♦	4♡	♆
♆	♅	♄	♃	♂	♀	☿	

28

Card #1: Your Birth Card 5♥

To be the Five of Hearts is to be born as a catalyst for emotional change. You are not here to simply feel what you feel and call it a day. You are here to *move* feeling. To loosen what is stuck. To bring the heart back into motion when it has become rigid, guarded, resigned, or afraid. There is a restlessness in this card, but it isn't random. It is the soul's way of saying, *there is more life in here than we have allowed ourselves to live.*

This is why freedom matters to you so much. You love beauty, color, play, connection, creativity. You love sharing your ideas with the world. You love the spark of beginnings and the pleasure of possibility. You often carry a naturally magnetic presence—people can feel your warmth and your aliveness. And yet, beneath all of that, the Five of Hearts can carry a very tender wound: the early pressure of being enough, the feeling of being left, the ache of not quite finding the kind of care you long for. Even when you are surrounded by people, there can be a subtle sense that something is missing—something you can't quite name, but can definitely feel.

Because of that tenderness, discernment becomes one of your core initiations. The Five of Hearts often becomes skilled at reading people, sensing misalignment, noticing when something doesn't add up. You learn quickly where love is real and where it is only a performance. And this is a gift for a healer, coach, or leader—because you can help others name what their heart has been trying to whisper for a long time. But this gift can also turn into a pattern of leaving. Leaving before you are left. Pivoting before you have to feel disappointment. Abandoning the thing you love the moment it becomes vulnerable enough to matter.

Your birth card is not asking you to give up freedom. It is asking you to discover a deeper kind of freedom—the freedom that comes from staying present with your own heart, even when it is disappointed. Even when it is scared. Even when it would rather disappear into the next beginning than face the tenderness of completion.

Card #2: Your Mars Card 9♥

Mars reveals how your passion moves, and for you it moves through the Nine of Hearts—the card of fulfillment, completion, and divine timing. This is where your chart begins to tell the deeper story: you are not only meant to create. You are meant to *finish*. You are meant to bring the beauty you imagine into a form that others can actually experience.

And this is precisely where the Five of Hearts can feel conflicted.

Because every completion carries an ending. Every fulfilled dream means the chapter closes. The project is done. The show ends. The single life changes. The "maybe" becomes a "yes," and in that yes, something else dies. And the Five of Hearts loves the open field of possibility so much that the nervous system can quietly resist the very thing it wants—because it doesn't want to feel the grief that comes with an ending. So you might find yourself creating and pivoting, creating and pivoting, creating and pivoting. Always moving. Always evolving. Always beginning again.

But the Nine of Hearts is not here to punish you with endings. It is here to mature you into devotion.

It teaches you that disappointment is not a sign you chose wrong. It is often simply the part of the process that asks you to deepen your craft, refine your message, strengthen your relationship with yourself. Mars in the Nine of Hearts is the passion to stay the course—not because it's easy, but because you love it. Not because you're being celebrated, but because the work is true.

When this card is aligned, you stop needing constant external affirmation to keep going. You learn to give yourself your own encouragement. You learn to let the natural endings of growth happen without interpreting them as failure. And this is where your freedom becomes real: you are no longer running from disappointment—you are moving through it.

Card #3: Your Neptune Card J♣

Neptune is the dream that pulls you forward, and with the Jack of Clubs, the dream is expression with impact. This is the card of the performer, the messenger, the one who carries ideas and brings them to life in a way people can actually *receive*. You are meant to be seen. You are meant to speak, share, teach, create, perform, lead, and transmit. You are not designed to hide your gifts in the back room and call it humility.

There is something magnetic about you, something that draws attention without you needing to force it. You may have noticed this your whole life: people are pulled toward you. They listen. They watch. They want to know what you think. The Jack of Clubs is the archetype of influence through personality and presence.

But Neptune also reveals the place where illusion can seduce you.

Because the Jack of Clubs can sometimes rely on natural charisma instead of disciplined skill. It can over-deliver confidence and under-deliver performance. It can want the spotlight without wanting the training. It can want the applause without wanting the repetition. And this is not a moral flaw—it is simply a crossroads in your growth as a leader.

Your Neptune card is asking you to love your gift enough to develop it.

To let yourself be initiated, trained, practiced, refined. To stop winging it as a way of protecting yourself from the vulnerability of really trying. Because when you truly develop your skills, your confidence becomes more than charm—it becomes authority. And your expression becomes something that can hold the weight of your calling.

Card #4: Your Pluto Card 9 ♦

Pluto is the crucible. It is the part of the chart that insists the soul become honest.

With Pluto in the Nine of Diamonds, your deep work is around fulfillment in the physical world —completion that can be measured, received, and sustained. This includes money, yes. But it also includes recognition, support, belonging, and the tangible feeling that what you are giving is landing. The Nine of Diamonds asks: *Will you allow your life to reward you?*

This can be a tender place for you, because part of you may carry the belief that the material world doesn't really reward your kind of heart. That your Diamond realm is "hard." That you have to work too much for too little. That people don't see you the way you want to be seen. And if those beliefs have been reinforced by experience, you may have learned to protect yourself by not expecting much—by keeping your dreams in a realm where they can't be taken from you, because they also can't be fully tested.

But Pluto doesn't let you stay there.

Pluto asks you to surrender to development. To accept that mastery is part of your devotion. That your gifts are meant to be trained, not only felt. That your creations are meant to complete, not only inspire. And when you stop avoiding the discomfort of being shaped, something opens: the Nine of Diamonds begins delivering fulfillment over and over again—payments, appreciation, resonance, the feeling of "this worked," "this landed," "this mattered." Not as a fantasy, but as a lived reality.

This Pluto placement is not taking your freedom away.

It is turning your freedom into a legacy.

Card #5: Your Cosmic Result Card 7 ♠

Your result is the Seven of Spades—the initiator of discernment through courage.

This is a profound outcome for a Five of Hearts, because it means your emotional freedom matures into spiritual and mental strength. The Seven of Spades is not here to drift. It is here to choose. It is here to face what is real, even when what is real is disappointing, uncomfortable, or inconvenient. It is here to stop confusing movement with growth, and start trusting the quiet power of commitment.

The Seven of Spades carries a kind of holy skepticism. It doesn't accept illusions, including the illusions we create about ourselves. It doesn't let you blame the audience when you didn't practice. It doesn't let you call something "not meant to be" when the deeper truth is that you were afraid of being fully seen. It is the part of your destiny that says: *Tell the truth. Stay with the truth. Let the truth shape you.*

And when you embody this, you become an extraordinary guide for others.

Because you can help people discern without becoming cynical. You can help them leave what is misaligned without turning leaving into a personality. You can help them face endings without collapsing into grief. You can help them build a relationship with discomfort that turns discomfort into evolution.

This is the mature heart: not the heart that never hurts, but the heart that refuses to abandon itself when it does.

Integration — Your Healer's Code in Motion

When we step back and look at your corrected chart, the arc tightens beautifully.

You are born a catalyst for emotional change. You crave freedom. You resist endings. You are asked to complete in the material world. And you ultimately develop profound spiritual discernment.

In distortion, you may pivot constantly. You may avoid finishing. You may repeat emotional cycles. You may call escape "evolution."

In alignment, something crystallizes.

You finish what you begin.

You stabilize financially.

You transform consciously rather than reactively.

You become sharp in discernment without losing heart.

So how do you know if you are living your chart?

Notice whether your life feels repetitive or progressive. Notice whether you complete or continuously restart. Notice whether your freedom feels grounded or frantic.

The 5 of Hearts is not here to run from endings.

It is here to master them.

Integration — Your Healer's Code in Motion

When we step back and take in your chart as a whole, we can see the story your life is trying to tell.

You begin as a heart that needs freedom and creative expression, and that learns discernment through disappointment. Your passion is asking you to complete—to embrace divine timing and understand that every creative cycle has an ending, and every ending is part of the fulfillment you seek. Your vision wants you in the spotlight, but not as a performance—as an offering that has been developed and earned through devotion. Your deep work is to allow tangible reward, to let your gifts be met in the physical world, and to surrender to the process of being shaped into mastery. And your result is the Seven of Spades: courage, honesty, and the capacity to choose your life with clarity.

In distortion, this chart loops.

You create, you pivot, you leave. You fall in love with the spark, then recoil at the vulnerability of completion. You feel disappointed, then you decide you must move on. You get good at discerning what is wrong, but you forget that your deepest lesson is learning how to stay with what you love long enough to let it mature.

In alignment, your whole system steadies.

You let endings be part of the beauty. You let devotion become your freedom. You train your gifts because you respect them. You allow reward because you are willing to receive. And you become the kind of healer, coach, or leader who can hold people through the uncomfortable middle—the place where most people quit—without losing heart.

So how do you know if you are living your chart?

Notice whether you are finishing what you begin. Notice whether you are willing to be seen even when the feedback isn't immediate. Notice whether your discernment leads to wise commitment —or constant escape. Notice whether you are allowing your life to meet you with support. And notice whether your courage is growing—not the loud kind, but the quiet kind that stays present with disappointment and still chooses love, truth, and creation anyway.

Your Healer's Code is not asking you to become less free.

It is asking you to become free enough to commit.

Affirmation of Alignment

I devote myself to what I love, even through the vulnerable middle, and I allow my gifts to be developed and rewarded. I choose truth with courage, and I let completion become part of my freedom.

6♥

	K♠	8♦	10♣			

A♠	3♦	5♣	10♠	Q♣	A♣	3♥	☿
2♥	9♠	9♣	J♥	5♠	7♦	7♥	♀
8♣	J♠ (HEALER'S CODE)	2♦	4♣	6♥ (HEALER'S CODE)	K♦	K♥	♂
JUPITER	*MARS*	*VENUS*	*MERCURY*	*BIRTHCARD*	*MOON*		
A♦	A♥	8♠ (HEALER'S CODE)	10♦ (HEALER'S CODE)	10♥ (HEALER'S CODE)	4♠	6♦	♃
TRANSFORMED SELF	*COSMIC LESSON*	*COSMIC RESULT*	*PLUTO*	*NEPTUNE*	*URANUS*	*SATURN*	
5♦	7♣	9♥	3♠	3♣	5♥	Q♦	♄
J♦	K♣	2♣	7♠	9♦	J♣	Q♠	♅
Q♥	6♠	6♣	8♥	2♠	4♦	4♥	♆
♆	♅	♄	♃	♂	♀	☿	

Card #1: Your Birth Card 6♥

To be the Six of Hearts is to carry a love that wants to *do something* with itself.

This is one of the first hearts that doesn't only wish for a more loving world—it looks at what's missing and feels a genuine impulse to step forward and participate. You can sense what would help. You can see what would improve. You often have a practical kind of compassion that says, *If I can make the environment kinder, safer, steadier… why wouldn't I?*

And because you can see what could change, you can feel an immense pressure to perform. To take tangible action again and again. To be productive, active, physically focused. Many Six of Hearts learn early that love is expressed through effort—through being useful, reliable, available, responsive. And you are often very good at it. You can build businesses. Impact families. Support communities. Step into roles where other people feel held simply because you are there.

But there is a tender distortion that can sneak in: you begin to give love outward so consistently that you forget to include yourself in the circle of care. You become skilled at harmonizing everyone else—making sure no one is upset, no one is angry, no one is frustrated—yet you quietly miss the importance of balancing your own experience. Your love becomes a service, but not always a nourishment.

The deeper invitation of the Six of Hearts is not to stop helping. It is to stop believing you must hold the world in order for love to exist inside it. You are not here to control reality into harmony. You are here to *demonstrate* harmony—by being grounded, discerning, and devoted, while also being well, rested, supported, and fully alive.

Card #2: Your Mars Card J♠

Mars reveals how your passion moves. With the Jack of Spades here, your passion is an initiation.

This is the part of you that is meant to awaken—not to more effort, but to a higher truth. The Jack of Spades does not inflate the ego. It purifies it. It gently challenges the belief that you are alone, that everything depends on you, that if you don't do it, it won't happen.

There is something incredibly relieving about this Mars card when you let it in.

Because the Six of Hearts can quietly live as if it is responsible for the emotional field of everyone around them. If the group is disoriented, you try to fix it. If the business is wobbling, you tighten your grip. If someone is unhappy, you over-function. The Jack of Spades offers another posture: humility before the Source that moves through you. Not religion. Not performance. Simply relationship.

This Mars card teaches you to say, in your own way, *Use me. Guide me. Let love move through me... and let me be included in that love.*

When that becomes your inner stance, your drive changes. You still take action. You still lead. But the pressure softens. The urgency becomes clarity. You stop pushing from fear, and you start moving from alignment.

Card #3: Your Neptune Card 10♥

Neptune is the dream that pulls you forward. With the Ten of Hearts, your dream is vast.

You can envision humanity changed. You can sense a more authentic world, a more awakened world, a more heart-led world—one that feels beyond the current limitations of what people think is possible. And because your vision is so big, it can intensify your desire to work harder, do more, carry more, fix more.

This is where the Ten of Hearts becomes both a gift and a test.

A gift, because it gives you purpose. It gives you a reason to devote yourself. It reminds you that you are not here for small love—you are here for meaningful love.

And a test, because it can tempt you into believing you see the whole picture. Sometimes the Six of Hearts can feel like, *I'm the one who understands what needs to happen.* The Ten of Hearts reminds you that you may indeed see far... but there is always a bigger perspective. A wiser timing. A more intelligent choreography at play than the mind can hold alone.

This is why the Jack of Spades in Mars is so essential. It keeps your vision open. It keeps your certainty surrendered. It helps you stay devoted without becoming rigid. It helps you hold the dream without turning it into a burden you must personally fulfill.

Card #4: Your Pluto Card 10♦

Pluto is the crucible. It's where your soul insists you become honest in the physical world.

With the Ten of Diamonds, the lesson is stewardship. It is the call to build financial structure, to understand what is happening in your systems, and to take responsibility for the material side of your mission. This chart can carry immense blessing with money and success—but it also carries a real vulnerability: when you are loving, charismatic, and devoted, people can assume you will carry things for them. Or they can try to steer your vision, manage your resources, or benefit from your generosity without meeting you in integrity.

The Ten of Diamonds doesn't ask you to become suspicious. It asks you to become sovereign.

To learn what you are building. To know your numbers. To understand your structures. To not hand your power away because you would rather stay in inspiration than deal with logistics. This is an initiation into grounded leadership: love that scales responsibly, love that endures because it is supported by clear agreements, wise systems, and discernment.

And there is something else here, too—something tender.

The Six of Hearts often wants to believe that if they are aligned with Source, everything will be taken care of. Pluto in Ten of Diamonds says: alignment is real… and so is responsibility. Devotion doesn't replace stewardship. It empowers it.

Card #5: Your Cosmic Result Card 8♠

Your result is the Eight of Spades: momentum with higher wisdom.

This is what you want most—not just to be loving, but to be *devoted to the highest truth*. To keep learning. To keep evolving. To keep aligning with a deeper intelligence. The Eight of Spades carries the longing for continual expansion, the desire to understand what's really going on in the world, and the hunger to stay close to what is true.

But this result is not only for you.

It's also what you give.

Because the Six of Hearts has a unique medicine: you can open hearts without letting people float away into spiritual fantasy. You can help highly idealistic people soften. You can help devoted seekers remember the heart. You can help the spiritually passionate stay human. And when your love becomes balanced—when you stop giving from pressure and start giving from overflow—you become a powerful catalyst for transformation.

The Eight of Spades is the meeting point of devotion and embodiment. It is wisdom that moves. Truth that acts. Spirituality that lands in the physical world as real change.

Integration — Your Healer's Code in Motion

When we take your chart as a whole, it tells a very clear story.

You begin as a lover of harmony who feels called to make a tangible difference. You are passionate enough to work hard, to show up, to build, to fix, to improve—but your Mars initiation is to stop believing it all depends on you, and to let a higher wisdom guide your action. Your Neptune vision is enormous, and it must be tempered by humility and openness to an even bigger perspective. Your Pluto work is stewardship—money, structure, responsibility, and the discernment that keeps your generosity from becoming a loophole others can exploit. And your result is momentum with truth: the Eight of Spades, a life devoted to higher purpose that still stays grounded in reality.

In distortion, this chart can feel like pressure without end. Like you are always carrying something. Like you are always fixing something. Like if you rest, the world falls apart. Like love is your job, and your nervous system is the payment.

In alignment, the feeling changes.

You still serve. You still lead. You still build.

But you are not forcing.

You are not alone.

You are not trying to edit reality into harmony through sheer will.

You are collaborating with something greater, while also honoring the practical steps that keep your life supported.

So how do you know if you are living your chart?

You can feel it in the quality of your effort. Your action feels guided, not frantic. Your leadership feels devotional, not performative. Your giving includes you, not only everyone else. You are building systems that protect your mission and your energy. You are less likely to be taken advantage of, because your boundaries are loving and clear. And your connection to truth is not just an interest—it's a lived relationship that keeps expanding you, even as you stay grounded.

This is the heart of the Six of Hearts: love that moves through the world as harmony… without abandoning the one who carries it.

Affirmation of Alignment

I allow a higher wisdom to guide my action, and I include myself in the love I give. I build with devotion and discernment, and my service is supported, sustainable, and true.

7♡

Matt & Joy Kahn

Life Chart

JOKER

		K♠	8♦	10♣		

A♠ MOON	3♦	5♣	10♣	Q♣	A♣	3♥	☿
2♥ URANUS	9♠ SATURN	9♣ JUPITER	HEALER'S CODE J♡ MARS	5♠ VENUS	7♦ MERCURY	HEALER'S CODE 7♡ BIRTHCARD	♀
8♣	J♠	2♦ TRANS-FORMED SELF	4♣ COSMIC LESSON	HEALER'S CODE 6♡ COSMIC RESULT	HEALER'S CODE K♦ PLUTO	HEALER'S CODE K♡ NEPTUNE	♂
A♦	A♡	8♠	10♦	10♡	4♠	6♦	♃
5♦	7♣	9♡	3♠	3♣	5♡	Q♦	♄
J♦	K♣	2♣	7♠	9♦	J♣	Q♠	♅
Q♡	6♠	6♣	8♡	2♣	4♦	4♡	♆
♆	♅	♄	♃	♂	♀	☿	

Card #1: Your Birth Card 7♥

If you are the Seven of Hearts, you were not born naïve about love. You were born perceptive.

You have the kind of heart that has watched love up close—close enough to notice where people say the right things while living a different truth. Close enough to recognize the subtle ways devotion can become manipulation. Close enough to feel how quickly someone's tenderness can disappear when their comfort is threatened. Because of what you have seen, you don't fall for sweetness alone. You're moved by integrity. You're moved by follow-through. You're moved when someone's actions match their words, not once, but consistently.

This is the turning point inside the Hearts kingdom. The Seven is where love stops being only a feeling and starts becoming a question. *What is love in practice? What does it look like when it has to show up on a hard day? What does it look like when it costs something—time, effort, humility, responsibility?* Your heart is learning to include discernment and reality, not as a defense, but as maturity.

And yet, this card holds a tender paradox. Because while you may appear skeptical, you are not loveless. You are deeply devoted. The reason you notice distortion is because you care. The reason you demand consistency is because you know how sacred love actually is. But if you've experienced enough disappointment, a quiet hardening can begin to form—not the loud kind, but the subtle kind that says, *Maybe I should expect less. Maybe wanting more is foolish. Maybe I should protect myself by needing less.*

Your mastery is not to become softer in the way people expect. Your mastery is to become truer in the way your soul requires. To refuse fantasy without losing hope. To demand embodied love without becoming suspicious. To hold standards without becoming closed.

As a healer, coach, or leader, this makes you extraordinary at naming what others feel but cannot articulate. You can sense relational imbalance quickly. You can feel where someone is abandoning themselves "to keep the peace." And because you've lived the lesson, you can guide people back to a love that is not performed, but practiced.

Card #2: Your Mars Card J♥

Mars reveals how your passion moves. For you, it moves through the Jack of Hearts—the expressive heart, the messenger of love.

This means your love is not meant to sit quietly inside you. It wants to move. It wants to reach. It wants to encourage, uplift, advocate, comfort, and remind people that tenderness still matters in a world that can feel sharp. You may find yourself drawn toward healing spaces, creative expression, caregiving roles, community leadership, or any place where emotional intelligence becomes medicine.

But because your birth card is discerning, your Mars card can become a compensating force. When the Seven of Hearts feels disappointed, the Jack of Hearts may try to *prove* love. You may give more than your share. You may become the one who texts first, checks in, carries the emotional tone, fills the gaps, smooths what is uncomfortable, and tries to keep everyone okay. Not because you are weak, but because you genuinely care—and because a part of you may believe that if you don't hold the love, it won't be held.

This is where passion can quietly turn into rescuing.

Your chart is asking you to learn the difference between supporting people and saving them. Between offering care and making yourself responsible for outcomes that are not yours. Between generosity and self-erasure.

When your Mars is aligned, your love becomes magnetic again. You give from overflow, not from fear. You encourage without managing. You show up with warmth while still honoring your own limits. And people don't feel indebted to you—they feel strengthened by you.

Card #3: Your Neptune Card K♥

Neptune is the dream that pulls you forward. With the King of Hearts here, your vision is emotional leadership.

This is not a small dream. It is the dream of a world that functions differently. A world where compassion is not a sentiment, but a structure. A world where families, organizations, and communities are built around care instead of control. You may feel called to build something meaningful—a business, a nonprofit, a container, a movement—where love becomes operational and people are supported in practical ways.

This Neptune placement speaks to your capacity to lead with heart without losing your authority. You can hold the emotional field of a room. You can guide difficult conversations. You can protect what is sacred. You can be the kind of leader people trust because they feel your sincerity.

And Neptune, by nature, can blur.

So one of your illusions to watch is the belief that you are responsible for the emotional weight of the world. That if you don't do it, no one will. That you must solve the biggest problem to justify your gifts. That you must carry more to be worthy of your vision. The King of Hearts doesn't ask you to shoulder everything. It asks you to embody your role and let your integrity be the influence.

When you release the pressure to save everyone, something becomes clear: your presence alone changes systems. Your example alone gives people permission to lead differently. Your steadiness alone is a form of revolution.

This is love as leadership—not dramatic, not performative, but lived.

Card #4: Your Pluto Card K♦

Pluto is the crucible. It is the place the ego would prefer to avoid—the place that insists you become real.

With Pluto in the King of Diamonds, your initiation is into the physical plane: money, systems, strategy, sustainability, competence, and the mature stewardship required to build something that lasts. This card does not diminish your heart. It stabilizes it.

You may naturally resist the material world if it has felt cold, transactional, or disappointing. You may prefer inspiration over logistics. You may want love to be enough. And in many ways, love *is* enough to inspire a mission. But Pluto teaches you that love must be able to endure reality.

If you want to change lives, you must understand structure. If you want your work to be trusted, you must understand stewardship. If you want love to scale, you must build it responsibly. The King of Diamonds asks you to become fluent in the language of the earth—plans, numbers, agreements, timelines, systems—so your compassion doesn't remain an idea, but becomes a living framework that can actually hold people.

This is where your Seven of Hearts becomes deeply empowered. Because your birth card already knows: words are not enough. Pluto makes that wisdom practical. It teaches you to build love in a way that cannot be easily undermined—because it is supported by clear choices, clear structures, and clear integrity.

When you integrate this card, you stop feeling like the physical world is what corrupts love. You realize it can also be what *protects* it.

Card #5: Your Cosmic Result Card 6♥

Your result is the Six of Hearts—harmony.

Not fantasy. Not martyrdom. Not cynicism.

Harmony that is lived.

The Six of Hearts is love that has found its balance point: love that is reciprocal, grounded, steady, and mature. Love that can give and receive without distortion. Love that doesn't have to prove itself, because it is consistent.

This is a beautiful completion for the Seven of Hearts, because it means the skepticism softens into wisdom. You no longer harden when love disappoints you. You no longer overextend to prove devotion. You no longer feel responsible for carrying the emotional field alone. Instead, you become what you have been searching for: embodied love with boundaries.

As a healer, coach, or leader, this becomes your signature. People feel safe in your presence because you're not performing care—you're practicing it. They can feel that your compassion is real because your standards are real. They can feel that your warmth is trustworthy because your follow-through is trustworthy.

The Six of Hearts is the experience of being able to love without losing yourself.

Integration — Your Healer's Code in Motion

When we step back and look at your chart as a whole, a clear pattern emerges.

You are a heart that learned discernment. You are a lover who refuses illusion. You are someone who wants compassion to become structure—and who is being trained to lead from love without turning love into self-sacrifice.

In distortion, love can feel heavy. You may feel disappointed in others. You may believe you have to carry emotional responsibility alone. You may try to compensate for inconsistency by giving more. You may dream of changing the world while quietly feeling overwhelmed by what is broken.

In alignment, everything softens and strengthens at the same time.

You hold high standards without hardening. You give generously without abandoning yourself. You build responsibly without losing heart. You stop trying to rescue people from their lessons and begin empowering those who are ready to rise. You move from *proving* love to *embodying* it.

So how do you know if you are living your chart?

Notice whether love feels draining or steady. Notice whether your giving feels like overflow or obligation. Notice whether your standards create clarity or isolation. Notice whether your leadership feels like a burden you carry alone—or a purpose you live with steadiness. And notice whether you are building structures that support your care, rather than relying on your nervous system to hold everything together.

The Seven of Hearts does not eliminate heartbreak.

It transforms heartbreak into discernment.

And discernment into harmony.

Your Healer's Code is not about becoming less sensitive.

It is about becoming more true.

Affirmation of Alignment

I lead with compassion and embodied integrity. I no longer chase love or prove it—I live it through my boundaries, my follow-through, and my steady heart.

8♡

Life Chart

		K♠	8♢	10♣			
		URANUS	SATURN	JUPITER			

				HEALER'S CODE	HEALER'S CODE	HEALER'S CODE	
A♠	3♢	5♣	10♣	Q♣	A♣	3♡	☿
		TRANS-FORMED SELF	COSMIC LESSON	COSMIC RESULT	PLUTO	NEPTUNE	
2♡	9♠	9♣	J♡	5♠	7♢	7♡	♀
8♣	J♠	2♢	4♣	6♡	K♢	K♡	♂
A♢	A♡	8♠	10♢	10♡	4♠	6♢	♃
5♢	7♣	9♡	3♠	3♣	5♡	Q♢	♄
J♢	K♣	2♣	7♠	9♢	J♣	Q♠	⛢
Q♡ (HEALER'S CODE)	6♠	6♣	8♡ (HEALER'S CODE)	2♠	4♢	4♡	♆
MARS	VENUS	MERCURY	BIRTHCARD	MOON			
♆	⛢	♄	♃	♂	♀	☿	

Card #1: Your Birth Card 8♥

To be the Eight of Hearts is to live with a very particular kind of devotion. You are not only sensitive. You are not only loving. You are *steady*. There is a momentum in you that knows how to show up, day after day, and keep building something meaningful—especially when other people lose heart, lose focus, or lose faith. You can hold a vision for community. You can feel what it would mean for a family, an organization, or a movement to rally around something true. And because you can feel that possibility so vividly, you often carry a deep desire to bring people together—into purpose, into belonging, into shared direction.

Yet the Eight of Hearts is also one of the first places in the Hearts kingdom where the heart begins to feel the weight of the world. Not because your love is flawed, but because the world often measures "importance" differently than you do. The world tends to praise financial success more loudly than emotional fulfillment. It celebrates output more than tenderness. It rewards what can be quantified. And when you're an Eight of Hearts, you can start to interpret your own worth through that external lens—almost without realizing it. You may find yourself doing all the right things, showing up, working hard, building stability… and still feeling a quiet question underneath it all: *Is this really it? Is this actually my purpose? Why don't I feel as fulfilled as I thought I would?*

This is one of the most tender paradoxes of your birth card. You may appear capable, strong, reliable, and determined, while privately carrying the ache of feeling misunderstood—especially in your emotional nature. The Eight of Hearts often learns to tone down their outpouring of affection because it can feel "too much" for a world that doesn't always know how to receive love without trying to leverage it. Over time, that suppression can create overwhelm. You can keep producing. You can keep serving. You can keep building. But the heart begins to ask for something deeper than success: it asks for *meaning*.

As a healer, coach, or leader, this is part of what makes you so powerful. You know what it is to do everything "right" and still feel empty. You understand the gap between accomplishment and fulfillment. And because you understand it, you can guide others back to the place where their life becomes an inside-out experience again—not measured by applause, but by alignment.

Card #2: Your Mars Card Q♥

Mars reveals how your passion moves, and for you it moves through the Queen of Hearts. This is the card that says your strategic advantage is not more effort. It is more *heart*. Not sentiment. Not performance. Heart as nourishment. Heart as nurturance. Heart as the willingness to include yourself in the very love you offer to everyone else.

Because when the Eight of Hearts is in distortion, you can start chasing fulfillment by chasing approval. You can fall into a loop that sounds like: *If I make enough people happy, I will finally feel successful. If I do enough, if I please enough, if I deliver enough, I will finally feel satisfied.* And yet, the more you chase, the more elusive it becomes—because your heart is not actually craving external validation. Your heart is craving permission to be what it is: deeply caring, deeply affectionate, deeply devoted, and worthy of rest, support, and tenderness.

The Queen of Hearts in Mars is a radical reorientation. It asks you to measure success internally. It asks you to prioritize self-appreciation, self-care, and self-love—not as indulgence, but as strategy. It reminds you that if your passion is to nurture, then you must become someone who nurtures yourself as faithfully as you nurture the world. Not later. Not once everything is done. Now, in the middle of the building.

And when this card is aligned, something beautiful happens: you become magnetic without trying. You stop chasing appreciation, and appreciation begins finding you—because your energy becomes fuller, softer, more grounded, and more real.

Card #3: Your Neptune Card 3♥

Neptune is the dream that pulls you forward. With the Three of Hearts here, your vision includes visibility. This is the part of you that wants to be seen, acknowledged, celebrated. And it's important to name this without shame, because the Three of Hearts isn't only about ego—it's about impact. It feels good when people say, *"That mattered. That helped me. I felt you."* The heart loves affirmation not because it is addicted to praise, but because praise can be evidence that love actually landed.

Yet this Neptune placement also reveals how easily your relationship with feedback can become distorted. If most of the recognition you've received has been tied to material accomplishments —what you built, what you earned, what you produced—then the nervous system starts to equate love with output. You can begin to feel like you're only "doing well" when you're being applauded. And when the applause quiets, you may feel uncertain again, like your purpose has slipped away.

But your chart keeps returning you to one central truth: fulfillment is an inside job.

When you focus on your Mars path—nurturing from the inside, honoring your heart, letting your passion flow as care rather than performance—you actually receive more meaningful feedback from the world. Not because you're trying harder, but because you're being truer. And the Three of Hearts becomes what it was always meant to be: joy. Connection. Warmth. The ability to light up the room without losing yourself in the room.

Card #4: Your Pluto Card — A♣

Pluto is the crucible. It is the place where your life insists you return to yourself.

With Pluto in the Ace of Clubs, your deepest breakthrough comes through self-inquiry. Through self-reflection. Through the willingness to see yourself as you are—your strengths, your gifts, your blind spots, your edges of growth—without flinching, and without outsourcing your self-definition to the opinions of others.

This is not a gentle Pluto. But it is a sacred one.

Because the Eight of Hearts can spend years building stability while secretly feeling unsure who they are beyond what they do for others. You may have learned to identify yourself through what you produce, what you provide, what you hold together. Pluto in Ace of Clubs says: *That is not who you are. That is what you do.*

Your life will keep inviting you back to the mirror until you become the one who decides whether you are successful. Until you become the one who knows what fulfillment means for you. Until you become the one who includes you in the community you keep trying to build. This is the initiation of self-responsibility—not in a harsh way, but in a liberating one. Because when you stop asking the world to tell you who you are, you finally have the space to be who you are.

Card #5: Your Cosmic Result Card — Q♣

Your result is the Queen of Clubs—the wise nurturer who can speak clearly.

This is one of the most beautiful destinations for an Eight of Hearts, because it turns your devotion into mentorship. It opens the gift of articulation. Of teaching. Of guiding. Of being able to share what you've learned in a way that helps other people feel seen, understood, and empowered—without needing them to affirm you in order for you to trust yourself.

The Queen of Clubs carries a particular kind of confidence: not the brittle kind that needs constant reassurance, but the grounded kind that comes from self-awareness. This result suggests that your life is shaping you into someone who can hold others with wisdom, because you have learned how to hold yourself. You become someone who can lead communities and families and organizations not by chasing success, but by transmitting clarity. By saying the thing that matters. By naming what is true. By helping people reconnect to their own hearts without turning your own heart into a hungry question mark.

This is the teacher who doesn't preach.

This is the guide who remembers.

This is the leader who nurtures with intelligence.

Integration — Your Healer's Code in Motion

When we take your chart as a whole, a very clear thread emerges.

You are a devoted builder of community who has been trained by life to question the difference between success and fulfillment. Your Mars strategy is to let love and nurturing be the primary focus—not as a personality trait, but as a lived devotion that includes you. Your vision longs for connection, joy, and meaningful recognition, yet your chart insists that you stop letting external feedback define your inner worth. Your Pluto work is self-inquiry: the courage to see yourself honestly and to become the one who decides what "success" actually means. And your result is the Queen of Clubs: the ability to articulate wisdom, teach clearly, and guide others back to themselves in a way that is both compassionate and strong.

In distortion, this chart can feel like a chase. You can do well, build well, succeed well—yet still feel unfulfilled. You can become a people-pleaser in leadership clothing. You can keep trying to make more people happy, hoping it will finally quiet the question inside you. You can suppress the tenderness of your heart because it feels "too much" for a world that only applauds output.

In alignment, you feel something different.

You feel internally resourced. You begin measuring your life by your own standards. Your passion becomes nurturance instead of performance. Your joy becomes authentic instead of strategic. Your work becomes meaningful not because everyone is praising you, but because you can feel your own fulfillment from within. And from that place, your leadership becomes even more impactful—because people can sense you are not seeking them for validation. You are serving from wholeness.

So how do you know if you are living your chart?

You can tell by where you look for your sense of "enough." If you need the world to applaud you before you can rest, you're still living from the outer lens. If you feel resentful that people don't appreciate you unless you're producing, you're still translating love into output. But when you are living your chart, you can feel your purpose in your body. You can feel your heart included. You can feel that your nurturing is not draining you, because it is also nourishing you. You can feel that your success is no longer a question mark, because you are the one who knows what it means.

This is the Eight of Hearts becoming what it was always meant to be: devoted, capable, and emotionally free.

Affirmation of Alignment

I measure my success from within, and I include myself in the love I give. I lead with nurturing wisdom and clear voice, and my devotion becomes true fulfillment.

9♡

Life Chart

		K♠	8♦	10♣			
A♠	3♦	5♣	10♠	Q♣	A♣	3♡	☿
2♡	9♠	9♣	J♡	5♠	7♦	7♡	♀
8♣	J♠	2♦	4♣	6♡	K♦	K♡	♂
A♦	A♡	8♠	10♦	10♡	4♠	6♦	♃
5♦ VENUS	7♣ MERCURY	HEALER'S CODE 9♡ BIRTHCARD	3♠ MOON	3♣	5♡	Q♦	♄
HEALER'S CODE J♦ COSMIC RESULT	HEALER'S CODE K♣ PLUTO	HEALER'S CODE 2♣ NEPTUNE	7♠ URANUS	9♦ SATURN	J♣ JUPITER	HEALER'S CODE Q♠ MARS	♅
Q♡	6♠	6♣	8♡	2♣	4♦ TRANS-FORMED SELF	4♡ COSMIC LESSON	♆
♆	♅	♄	♃	♂	♀	☿	

Card #1: Your Birth Card 9♥

To be the Nine of Hearts is to carry the ache and the promise of fulfillment in the same breath.

You are not indifferent to love. You are not casual about connection. You feel responsible for it. Responsible for the emotional temperature of a room. Responsible for whether people feel cared for. Responsible for whether harmony is restored. There is something in you that wants to experience love at the highest scale—to know it deeply, to give it generously, to receive it fully. And beneath that longing is an even deeper desire: to finally feel cared for yourself.

The Nine of Hearts can begin life with a heaviness that is difficult to articulate. You may have felt responsible for others very early. You may have felt that your capacity to love was greater than what was reflected back to you. You may have sensed that if you just loved enough, gave enough, stayed enough, endured enough, someone would eventually take care of you in return. And so you may have overgiven. You may have stayed in relationships that were unkind but materially secure. You may have confused being provided for with being cherished.

This is not weakness. It is an initiation.

Because the Nine of Hearts is not here to beg for fulfillment. It is here to embody it. You are not here to secure love through sacrifice. You are here to discover that your value does not depend on how indispensable you are to someone else's life. The higher expression of this birth card is a profound one: *I love because I am love. I give because it is natural to me. But I do not need to smother others with my devotion in order to be worthy of care.*

As a healer, coach, or leader, you understand unrequited love. You understand what it feels like to pour yourself into something and wonder if it will ever return in equal measure. And because you understand it, you can guide others out of that pattern—not by hardening them, but by helping them reclaim their self-worth.

Card #2: Your Mars Card Q♠

Mars reveals your strategic advantage—how your passion moves most effectively. For you, that advantage flows through the Queen of Spades: intuition, discernment, and spiritual clarity.

You have always known.

You have known when a relationship was not right for you. You have known when a job was misaligned. You have known when someone's affection was conditional. You have known when something was over. Your intuition is not faint. It is direct. It is instinctual. It feels like information arriving from somewhere beyond logic.

And yet, the Nine of Hearts sometimes ignores what the Queen of Spades knows.

Why? Because when your heart is craving care, it can override your discernment. When you fear losing financial support, companionship, or approval, you may choose comfort over truth. But every time you look back on a situation that drained you, you can hear yourself saying, *I knew. I knew that long ago.*

The breakthrough of this chart begins the moment you decide to trust that knowing.

The Queen of Spades in Mars gives you the capacity to sever ties cleanly when something is complete. Especially in career, health, or financial matters, you can walk away with surprising strength. It is only when love feels scarce that leaving becomes difficult.

When your Mars energy is aligned, you move with spiritual authority. You act from faith in what cannot yet be seen. You trust the unseen wisdom that guides you toward stability that does not require self-sacrifice. Your strategy for fulfillment is not clinging. It is clarity.

Card #3: Your Neptune Card 2♣

Neptune represents the dream that pulls you forward—and also the illusion that can distort it. With the Two of Clubs, your dream is expression through truth. You are here to speak what you see. To articulate wisdom that others are afraid to say out loud. To connect ideas in a way that changes lives.

You have a gift with words. You can communicate insight that was born from loss, from intuition, from lived experience. You understand how fear shapes decisions. You understand how silence can cost someone their freedom. And you are meant to use your voice to interrupt those patterns.

But this is also where fear can become a shadow.

Because if speaking your truth might cost you love, security, or financial stability, you may hesitate. You may withhold. You may convince yourself that silence is safer. The distortion of this Neptune card whispers, *If you speak, you will be punished.*

And yet the higher expression says something very different: *When you speak, you fulfill your vision.*

The Two of Clubs matures when you realize that truth is not what costs you stability—it is what creates it. When you honor your intuition and articulate what you know, you begin attracting people and opportunities aligned with your integrity. Your voice becomes the bridge between your spiritual knowing and your material future.

Card #4: Your Pluto Card K♣

Pluto is the crucible. It is the place where wisdom must become embodied leadership.

With Pluto in the King of Clubs, your life insists that you step into intellectual authority. You are not meant to simply survive your lessons—you are meant to translate them. To digest your pain. To refine your insight. To teach what you have learned in a way others can understand and apply.

This may show up as teaching, mentoring, writing, leading teams, running organizations, or guiding others through transformation. The King of Clubs is the leader who commands respect not through dominance, but through clarity. Your ideas matter. Your discernment matters. Your voice carries weight because it has been forged through experience.

But Pluto does not allow shortcuts.

You cannot bypass your self-responsibility and still step into this leadership. You must confront your fear of abandonment. You must confront your patterns of overgiving. You must confront your avoidance of the material world. And when you do, something extraordinary happens: your wisdom becomes undeniable.

The King of Clubs in Pluto transforms your intuitive knowing into structured knowledge. It asks you to own your mind as much as your heart.

Card #5: Your Cosmic Result Card J◆

Your result is the Jack of Diamonds—initiation into the material world with charisma and integrity.

This is where the entire arc of your chart becomes visible. The Nine of Hearts begins life believing someone else must provide safety. The Jack of Diamonds ends that story. It says: you can create your own stability. You can attract prosperity through your own gifts. You can become magnetic not because you cling, but because you stand.

The Jack of Diamonds is charm grounded in self-awareness. It is the ability to attract wealth, opportunity, and influence because you are aligned. It is material prosperity initiated through higher truth.

And this result is not only for you—it is who you came to help.

You are uniquely positioned to guide people who struggle with money, worth, charisma, or confidence. You understand the fear of being left. You understand the temptation to trade integrity for security. And because you have walked through that fire, you can teach others how to build wealth without losing themselves.

The Jack of Diamonds is the integration of heart and structure. It is prosperity that does not require self-abandonment.

Integration — Your Healer's Code in Motion

When we step back and feel your chart as a whole, a powerful story emerges.

You begin as a heart that feels responsible for everyone's well-being and longs to experience total fulfillment. Your strategy is intuition—the Queen of Spades reminding you that you always know the truth. Your dream is voice—the courage to speak what you see and to use your lived wisdom as medicine. Your crucible is leadership—owning your knowledge and refusing to diminish your authority. And your result is material initiation—the ability to generate prosperity through aligned action.

In distortion, this chart can create cycles of unrequited love, financial dependence, silence, and self-doubt. You may settle for relationships that provide security but not kindness. You may overgive hoping to be chosen. You may mute your truth to avoid loss.

In alignment, everything shifts.

You trust your intuition even when it asks you to walk away. You speak your truth even when it trembles. You build your own stability instead of waiting to be rescued. You lead with clarity instead of emotional obligation.

So how do you know if you are living your chart?

Notice whether you are staying in situations that your intuition has already outgrown. Notice whether you are silent when you know you should speak. Notice whether you measure your worth by who chooses you—or by the integrity with which you choose yourself. Notice whether you are building your own foundation in the physical world. And notice whether love feels expansive rather than desperate.

The Nine of Hearts does not eliminate longing.

It transforms longing into sovereignty.

Your Healer's Code is not about loving less.

It is about loving without losing yourself.

Affirmation of Alignment

I trust my intuition and speak my truth with courage. I create stability through aligned action, and I allow fulfillment to arise from within rather than waiting to be rescued.

10♥

Matt & Joy Kahn — *Life Chart*

	K♠	8♦	10♣				
A♠	3♦	5♣	10♣	Q♣	A♣	3♥	☿
2♥	9♠	9♣	J♥	5♠	7♦	7♥	♀
8♣	J♠	2♦	4♣	6♥	K♦	K♥	♂
A♦	A♥ *(HEALER'S CODE)*	8♠	10♦	10♥ *(HEALER'S CODE)*	4♠	6♦	♃
JUPITER	MARS	VENUS	MERCURY	BIRTHCARD	MOON		
5♦	7♣	9♥ *(HEALER'S CODE)*	3♠ *(HEALER'S CODE)*	3♣ *(HEALER'S CODE)*	5♥	Q♦	♄
TRANS-FORMED SELF	COSMIC LESSON	COSMIC RESULT	PLUTO	NEPTUNE	URANUS	SATURN	
J♦	K♣	2♣	7♠	9♦	J♣	Q♠	♅
Q♥	6♠	6♣	8♥	2♠	4♦	4♥	♆
♆	♅	♄	♃	♂	♀	☿	

Card #1: Your Birth Card 10♥

To be the Ten of Hearts is to carry the blueprint of the world you wish existed.

You don't simply hope for peace—you believe it is the natural operating system of reality. You value love as a structure, not a sentiment. You believe community should feel nourishing. You believe connection should feel safe. You believe fulfillment should be possible, not rare. And somewhere inside you, there is a quiet knowing that humanity is capable of more tenderness than it currently expresses.

This makes you idealistic—but not in a naïve way. It makes you visionary. You can see what is possible when love becomes the foundation rather than the afterthought. And because you can see it, you feel called to embody it.

Yet here is the tension you live with.

The world around you often measures importance through financial success, material output, or visible achievement. And while you deeply value peace, love, and emotional fulfillment, you are not immune to the pull of prosperity. You want stability. You want comfort. You want your physical needs met without constant strain. But you may quietly feel guilty for that desire—as though wanting financial abundance somehow contradicts your devotion to love.

So you stand in the middle of two currents.

One says, *Peace is everything.*

The other says, *Security matters too.*

And if you have overgiven, overworked, or overextended yourself in the name of being loving, you may feel unappreciated. You show up. You build. You serve. You give. And instead of gratitude, you're often met with expectation. Instead of "thank you," you're handed more responsibility.

This can be a frustrating chart to inhabit early in life. You may feel like you are holding a vision that others do not value in the same way you do. You may feel misunderstood in your depth of care. You may feel like you are always giving more than you receive.

But you are not here to abandon your vision.

You are here to refine how you live it.

Card #2: Your Mars Card A♥

Mars reveals your strategic advantage—the way your passion becomes most powerful.

For you, it flows through the Ace of Hearts.

This is the return to simple love.

Not dramatic love. Not sacrificial love. Not love that exhausts itself trying to prove its worth. But love as a seed. Love as a beginning. Love as something that grows naturally when nurtured gently.

The Ace of Hearts in Mars reminds you that you do not have to carry the emotional world for everyone. You do not have to overempath. You do not have to overextend. You do not have to give until you are empty.

Instead, you point people back to the love within themselves.

You give just enough to inspire their own growth. You encourage without rescuing. You nurture without smothering. You create space for love to awaken in others rather than trying to manufacture it for them.

And this is where your Ten of Hearts begins to soften.

Because when you stop trying to engineer peace for everyone, you begin to experience it within yourself. When you stop overfunctioning to secure appreciation, you begin to feel internally resourced. When you allow love to be reciprocal rather than one-directional, your passion becomes sustainable.

The Ace of Hearts is your strategy: begin with love, include yourself, and let it grow from there.

Card #3: Your Neptune Card 3♣

Neptune represents the dream that pulls you forward—and the illusion that can distort it.

With the Three of Clubs here, your dream is creative problem-solving. You want to engineer solutions. You want to take your ideas and bring them into tangible systems that make life easier for others. You love organizing concepts. You love refining structures. You love seeing how a well-designed idea can ripple through communities and change outcomes.

You may dream of building something that shifts how people experience the world. A program. A company. A movement. A framework. A work of art. A process that simplifies what feels chaotic.

And there can be a subtle illusion woven into that dream: *If I can solve the problem perfectly, then I will finally experience peace. If I build the right system, the world will harmonize. If I create the perfect solution, I will fulfill my purpose and be secure.*

But your chart is not asking you to find the perfect idea.

It is inviting you to create.

The Three of Clubs thrives when you let creativity move through you without demanding that it solve everything. You are inspired to build, to design, to organize—not to carry the weight of fixing humanity. When you release the pressure to produce the flawless answer, your ideas become lighter. More playful. More innovative. More alive.

And ironically, that is when they land most powerfully.

Card #4: Your Pluto Card 3♠

Pluto is the crucible—the place where pressure becomes transformation.

With the Three of Spades here, your initiation is mental refinement. You are asked to look at your creations, your ideas, your systems, and be willing to let them evolve. To let go of what no longer fits. To pivot when necessary. To integrate higher wisdom into the structure you've built.

This card asks you to release anxiety around "getting it right."

You do not need the perfect idea. You need the willingness to refine.

The Three of Spades says: create, then listen. Build, then observe. Adjust without shame. Let the idea teach you how it wants to grow. You are not responsible for holding the entire vision at once. The vision is moving through you, not resting on your shoulders.

When Pluto is integrated, you become someone who can hold innovation without spiraling into overwhelm. You can let go of outdated strategies without feeling like you failed. You can trust the unfolding process.

And this steadiness is what opens your result.

Card #5: Your Cosmic Result Card 9♥

Your result is the Nine of Hearts—fulfillment through emotional maturity.

This is beautiful.

Because the Ten of Hearts begins with the longing for a peaceful, loving world. The Nine of Hearts arrives at the experience of fulfillment—not through external perfection, but through inner responsibility.

You learn that you are not here to sacrifice your prosperity for love. Nor are you here to sacrifice love for prosperity. You are here to integrate them.

The Nine of Hearts represents the moment when you stop carrying the world's emotional burden and begin living from embodied fulfillment. You allow yourself to receive care. You allow yourself to build stability without shame. You allow love and money to coexist in integrity.

And as a healer, coach, or leader, this becomes your medicine.

You help people who feel perpetually disappointed. You help those who overgive. You help those who secretly believe they must choose between peace and prosperity. Because you have walked that tension yourself.

You become a guide into wholeness.

Integration — Your Healer's Code in Motion

When we step back and see your chart as a whole, a profound arc emerges.

You begin as someone who believes in a world organized by love. You wrestle with the tension between peace and prosperity. You work hard. You give generously. You sometimes feel unappreciated. Your Mars card teaches you to begin with self-love and stop overextending. Your Neptune invites you to create without needing perfection. Your Pluto refines your ideas without anxiety. And your result becomes emotional fulfillment that no longer depends on external validation.

So how do you know if you are living your chart?

Notice whether you feel resentful or steady. Notice whether you are overgiving in order to secure appreciation. Notice whether you are chasing the "perfect solution" to justify your existence. Notice whether your love includes you. Notice whether prosperity feels shameful or integrated.

When you are aligned, you feel something different.

You feel peaceful without pretending.

You feel prosperous without guilt.

You create without pressure.

You give without depletion.

You receive without embarrassment.

The Ten of Hearts is not here to save the world.

It is here to demonstrate that love and stability can live in the same body.

Affirmation of Alignment

I honor my vision of peace while allowing myself to prosper. I create with love, refine with wisdom, and embody fulfillment without sacrifice.

J♥

Matt & Joy Kahn — *Life Chart*

		K♠	8♦	10♣			
A♠	3♦	5♣	10♠	Q♣	A♣	3♥	☿
2♥ HEALER'S CODE MARS	9♠ VENUS	9♣ MERCURY	J♥ HEALER'S CODE BIRTHCARD	5♠ MOON	7♦	7♥	♀
8♣ COSMIC LESSON	J♠ HEALER'S CODE COSMIC RESULT	2♦ HEALER'S CODE PLUTO	4♣ HEALER'S CODE NEPTUNE	6♥ URANUS	K♦ SATURN	K♥ JUPITER	♂
A♦	A♥	8♠	10♦	10♥	4♠	6♦ TRANSFORMED SELF	♃
5♦	7♣	9♥	3♠	3♣	5♥	Q♦	♄
J♦	K♣	2♣	7♠	9♦	J♣	Q♠	♅
Q♥	6♠	6♣	8♥	2♣	4♦	4♥	♆
♆	♅	♄	♃	♂	♀	☿	

Card #1: Your Birth Card J🩶

To be the Jack of Hearts is to stand at the very center of the emotional kingdom.

This is not a light placement. It carries a gravity that you likely felt long before you had language for it. There is a quiet imprint in this chart that says, *If something matters, I will sacrifice for it.* If someone is hurting, I will carry some of that pain. If love is needed, I will give it—even if it costs me.

This is why this archetype has long been associated with the martyr. There is an instinctual willingness to put yourself on the line for what you believe in. To take on the project no one else wants. To stay up later. To give more. To absorb the emotional weight so others don't have to. And if you look back across your life, you may see how early this pattern began.

You likely witnessed sacrifice. You likely internalized the belief that everything meaningful requires loss. That if you want love, you must earn it. That if you want impact, you must exhaust yourself. That if you want connection, you must give more than you receive.

And yet, this is only the distorted side of your initiation.

The awakened Jack of Hearts does not disappear into sacrifice. They transform through love. They allow the losses, the disappointments, the heartbreaks to deepen their capacity for compassion without erasing themselves in the process. They crave a tactile, embodied experience of life. They want to be in it. Hands in the dough. Feet in the water. Fully present. Fully engaged. Fully transformed by what they touch.

As a healer, coach, or leader, you are capable of sitting in the rawest human experiences without flinching. You can hold grief. You can hold shame. You can hold regret. You can witness people at their most vulnerable and remain steady. But your mastery lies in learning that your life is not meant to be a perpetual altar of sacrifice. It is meant to be a living channel of love.

Card #2: Your Mars Card 2🩶

Mars reveals your strategic advantage—the way your passion moves most effectively.

For you, it moves through the Two of Hearts.

This is sacred partnership energy. It is the ability to truly be with another. Not to fix them. Not to preach to them. Not to dominate the space with your own emotional intensity—but to sit beside them and witness their humanity.

Your passion expresses itself in one-on-one spaces. In deep conversations. In moments of shared vulnerability. In holding someone's story without rushing to rewrite it. You can help people see themselves in ways they have never allowed themselves to be seen. You can sit with someone for hours while they untangle distortions they have carried for decades.

This is one of the strongest placements in the deck for relational healing.

But here is where awareness matters.

If your birth card leans toward martyrdom, your Mars card can reinforce over-attachment. You may begin to define yourself by who needs you. You may feel indispensable in someone's transformation. You may blur the line between support and emotional entanglement.

When your Mars energy is aligned, partnership becomes empowerment. You hold space without absorbing. You love without collapsing. You support without becoming responsible for outcomes that are not yours.

And in that alignment, you become magnetic—not because you sacrifice, but because you witness with strength.

Card #3: Your Neptune Card 4♣

Neptune represents the dream that pulls you forward—and the illusion that can distort it.

With the Four of Clubs here, your dream includes structure. You are inspired by systems. By frameworks. By plans that make expression possible. You are not chaotic in your creativity—you are methodical. You like to know where the ingredients are before you cook. You like to see the architecture before you build.

You dream of creating something organized. Something stable. Something that holds the love you want to give.

And yet, Neptune can exaggerate.

You may believe you need the perfect structure before you can begin. You may overcomplicate the plan. You may freeze in the face of your own grand vision because it feels too large to execute. Or, on the other side, you may build such rigid systems that your creativity feels boxed in.

The higher expression of the Four of Clubs is simple: structure exists to support freedom.

You do not need the perfect plan. You need enough structure to hold your expression. When you lean into structure as a gentle guide rather than a controlling force, your creativity flows more powerfully. You begin building things that are both stable and alive.

And your love becomes operational—not theoretical.

Card #4: Your Pluto Card 2♦

Pluto is the crucible. It is the place where your ego feels most uncomfortable—and where your greatest breakthrough waits.

With Pluto in the Two of Diamonds, your initiation revolves around value in the material world.

Money feels complicated here.

You understand your emotional worth. You understand your spiritual depth. You understand the intellectual brilliance of what you offer. But equating your gifts to financial compensation can feel foreign, even wrong. There can be a deep discomfort with charging. With naming your price. With asserting that your time, your wisdom, your presence carries tangible value.

You may avoid conversations about money. You may circle around pricing. You may feel guilt when you ask to be paid. You may believe that if you truly love people, you should make yourself accessible to everyone.

And this is where Pluto insists on growth.

Because avoiding money does not make you more loving. It makes you more depleted. Refusing compensation does not make you more virtuous. It often keeps you small.

The Two of Diamonds asks you to see your reflection in the material world and say, *I am worthy of exchange.* Not because your worth can be quantified, but because value must circulate in order to sustain what you are building.

When you integrate this card, money stops feeling like betrayal. It becomes stewardship. It becomes an agreement of mutual respect. It becomes the bridge that allows your love to endure.

Card #5: Your Cosmic Result Card J♠

Your result is the Jack of Spades—initiation into higher wisdom through the mind and spirit.

This is powerful.

The Jack of Spades carries a longing for something beyond material success. They may achieve financially. They may be respected. They may be positioned as leaders. And yet, there is a hunger for deeper initiation—for spiritual integration, for higher awareness, for a love that transcends surface achievement.

Who better to guide them than the Jack of Hearts?

Because you understand that the path to higher wisdom runs through the heart.

Your journey through martyrdom, relational healing, structural refinement, and material worth equips you to help others integrate empathy into their intellect. To soften rigidity with compassion. To remind ambitious minds that love is not weakness—it is the missing dimension of their leadership.

You become the initiator of empathy.

You help those who crave higher wisdom realize that knowing more is not enough. They must embody more.

And that embodiment begins in the heart.

Integration — Your Healer's Code in Motion

When we step back and feel your chart as a whole, we see a profound arc.

You begin with a willingness to sacrifice for love. Your passion expresses through intimate partnership and deep witnessing. Your dream is structured creativity. Your crucible is material worth. And your result is spiritual initiation through the heart.

In distortion, this chart can feel heavy. You may overgive. You may exhaust yourself. You may undercharge. You may avoid financial conversations. You may feel perpetually responsible for everyone else's transformation.

In alignment, something steadies.

You still love deeply—but you do not disappear. You still serve—but you are compensated. You still build—but your structure supports your freedom. You still initiate others—but you are not the altar.

So how do you know if you are living your chart?

Notice whether your service feels sustainable or sacrificial. Notice whether you can talk about money without shrinking. Notice whether your partnerships feel mutual rather than dependent. Notice whether your structure supports your creativity instead of suffocating it. Notice whether your love transforms you instead of depleting you.

The Jack of Hearts is not here to suffer for love.

You are here to demonstrate that love transforms without destroying the one who carries it.

Affirmation of Alignment

I serve from love without sacrificing myself. I honor my worth in every exchange, and I allow my heart to initiate wisdom in the world.

Q♥

Matt & Joy Kahn

Life Chart

HEALER'S CODE		HEALER'S CODE	HEALER'S CODE				
A♠	**3♦**	**5♣**	**10♥**	**Q♣**	**A♣**	**3♥**	☿
COSMIC LESSON	COSMIC RESULT	PLUTO	NEPTUNE	URANUS	SATURN	JUPITER	
2♥	**9♠**	**9♣**	**J♥**	**5♠**	**7♦**	**7♥** TRANS-FORMED SELF	♀
8♣	**J♠**	**2♦**	**4♣**	**6♥**	**K♦**	**K♥**	♂
A♦	**A♥**	**8♠**	**10♦**	**10♥**	**4♠**	**6♦**	♃
5♦	**7♣**	**9♥**	**3♠**	**3♣**	**5♥**	**Q♦**	♄
J♦	**K♣**	**2♣**	**7♠**	**9♦**	**J♣**	**Q♠**	♅
Q♥ BIRTHCARD	**6♠** MOON	**6♣**	**8♥**	**2♠**	**4♦**	**4♥**	♆
♇	♅	♄	♃	♂	♀	☿	

HEALER'S CODE: **K♠** MARS · **8♦** VENUS · **10♣** MERCURY

Card #1: Your Birth Card Q♥

To be the Queen of Hearts is to live with your heart right at the surface of your life.

You don't merely feel love—you *radiate* it. You want people to feel cared for in your presence. You want tenderness to be the atmosphere. You want the people around you to soften, to exhale, to remember they are safe. There is a maternal current in this card, a nurturing force that can hold others in ways they have rarely been held. You are often the one who notices what someone needs before they ask. You feel the unspoken. You sense the quiet ache behind someone's smile.

And because your love is so accessible, your chart carries a very specific temptation: to push love onto others.

Not because you are manipulative, but because your devotion is intense. When you care, you want it returned. When you rescue, you want appreciation. When you show up, you want recognition. And if you have been pouring yourself into people who cannot reciprocate, the Queen of Hearts can become confused and frustrated. *Why doesn't the world mirror back what I give? Why can't people love as deeply as I do?*

This is where the Queen of Hearts can begin living from entitlement without realizing it— entitlement not as arrogance, but as emotional desperation wearing a crown. It can sound like: *I have done so much. I have sacrificed so much. Surely this means I should finally be met.* And when you aren't met, the heart can tighten. Love can start to feel like a bargain rather than a gift.

But the higher expression of this card is one of the most beautiful archetypes in the deck.

It is the nurturer who loves without needing to control reality into affirmation. It is the healer who serves without insisting the world say thank you. It is the leader who learns that love is not something you force people to return—it is something you embody, and then you discern who is capable of honoring it.

This is the Queen of Hearts at her highest: an infinite stream of love flowing through someone who has learned to include themselves in that stream.

Card #2: Your Mars Card K♠

Mars reveals your strategic advantage—how your passion moves most effectively.

For you, it moves through the King of Spades: authority with wisdom.

This is a dramatic shift from pure nurturance, and it is exactly what your chart requires. Because your love is strong, but love without authority becomes vulnerable. You can become passive. You can become background. You can become the one who holds everyone while no one truly holds you. The King of Spades in Mars says: *No more hiding behind caretaking. Step forward. Lead.*

This is not ego.

It is loving confidence.

It is the kind of authority that allows a firefighter to run into a burning building. It is the kind of conviction that allows someone to build a mission big enough to feed people across the world. It is the kind of steadiness that says, *I know what I'm here to do, and I'm willing to go first.*

When this Mars is aligned, your nurturance becomes even more powerful because it is protected by clarity. You can say no. You can set boundaries. You can direct the room. You can lead with a calm voice that others naturally trust. And you stop shrinking your contribution in order to remain liked.

This is how your love becomes respected.

Card #3: Your Neptune Card 10♠

Neptune is the dream that pulls you forward—and the illusion that can distort it.

With the Ten of Spades here, your dream is to fulfill something big. This is the vision of responsibility, legacy, and meaningful contribution. You can sense that your capacity is larger than a "small life." You can hold projects that require endurance. You can carry missions that unfold over years. You can do what many people can't: show up again and again and keep moving the vision forward.

But this Neptune placement can swing between two poles.

On the higher side, it is the deep trust that you can accomplish anything by taking one step at a time—especially when you allow support, allies, delegation, and spiritual guidance to be part of your process.

On the distorted side, it becomes burden and expectation. *Everyone should support me because my vision is important.* Or, *Why am I the only one carrying this?* Or, *If people loved me, they would make space for my dreams.*

This is a tender place for the Queen of Hearts, because your heart can confuse support with love.

So Neptune teaches you something more mature: support is co-created. It isn't demanded. It isn't assumed. It is built through relationships, agreements, and the willingness to both receive help and participate in the system that makes help possible.

This is how your dream becomes real without becoming heavy.

Card #4: Your Pluto Card 5♣

Pluto is the crucible—the place where your life insists you evolve.

With Pluto in the Five of Clubs, your initiation is decisiveness.

You must choose.

You cannot do it all. You cannot do it with everyone. You cannot pour love in every direction and hope your life will somehow feel clear.

The Queen of Hearts wants to care for everyone. To hold everyone. To be part of everything. To keep the circle wide enough that no one feels excluded. And Pluto says: *That will become your burden unless you learn discernment.*

The Five of Clubs asks you to decide what you want. To commit to what matters. To say yes with your whole heart—and to say no without guilt. It teaches you that freedom is not created by keeping every option open. Freedom is created through aligned choice.

And this Pluto can feel uncomfortable, because choosing means someone might be disappointed. Someone might not understand. Someone might not be included. But this is where your authority develops.

Because when you choose, your love gains direction.

And direction is what turns love into impact.

Card #5: Your Cosmic Result Card 3 ◆

Your result is the Three of Diamonds—creative force in the physical world.

This is the gift that arrives when you master your chart: your love becomes *productive* in the most sacred way. You build things. You bring things to life. You create solutions. You contribute tangibly. You become an embodied creator—someone whose care is not only emotional support, but real-world change.

And this result also reveals who you came here to help.

The Three of Diamonds carries enormous creative impulse. They are builders, makers, creators, doers. But they can get trapped in the belief that their creativity only matters if it is financially rewarded. They can chase money and lose love. They can create constantly and still feel empty.

Your medicine is that you help them remember: fulfillment is born when creation is fueled by love. And prosperity becomes sustainable when the heart is included.

So you guide creators back into purpose. You help builders find meaning. You help ambitious people remember that success is hollow if it costs them their soul.

And in doing so, you get to live your own truth: a life built from love that is also physically sustaining.

Integration — Your Healer's Code in Motion

Your chart is the story of love becoming leadership.

You begin as the nurturer who longs to be met and understood. Your Mars card teaches you authority so your love is not exploited or diminished. Your Neptune card pulls you toward a big mission, while also asking you to release the belief that support should be automatic. Your Pluto card insists you choose—because without choice, your love becomes burden. And your result is creation: bringing love into the physical world as tangible change.

In distortion, this chart can feel like overgiving, underreceiving, and quietly resenting the world for not recognizing how much you care. It can feel like expecting others to prove their love through support. It can feel like carrying an enormous vision and wondering why you are alone in it.

In alignment, something becomes simple.

You love freely, but you do not push love onto others. You lead with authority, but you do not harden. You receive support, but you co-create it. You choose your direction, and that choice frees you. And you create, not from pressure, but from devotion.

So how do you know if you are living your chart?

Notice whether your love feels like giving from overflow—or giving to get. Notice whether your leadership feels clear—or emotionally entangled. Notice whether your vision feels like inspiration—or burden. Notice whether you are trying to include everyone—or choosing what truly matters. And notice whether you are creating tangible results from love, rather than hoping love will someday be returned as reward.

The Queen of Hearts is not here to force the world to love them.

You are here to embody love so fully that it becomes unmistakable—and then to build a life that honors it.

Affirmation of Alignment

I lead with loving authority and clear discernment. I choose what matters, receive support with humility, and create tangible impact from the love I embody.

K♡

Matt & Joy Kahn — *Life Chart*

		K♠	8♦	10♣			
A♠	3♦	5♣	10♠	Q♣	A♣	3♡	☿
2♡ (MOON)	9♠	9♣	J♡	5♠	7♦	7♡	♀
8♣ (URANUS)	J♠ (SATURN)	2♦ (JUPITER)	4♣ (HEALER'S CODE / MARS)	6♡ (VENUS)	K♦ (MERCURY)	K♡ (HEALER'S CODE / BIRTHCARD)	♂
A♦	A♡	8♠ (TRANSFORMED SELF)	10♦ (HEALER'S CODE / COSMIC LESSON)	10♡ (HEALER'S CODE / COSMIC RESULT)	4♠ (HEALER'S CODE / PLUTO)	6♦ (HEALER'S CODE / NEPTUNE)	♃
5♦	7♣	9♡	3♠	3♣	5♡	Q♦	♄
J♦	K♣	2♣	7♠	9♦	J♣	Q♣	♅
Q♡	6♠	6♣	8♡	2♣	4♦	4♡	♆
♆	♅	♄	♃	♂	♀	☿	

Card #1: Your Birth Card K♥

To be the King of Hearts is to live as a visionary of love.

You can see creative potential as if it's already real. You can hear someone describe an idea and immediately picture the entire blueprint—how it would look, how it would feel, how it would function, how it would land in the world. It's almost like breathing for you. Imagination is not a hobby. It is a native language.

And because you can see so much, so quickly, one of the most tender challenges of your chart is that people don't always understand what you're saying. You may feel as if you're describing something obvious, something vivid, something already formed, and others look back at you blankly or underestimate what you're articulating. This can create a quiet frustration. Not because you need applause, but because you know what you see is real—and you want others to trust it too.

The King of Hearts carries a kind of closeness to Source: the feeling-sense of what's possible arriving before words can capture it. And your chart asks you to trust this. Not by trying to convince people with more explanation, but by letting your vision integrate long enough to become demonstrable.

As a healer, coach, or leader, this is one of your great gifts. You can help people dream again. You can help them remember possibility. You can feel the "next chapter" of their life before they can. But your leadership becomes most powerful when you learn that articulation isn't the goal. Embodiment is. You are here to make love visible through what you build.

Card #2: Your Mars Card 4♣

Mars reveals your strategic advantage—how your passion moves most effectively.

For you, it moves through the Four of Clubs: structure that communicates.

Because you can see so much so quickly, your instinct may be to speak it into existence. To explain it right away. To persuade people to understand what you already know. But your Mars card says: slow down. Create a container. Put it on paper. Draft it. Sketch it. Prototype it. Let your work speak for you.

The Four of Clubs is not asking you to become rigid. It's asking you to give your vision a place to land.

This card reminds you that structure is not the enemy of creativity—it's the ally. When you have a plan, even a simple one, you become far more effective. You create space for play without drowning in possibility. You create a framework that others can follow, even if they can't initially see what you see. And the more your vision moves into form, the more easily people trust it.

This is also why you need time.

Time to integrate. Time to test. Time to let the idea reveal itself. When you honor this Mars card, you stop burning energy trying to be understood, and you start building something that cannot be dismissed.

Card #3: Your Neptune Card 6 ♦

Neptune is the dream that pulls you forward—and the illusion that can distort it.

With the Six of Diamonds, your dream includes prosperity. And for the King of Hearts, prosperity often comes naturally. You are creative in a way that generates value. You can bring beauty, art, solutions, and meaningful structures into the world, and money tends to follow.

Yet this is where the illusion can sneak in.

Because it's easy to confuse "being able to generate money" with "mastering money." The Six of Diamonds can whisper: *Don't worry about details. You'll be successful. Everything will work out.* And often, in some sense, it does—until it doesn't. Until the lack of stewardship catches up. Until the flow becomes chaotic. Until the value you generate isn't being cared for with the same devotion you give to creating it.

This Neptune placement is asking you to be both artist and steward.

To let prosperity be part of your dream, but not the part that is outsourced. To understand that financial responsibility is not a distraction from your purpose. It is one of the ways your purpose becomes sustainable. When you care for your resources, you are caring for your mission. When you honor the details, you are honoring the beauty you bring into the world.

And when you integrate this, money stops being a side effect and becomes a stable ally— something that supports your ability to keep creating.

Card #4: Your Pluto Card 4 ♠

Pluto is the crucible. It is where your life insists that your foundation be real.

With Pluto in the Four of Spades, your challenge is to never take shortcuts in what you build. Not in systems. Not in relationships. Not in your health. Not in the core structures that hold your life.

This can be a surprising initiation for the King of Hearts, because your gift is vision. You can see the end result so clearly that the "slow work" of building the foundation can feel tedious. You may be tempted to rush. To assume the structure will hold because your intention is pure. To bypass certain steps because you can already see what it will become.

But the Four of Spades is uncompromising in its love.

It says: the foundation matters.

If you shortcut the foundation, you will spend your life repairing what could have been stable from the start. If you shortcut relationships, you will lose what could have become deeply nourishing. If you shortcut your own self-care, your body will eventually demand the attention you refused to give it.

Pluto here is asking you to build with reverence.

To give time and attention to what lasts.

And when you do, you become unstoppable—not because you push harder, but because your life is held by something stable enough to carry your vision.

Card #5: Your Cosmic Result Card 10♥

Your result is the Ten of Hearts—fulfillment.

This is what the King of Hearts truly wants: the experience of love, appreciation, acceptance, affection, community, and connection—not as an idea, but as a lived reality. The Ten of Hearts is the feeling of being met. Being celebrated. Being surrounded by people who genuinely want to be part of what you are building. It is the fulfillment of your art coming to life over and over again.

And this result is not just for you—it's who you came here to help.

You help people experience the life they dreamed of. You can build the house of their dreams. You can create the art they have always wanted to see. You can guide a family into the harmony they didn't think was possible. You can take someone's longing and translate it into something tangible.

But you can only do this consistently when you honor your Mars, your Neptune, and your Pluto.

Because fulfillment is not only a feeling. It is a structure that holds the feeling.

And your chart teaches you how to build it.

Integration — Your Healer's Code in Motion

Your chart is the story of vision becoming fulfillment.

You begin as someone who can see possibility without limit. You can imagine what could be in breathtaking detail. Your strategic advantage is structure—letting your vision integrate, drafting it, giving it form so your work can speak for itself. Your dream includes prosperity, but your lesson is stewardship: to care for what you generate. Your crucible is foundation—no shortcuts, no fragile systems, no rushed relationships. And your result is the Ten of Hearts: a life where love, community, and fulfillment are not only hoped for, but actually experienced.

In distortion, this chart can feel frustrating. You see what's possible, yet feel misunderstood. You generate money, yet avoid the details. You build quickly, yet later discover what wasn't stable. You crave deep fulfillment, yet your foundations don't always hold enough to receive it.

In alignment, something becomes beautifully simple.

You stop trying to convince people with words and start showing them through what you build. You let structure support your creativity. You treat prosperity as something worthy of care. You build foundations slowly enough to last. And then fulfillment arrives—not as a miracle you chase, but as the natural consequence of your devotion.

So how do you know if you are living your chart?

Notice whether you feel rushed to explain yourself, or whether you're willing to let your work speak. Notice whether your structures feel supportive, or improvised. Notice whether you are stewarding the resources you generate, or hoping they manage themselves. Notice whether your relationships and foundations are being built with patience. And notice whether fulfillment feels like a rare event—or a repeatable experience.

The King of Hearts doesn't need to shout their vision into the world.

You are here to build it—slowly enough to last, beautifully enough to inspire, and lovingly enough to fulfill.

Affirmation of Alignment

I honor my vision by giving it structure, stewardship, and a foundation that lasts. I allow fulfillment to meet me through the love I build into form.

THE CLUBS SUIT

The Clubs Suit governs the realm of thought, communication, and creative intelligence, guiding us through the full maturation of the mind:

> From the inspired spark of the Ace,
> to the duality of perspective in the Two,
> to the expressive articulation of the Three,
> to the organizing logic of the Four,
> to the stimulating disruption of the Five,
> to the integrative harmony of the Six,
> to the analytical discernment of the Seven,
> to the influential persuasion of the Eight,
> to the expansive synthesis of the Nine,
> to the masterful expression of the Ten,
> and finally the Court —
> where it transforms into
> the Messenger as the Jack,
> the Strategist as the Queen,
> and the Architect of Ideas as the King.

If your Birth Card lives in the Clubs Suit, your life is shaped by thought — not only what you think, but how you communicate, teach, question, and innovate. Your journey is not simply to gather information, but to refine perception, to use language responsibly, and to recognize that ideas carry creative power. Clubs remind us that the mind can divide or unite — and that mastery comes when thought becomes aligned with truth rather than ego.

On the following pages, you will find all cards contained within the suit of Clubs. The Clubs have been organized from Ace to King. Each card begins with a snapshot of its chart followed by a detailed description. While the charts have been offered for reference, the descriptions provide a chance to feel into their specific energy and purpose.

A♣

JOKER

Matt & Joy Kahn

| | | K♠ | 8◇ | 10♣ | *Life Chart* |

A♠ SATURN	**3◇** JUPITER	HEALER'S CODE **5♣** MARS	**10♠** VENUS	**Q♣** MERCURY	HEALER'S CODE **A♣** BIRTHCARD	**3♡** MOON
2♡	**9♠** TRANS-FORMED SELF	HEALER'S CODE **9♣** COSMIC LESSON	HEALER'S CODE **J♡** COSMIC RESULT	HEALER'S CODE **5♠** PLUTO	**7◇** NEPTUNE	**7♡** URANUS
8♣	**J♠**	**2◇**	**4♣**	**6♡**	**K◇**	**K♡**
A◇	**A♡**	**8♠**	**10◇**	**10♡**	**4♠**	**6◇**
5◇	**7♣**	**9♡**	**3♠**	**3♣**	**5♡**	**Q◇**
J◇	**K♣**	**2♣**	**7♠**	**9◇**	**J♣**	**Q♣**
Q♡	**6♠**	**6♣**	**8♡**	**2♣**	**4◇**	**4♡**
♆	⛢	♄	♃	♂	♀	☿

Right-column planet symbols (top to bottom): ☿ (Mercury), ♀ (Venus), ♂ (Mars), ♃ (Jupiter), ♄ (Saturn), ⛢ (Uranus), ♆ (Neptune)

Card #1: Your Birth Card A♣

If you are an Ace of Clubs, you were born with a mind that wakes up early. You don't just think —you *initiate* thought. You bring fresh ideas, new angles, and unexpected solutions into the rooms you walk into, often without even trying. There's a bright, catalytic quality to you, like you're here to start things that other people didn't yet realize were possible.

And yet, your chart isn't only mind. There is heart here too—an undeniable desire to belong, to connect, to be part of the living pulse of community. You may feel two instincts moving through you at once: a fierce independence that needs space, and a deep relational pull that wants celebration, family, friendship, and shared life. You're not meant to choose one over the other. You're meant to learn the art of honoring both without abandoning yourself.

In the earlier chapters of your life, this card can feel like identity is something you have to *earn*. You may have measured yourself through the eyes of others—how you're received, whether you're accepted, whether you "matter" in the ways you hope to matter. Not because you're shallow, but because the Ace is the beginning. It is the first step of self-definition. And for you, that self-definition is powerful enough that it can become vulnerable: when you don't know who you are yet, you can reach for external feedback to steady your sense of self.

But you are not here to be defined by approval. You are here to be defined by truth.

As a healer, coach, or leader, this becomes one of your greatest gifts. You can help people name what they haven't been able to name. You can help them locate their own clarity. You can translate complexity into insight. And when you're aligned, your mind doesn't become a weapon or a defense—it becomes a lantern. You don't use intellect to distance yourself from feeling. You use intelligence to bring people home to themselves.

Still, there's an edge to this Ace. You love new ideas… but you may struggle when someone else brings a new idea that challenges yours. This is not a flaw—it's a growth point. The Ace wants to *lead*. The initiation energy wants to be the one that sets direction. Your work is not to stop leading. It's to lead without needing to be the only light in the room.

Because the most mature expression of the Ace of Clubs is not control.

It's confidence.

It's the kind of confidence that can stay open, curious, and collaborative—without losing its center.

Card #2: Your Mars Card 5♣

Mars reveals how your passion moves, and what you're willing to fight for. For you, passion is not only personal—it's protective. The Five of Clubs carries devotion to the people you love, to the "home base" of your life, and to the structures that keep what matters safe. You're not just driven to build something inspiring. You're driven to build something that lasts.

This is the part of you that thinks in terms of foundation—financial, practical, familial. You tend to care deeply about stability, saving, investing, planning, and creating a life that doesn't feel fragile. You may be the one in your world who is quietly tracking what others don't want to look at. Not because you're fearful, but because you understand that love without structure can become uncertain. You want the people you love to be held by something real.

And then—right alongside that devotion—comes another equally strong need: freedom.

The Five of Clubs doesn't just build. It challenges. It tests. It wants room to move. So you may find yourself in a lifelong dance: "How do I support my people without losing myself?" "How do I stay connected without feeling trapped?" "How do I create stability without becoming imprisoned by routine?" You may love your family and community deeply, and still need solitude to recharge. You may be highly capable in public, and yet privately protective of your inner world.

Mars here asks you to claim your independence as a sacred requirement, not a guilty secret.

Because when you don't honor your need for space, you don't become more loving—you become more resentful. And when you *do* honor it, something beautiful happens: your devotion becomes clean and wholehearted, your support becomes sustainable, and your leadership becomes rooted instead of reactive.

Card #3: Your Neptune Card 7 ◆

Neptune is your vision—what pulls you, what shimmers in the distance, what you sense you're meant to grow into. With the Seven of Diamonds here, your vision is tied to the physical world: wealth, well-being, embodiment, security, sustainability. You are not here to float above reality. You are here to master life *in form*.

This card often creates a magnetic pull toward financial stability and a stronger foundation. You may find that your dreams naturally include practicality. You don't just want an inspired life— you want a resourced life. You want to feel supported. You want to know that what you build can carry you, your family, your future, and the people you're meant to serve.

And Neptune, as always, can bring a fog if you're not careful.

The shadow here is the subtle illusion that the physical world will "handle itself," or that you don't need to stretch in the material realm because you're already capable in other realms. But your chart doesn't let you bypass this. It keeps calling you back to embodiment—to the reality that money, health, and stability are not separate from spirituality. They are part of the same integration.

This is also why, when you ignore your physical needs—movement, care, building, investing—your system may start speaking to you through the body. Not as punishment. As guidance. As an awakening signal that says: "Come back. Get present. Build what supports you."

Neptune in the Seven of Diamonds is not asking you to chase wealth as proof of worth.

It's asking you to become someone who can hold abundance responsibly—so your life, your work, and your love can expand without strain.

Card #4: Your Pluto Card 5♠

Pluto is your deep transformation. The place where you would rather stay comfortable—but where your soul insists on evolution.

For you, Pluto is the Five of Spades, and this is not gentle medicine. This is the card that says: you are not meant to stay the same. You are not meant to repeat the same year again and again just because it feels familiar. You are not meant to "figure life out" once and then maintain it forever.

And yet… you may try.

Because the mind can become loyal to what it already understands. Because the family protector in you can resist disruption. Because a part of you may believe that stability means sameness.

But Pluto doesn't agree.

This transformation is about identity. It's about allowing your self-definition to evolve. It's about letting life reshape you, not just validate you. It's about choosing change before change chooses you.

When this Pluto card is resisted, you can begin to live in a quiet stagnation. You keep things predictable. You keep giving your power away to what others expect. You keep hoping that if you stay palatable, if you stay consistent, if you stay "acceptable," love will remain close and life will stay stable.

But Pluto's invitation is the opposite:

It says your stability is not found in staying the same.

It's found in becoming brave enough to transform.

When you say yes to this card—consciously, intentionally—your entire life opens. Your mind becomes more alive. Your relationships become more honest. Your work becomes more potent. You stop shaping yourself around other people's comfort, and you start shaping your life around your own truth.

And then love doesn't have to be earned.

It arrives naturally, because you are finally inhabiting yourself.

Card #5: Your Cosmic Result Card J♥

Your cosmic result reveals what your chart is trying to deliver you into—the lived outcome of your growth. And for you, it is the Jack of Hearts: love, connection, belonging, warmth, emotional openness, and a life that feels surrounded by genuine affection.

This is what you want more than you may admit.

Not performance. Not approval. Not being "respected" from a distance.

You want to be loved and adored as you are.

You want to give love freely, and receive it without bargaining for it. You want your life to feel relational, alive, connected—without self-sacrifice.

But here is the hinge point: that Jack of Hearts doesn't fully activate through pleasing people.

It activates through transformation.

If you avoid Pluto, you can fall into a pattern of repeating yourself—showing up, accommodating, serving, staying steady—hoping that consistency will finally be rewarded with the kind of love you long for. And sometimes you will receive *some* love that way… but it may not be as deep as you want. It may feel conditional, or thin, or tied to who you are "being" for others.

When you lean into the Five of Spades, everything changes.

Because as you transform, your heart opens in a new way. Not a naive heart—a brave heart. A heart that isn't trying to secure love through predictability. A heart that's willing to be seen in your evolution.

And then the Jack of Hearts becomes your lived atmosphere.

Love becomes less of a pursuit, and more of a reality you allow.

Integration — Your Healer's Code in Motion

When we step back and look at your chart as a whole, a clear rhythm emerges.

You are here to initiate with the mind, build for the people you love, and evolve beyond the version of you that depends on being understood. You are here to live as both independent and connected—without treating either as a threat. You are here to stop using sameness as safety, and start using truth as your foundation.

Your Ace of Clubs gives you brilliance and leadership. Your Five of Clubs gives you devotion and responsibility. Your Seven of Diamonds keeps calling you into embodied stability. Your Pluto Five of Spades demands transformation. And your cosmic result Jack of Hearts promises that love becomes abundant when you stop negotiating your identity.

So how do you know if you are living your chart?

Notice what happens when change appears. Do you meet it with curiosity, or do you tighten your grip on what's familiar? Notice whether you're building your life from authentic desire, or from the pressure to remain acceptable. Notice whether you feel loved for who you are becoming, or merely tolerated for how well you maintain the old version of yourself.

If you are living your chart, your mind feels inspired rather than defensive. Your independence feels honorable rather than secretive. Your devotion feels steady rather than resentful. Your body feels like an ally you listen to, not a signal you override. And love—real love—starts to gather around you, not because you performed for it, but because you finally let yourself be real inside of it.

Your transformation is not a detour from love.

It is the doorway into the depth of love you were always meant to know.

Affirmation of Alignment

I let myself evolve without guilt, and I allow love to meet me in my truth. I build a life that supports my freedom, my devotion, and my heart.

2♣

Matt & Joy Kahn

Life Chart

	K♠	8♦ TRANS-FORMED SELF	10♣ COSMIC LESSON			

A♠	3♦	5♣	10♠	Q♣	A♣	3♥	☿
2♥	9♠	9♣	J♥	5♠	7♦	7♥	♀
8♣	J♠	2♦	4♣	6♥	K♦	K♥	♂
A♦	A♥	8♣	10♦	10♥	4♠	6♦	♃
5♦	7♣	9♥	3♠	3♣	5♥	Q♦	♄
J♦ VENUS	K♣ MERCURY	HEALER'S CODE 2♣ BIRTHCARD	7♠ MOON	9♦	J♣	Q♣	♅
HEALER'S CODE Q♥ COSMIC RESULT	HEALER'S CODE 6♠ PLUTO	HEALER'S CODE 6♣ NEPTUNE	8♥ URANUS	2♠ SATURN	4♦ JUPITER	HEALER'S CODE 4♥ MARS	♆
♆	♅	♄	♃	♂	♀	☿	

Card #1: Your Birth Card 2♣

If you are a Two of Clubs, you were born with a mind that understands consequence.

This is not a light, carefree mental energy. This is the mind that sees both sides, anticipates outcomes, tracks ripple effects, and quietly asks, *"If I choose this… what might it cost?"* Of all the Twos, yours carries one of the deepest senses of responsibility. You are not naïve about choice. You understand that every decision shapes a path, and every path closes another.

Because of this, you may have grown up feeling the weight of decision long before others did. You might have hesitated when others leapt. You might have overthought when others acted impulsively. Not because you are incapable—but because you are aware. You see endings inside beginnings. You feel the echo of consequence before the action is even taken.

At times, this awareness can slow you down. You may find yourself circling decisions, analyzing outcomes, imagining what could go wrong. The mind becomes protective. It says, *"If I can predict every ripple, I can prevent pain."* And yet, the paradox of your chart is this: overthinking does not eliminate risk. It simply delays movement.

As a healer, coach, or leader, this can be both your brilliance and your burden. You are thoughtful. You do not move recklessly. You consider impact. You understand that your voice carries weight. But if fear of consequence becomes louder than desire, you can begin to live cautiously instead of courageously.

Your path is not about eliminating doubt. It is about choosing in spite of it.

The Two of Clubs is here to unlock decisive devotion. To teach you that what you want—truly want—is worth the discomfort of uncertainty. To help you fall in love with your purpose so deeply that the fear of what *might* happen becomes smaller than the call of what *wants* to happen.

You are not here to avoid consequence.

You are here to choose consciously—and move forward anyway.

Card #2: Your Mars Card 4♥

Your Mars card reveals how your passion moves. And for you, passion is not fiery or chaotic. It is devotional.

The Four of Hearts asks you to fall in love with a path.

To commit.

To root.

To anchor yourself in something meaningful enough that you stop wavering.

Where your Birth Card can hesitate, your Mars card whispers, *"Choose what you love and devote yourself to it."* Not casually. Not halfway. But wholeheartedly. Because once your heart is aligned, your mind becomes steady.

This card is about self-love as fuel. It is about knowing who you are, what you want, and why you want it—so clearly that even if others misunderstand you, you remain grounded. The fear for you is often relational: *What if they don't like me? What if I'm judged? What if I disrupt harmony?*

The Four of Hearts responds gently but firmly: love yourself enough to move anyway.

As a leader, this becomes magnetic. When you speak from devotion rather than defense, people feel the difference. When you take action because you are in love with your purpose—not because you are trying to prevent criticism—your energy stabilizes. You stop trying to manage perception. You start embodying conviction.

The Four of Hearts does not promise that everyone will approve of your choices. It promises that when you choose from love, the experience of walking your path will feel aligned and alive.

Your passion is not meant to be cautious.

It is meant to be committed.

Card #3: Your Neptune Card 6♣

Neptune reveals your vision—the dream that pulls you forward. And with the Six of Clubs, your dream is purpose.

You feel that life is not random. That your thoughts, your voice, your contributions matter. You sense that everything has meaning. That your existence is not accidental. This gives you a deep inner compass. You may feel called to express something that only you can express. To think something that only you can think. To say something that needs your voice.

But there is a subtle temptation here.

When you believe everything has purpose, you can slip into waiting. You can tell yourself that life will unfold as it should… that if something is meant to happen, it will. And while there is truth in that, your chart reminds you of something essential:

You are part of the unfolding.

Purpose does not move around you.

It moves through you.

The Six of Clubs asks you to see yourself not only as someone guided by meaning—but as someone who *creates* meaning through choice. Your thoughts shape your reality. Your words shift environments. Your decisions open or close doors.

As a healer or leader, this becomes profound. When you understand that you are not just witnessing purpose but embodying it, you stop shrinking. You stop deferring your voice. You begin co-creating with life instead of waiting for it to carry you.

Your purpose is not a distant calling.

It is a living current that requires your participation.

Card #4: Your Pluto Card 6♠

Pluto brings you to the Six of Spades.

This is deeper surrender. The recognition that your purpose is larger than your personal comfort. Larger than your timeline. Larger than your need for visible validation.

There may be seasons where you feel you are walking ahead of others. Where you are the first to speak. The first to choose differently. The first to disrupt a pattern.

This can feel lonely.

You may wonder why you must be the brave one. Why you must take the risk. Why the weight of impact feels so personal.

The Six of Spades reminds you: the impact is not yours alone to carry.

There is a current larger than your personality that desires resolution, healing, evolution. You are participating in it. Not orchestrating it.

When you try to hold the entire outcome on your shoulders, pressure builds. When you remember that your role is simply your part, relief returns.

As a leader, this is maturity. You focus on the step in front of you. You take responsibility for your choices. You release attachment to controlling the larger arc.

Your courage is not about being fearless. It is about trusting that the greater picture can hold what you cannot see.

And when you surrender the need to manage the whole, your energy steadies.

Card #5: Your Cosmic Result Card Q♥

The result of your journey is embodied love.

The Queen of Hearts represents emotional maturity, compassion, and relational sovereignty. The Queen does not love timidly or strategically. The Queen loves wisely.

When you learn to choose despite fear, something opens in you. You experience love not as something fragile that must be protected, but as something strong that can be expressed. You no longer guard yourself from decisions that might lead to deeper intimacy. You no longer hide from commitments that require bravery.

Instead, you become a safe place for others to land.

As a healer, coach, or leader, this is magnetic. People feel your steadiness. They feel your warmth. They sense that you are not performing love — you are embodying it. Your courage to choose allows others to trust their own hearts.

You show that love is not passive. It is chosen.

The Queen of Hearts helps embody a love that is not passive, but the result of your choices.

Integration — Your Healer's Code in Motion

When we step back and look at your chart as a whole, we see a mind that feels the weight of choice and a heart that longs for devotion.

In distortion, you may stall at the edge of decision. You may convince yourself that thinking longer will make the risk disappear. You may feel responsible for preventing every possible negative outcome.

But life does not ask you to eliminate uncertainty. It asks you to participate despite it.

So how do you know if you are living your chart?

Notice whether your decisions are driven by fear of consequence or love of purpose. Notice whether your mind feels trapped in analysis or anchored in devotion. Notice whether leadership feels like pressure on your shoulders or a path beneath your feet.

When you are aligned, your thoughts become clear instead of circular. Your choices feel intentional instead of reactive. Your heart feels open instead of guarded.

You stop asking, "What if this goes wrong?" and begin asking, "Is this aligned with who I am?"

You realize that consequence is not punishment. It is movement.

And you begin to trust yourself enough to move.

Affirmation of Alignment

I trust my choices and devote myself to what I love.

My courage to decide creates the love and impact I am here to embody.

Matt & Joy Kahn

Life Chart

		K♠	8♦	10♣			
A♠	3♦	5♣	10♣	Q♣	A♣	3♥	☿
2♥	9♠	9♣	J♥	5♠	7♦	7♥	♀
8♣	J♠	2♦	4♣	6♥	K♦	K♥	♂
A♦	A♥	8♠	10♦	10♥	4♠	6♦	♃
5♦	7♣ (HEALER'S CODE)	9♥	3♠	3♣ (HEALER'S CODE / BIRTHCARD)	5♥	Q♦	♄
JUPITER	MARS	VENUS	MERCURY	BIRTHCARD	MOON		
J♦ (TRANSFORMED SELF)	K♣ (COSMIC LESSON)	2♣ (HEALER'S CODE / COSMIC RESULT)	7♠ (HEALER'S CODE / PLUTO)	9♦ (HEALER'S CODE / NEPTUNE)	J♣ (URANUS)	Q♠ (SATURN)	♅
Q♥	6♠	6♣	8♥	2♣	4♦	4♥	♆
♆	♅	♄	♃	♂	♀	☿	

Card #1: Your Birth Card 3♣

If you are a Three of Clubs, you carry a mind that does not merely think — it constructs. You see patterns where others see noise. You sense structure inside chaos. Complex systems do not intimidate you; they intrigue you. There is something in you that delights in refinement — in taking what feels scattered and shaping it into something coherent, usable, and elegant.

You are a natural architect of ideas. Not just creative, but constructive. You can receive a flood of information and distill it into something digestible. You can translate abstraction into process. You can write, speak, build, or design in a way that helps others finally understand what once felt overwhelming. This is not accidental. This is the signature of your chart.

And yet, with this brilliance comes pressure.

Because you do not just want to create. You want to get it right. You want the right answer. The most elegant solution. The refined expression. There is a quiet intensity in you that says, "If I am going to do this, it must be done well." Over time, that intensity can turn into weight. You may begin to equate your value with what you produce. With how well you solve problems or with how efficiently you respond.

People sense your capability. They rely on you. They invite you into projects. They expect clarity from you. And because you can deliver, you often do. But if you are not careful, you begin creating not for the joy of it — but for the affirmation of it. For the reassurance that you are valuable.

Here is the deeper truth of your chart: it is the act of creation itself that fulfills you. Not the applause. Not the outcome. Not even the usefulness. The process.

You are here to create because creating stabilizes your spirit. When you build for the love of building, when you refine because it delights you, when you write or design or teach because it feels alive in your body — that is when you are most aligned.

Card #2: Your Mars Card 7♣

Your Mars card intensifies your mental strength. The Seven of Clubs adds discernment, depth, and a relentless drive toward truth. It reinforces that voice in you that says, "I can see how this could be better."

You do not look at what exists and accept it at face value. You immediately perceive potential. You see the upgrade. The optimization. The more precise articulation. This is a gift. It is the mark of a visionary mind.

But the Seven of Clubs also carries a subtle edge. Improvement can become requirement.

Discernment can become judgment. And the desire for refinement can quietly transform into dissatisfaction.

You may find yourself thinking, "This works… but it could work better." And sometimes that is wisdom. But sometimes, it is your own inner standard tightening around you.

This Mars energy asks you to deepen your relationship with truth — not perfection. Truth does not always demand enhancement. Sometimes truth simply says, "This is sufficient." Sometimes the highest wisdom is recognizing when something has reached its natural form.

There may also be moments of insecurity here. A double-checking. An over-verifying. A subtle questioning of whether you truly know what you know. That doubt can slow you down or tighten your chest. Or — if matured — it can humble you into mentorship. Into teaching. Into sharing not just the conclusion, but the path you walked to reach it.

When the Seven of Clubs is integrated, you become an extraordinary guide. Not someone who critiques from a distance, but someone who reveals process. Someone who says, "Here is how I see it. Let me show you."

Your Mars is not here to sharpen you against the world. It is here to refine your discernment until it feels steady instead of strained.

Card #3: Your Neptune Card 9 ◆

Your Neptune card gives you vision.

The Nine of Diamonds allows you to see something in its completed form before it exists. You can hold an idea and instantly glimpse its manifestation. You reverse-engineer naturally. You understand how a seed becomes a structure.

This is why you can build so effectively. You are not guessing. You are envisioning.

But Neptune can distort vision just as easily as it inspires it.

If you can see the finished product so clearly, you may hesitate to begin unless it matches your internal image perfectly. If the outcome does not excite you fully, you may not start at all. Or you may restrict yourself to projects that feel guaranteed.

This is where your expansion lies.

The Nine of Diamonds invites you to loosen your grip on certainty. You do not need to know exactly how it will end in order to begin. You do not need the final form to be flawless before you step forward.

Vision is meant to inspire movement — not control it.

When Neptune is balanced, you allow the future to evolve as you build. You permit the project to change shape. You trust that clarity will grow alongside action. And you begin to experience prosperity not just as material success, but as expansion of possibility.

You are not here to create only what is safe. You are here to create what is alive.

Card #4: Your Pluto Card 7♠

Pluto is where transformation becomes unavoidable.

For you, Pluto sits in the Seven of Spades — the card of spiritual insight through lived experience. This card shifts your relationship with outcome.

You may enter a project believing the result is what matters. Yet time and again, you will discover that the journey itself transforms you more than the final product ever could. The real meaning is not in the achievement. It is in who you become while building it.

The Seven of Spades softens your attachment to perfection. It teaches you that process is sacred. That exploration is valuable even if the end result is discarded. That creative expression is not wasted simply because it evolves.

This card also confronts your deeper fears — fear of getting it wrong, fear of disappointing others, fear of miscalculation. These fears can keep you from acting decisively. They can trap your brilliance in preparation rather than execution.

But when you allow the process to change you, something loosens. You begin to move more freely. You begin to create without the heavy burden of finality. You understand that nothing is truly lost. Every attempt refines you.

Card #5: Your Cosmic Result Card 2♣

Your Cosmic Result is integration through connection.

The Two of Clubs brings decisiveness and alignment between thought and action. It is the energy of saying, "I choose this," without spiraling into over-analysis. It is collaborative intelligence. It is shared creativity. It is your brilliant mind working in harmony with others rather than in isolation.

When you embrace the journey, when you release perfection as your metric of worth, when you allow meaning to unfold through experience — your mind softens. It becomes more relational. More fluid. Less burdened.

The Two of Clubs is not about thinking alone. It is about thinking together. It is about building with others who respect your vision and contribute their own. It is about allowing support.

And in that support, your creativity multiplies.

You are no longer creating to prove. You are creating to participate.

Integration — Your Healer's Code in Motion

The essence of your chart is this: your mind is powerful, but it is not meant to imprison you.

You are here to create, refine, build, teach, and innovate. But you are not here to carry the weight of perfection on your shoulders. Your anxiety lessens the moment you remember that creation itself is the fulfillment.

So how do you know if you are living your chart?

You know because creating feels playful again. You begin projects without demanding that they justify themselves. You make decisions without rehearsing every possible consequence. You collaborate instead of isolating. You share your process instead of hoarding it until it is flawless.

You also notice that your nervous system softens. The constant pressure to get it exactly right fades. You still care about excellence — but excellence no longer defines your worth.

When you are living your chart, you allow yourself to evolve through what you build. You trust that even "imperfect" action carries wisdom. You recognize that your value is not in what you deliver — it is in who you are while delivering it.

And that shift changes everything.

Affirmation of Alignment

I create because it fulfills me, not because it proves my worth.

My mind is a gift, and I allow it to serve without carrying the weight of perfection.

4♧

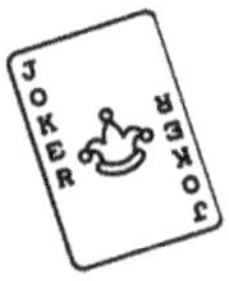

Matt & Joy Kahn

Life Chart

		K♤	8♢	10♧			
A♤	3♢	5♧	10♤	Q♧	A♧	3♡	☿
2♡	9♤	9♧	J♡	5♤	7♢	7♡	♀
HEALER'S CODE 8♧ MARS	J♤ VENUS	2♢ MERCURY	HEALER'S CODE 4♧ BIRTHCARD	6♡ MOON	K♢	K♡	♂
A♢ COSMIC LESSON	HEALER'S CODE A♡ COSMIC RESULT	HEALER'S CODE 8♤ PLUTO	HEALER'S CODE 10♢ NEPTUNE	10♡ URANUS	4♤ SATURN	6♢ JUPITER	♃
5♢	7♧	9♡	3♤	3♧	5♡	Q♢ TRANS-FORMED SELF	♄
J♢	K♧	2♧	7♤	9♢	J♧	Q♤	♅
Q♡	6♤	6♧	8♡	2♤	4♢	4♡	♆
♆	♅	♄	♃	♂	♀	☿	

Card #1: Your Birth Card 4♣

If you are a Four of Clubs, your mind is always working – always imagining what comes next. You carry an inner engine that turns ideas into structures, visions into systems, and inspiration into something real enough to hold, share, teach, and build upon. You don't just imagine what could be — you can see the steps. You can sense the sequence. You can feel the architecture of success as if it's already laid out in front of you.

This is one of the great gifts of your chart: you translate. You take what is invisible and give it form. You can gather wisdom from many places and package it in ways that actually reach people. You can hear a complex idea and see how it can be brought to life – literally. And because you can do this, you often find yourself synthesizing ideas for others. You can see frameworks, communities, family structures, teams, missions, businesses, movements. You don't just hold the vision; you hold the drive to fulfill it.

You also move faster than most. You can accomplish in a week what others would need a season to complete. There's a natural momentum in you — a willingness to do the work, to follow through, to keep going, to keep refining. And the world tends to respond to that. When you are aligned, success is not mysterious to you. You can see what will work, and you are willing to do what it takes to make it work.

But this is also where your edge lives.

Because with all this capacity, you can start to believe you are the one who must implement everything you see. You can start carrying the whole vision alone simply because you're capable. You can overwork, overbuild, and overcommit yourself into exhaustion — not because you don't love what you're doing, but because it can be hard to slow down when you are doing what you love. And because you can see every detail so clearly, it can feel easier to do it yourself than to slow down and bring others into the build.

Your fulfillment, though, does not live in solitary achievement. It lives inside a group dynamic. Your chart is deeply team-oriented. You are meant to lead within a collective — whether that is a family, a business, a community, or a creative partnership — where the vision is shared and the weight is distributed. Your brilliance expands when you let yourself be supported.

Card #2: Your Mars Card 8♣

Your Mars card, the Eight of Clubs, is where your discipline becomes undeniable. This is devotion as an inner force. When you choose something, you can stay with it. You can commit. You can build steadily, consistently, and with extraordinary stamina. This is one of the reasons your visions actually come to life — you don't just get inspired. You follow through.

And yet, this devotion comes with an important lesson: commitment is sacred, but it is not meant to become captivity.

The Eight of Clubs can sometimes stay longer than it truly wants to. You might sense the writing on the wall — a project is complete, an era is ending, your interest has moved — but your commitment keeps you there anyway. You may keep building simply because you already started. You may keep holding simply because others depend on you. You may keep pushing because you can.

This is where your Mars refinement begins: learning when to stay, and learning when to walk away. Not as a failure — as wisdom.

There is also a subtle attachment pattern that can show up here, especially because your mind sees outcomes so clearly. You might become attached to how something "should" unfold. You might grip the process, trying to ensure it lands exactly as you envision. But your Mars power grows when you remain committed to the vision without becoming rigid about the outcome.

Your devotion is meant to serve your life — not consume it.

Card #3: Your Neptune Card 10 ◆

Your Neptune card, the Ten of Diamonds, gives you an ability that many people secretly long for: you can see results in the physical world. You can envision completion. You can sense how something will turn out. You tend to attract stability when your energy is aligned, because your mind understands how to bring things to fruition.

But Neptune is also where a quiet illusion can form.

The Ten of Diamonds can begin to believe that if you just keep doing the same things, you will keep getting the same result. And sometimes that is true — when your mind, heart, and actions are moving together in one direction. But when your inner alignment shifts, repeating old behaviors doesn't recreate old success. It creates strain.

This is where your chart asks you to get honest about what your attention is truly devoted to right now.

Because your success moves with your attention. If your mind is leaning toward a new vision, but your actions are still chained to an old structure, you will feel disconnected — like your body is working for something your spirit is no longer choosing. And that disconnection can quietly drain you, even while everything "looks fine" on the outside.

The Ten of Diamonds invites a deeper kind of prosperity — one that comes from coherence. When your mind is focused. When your heart is in it. When your actions match what you actually want to create. And if your heart has moved, the solution isn't forcing yourself to keep producing — it may be allowing others to carry the old structure while you reorient toward what is calling you now.

This is the difference between wealth that sustains you and success that slowly depletes you.

Card #4: Your Pluto Card 8♠

Your Pluto card, the Eight of Spades, is a profound invitation into conscious transformation.

This card speaks to momentum — the life-force that builds when you've been walking a path for a while. You've created movement. You've built something. You've generated traction. Now Pluto asks: are you willing to let that momentum evolve into its next form?

Because the Eight of Spades reveals something crucial: transformation is already on the path. It is not always separate from what you're doing. Sometimes the path is meant to deepen. Sometimes it is meant to shift. Sometimes it is meant to end so a new direction can begin.

And the most important part is this: you get to choose it consciously.

The Eight of Spades offers you the opportunity to redirect your focus before the universe redirects it for you. Before life has to break something down to get your attention. Before the structure collapses under the weight of misalignment. This is not a threat — it's grace. It is your chart saying, "You are wise enough to pivot before force is required."

So when you feel the nudge — when you sense that your path is transforming — your work is to lean in early. To choose the change. To invest your attention into the new direction while it still feels fluid, while your spirit is still engaged, while the transition can be spacious instead of abrupt.

This is how your chart stays in ease.

Card #5: Your Cosmic Result Card A♥

Your Cosmic Result is the Ace of Hearts, and it is one of the most beautiful outcomes a mind like yours can reach: a new beginning rooted in joy, connection, and genuine fulfillment.

When you stop trying to carry everything alone, when you release attachment to outcomes, when you let your alignment lead the way — something opens. New people arrive. New opportunities surface. New ideas find you. Not because you chased them, but because your energy becomes available for what is next.

The Ace of Hearts is the return of play.

It is the return of love.

It is the feeling that you are not just building a mission — you are building a life that feels good to live inside. It is the moment when creation becomes relational again, when the work becomes a doorway to connection rather than a burden of responsibility.

And perhaps most importantly, it is the reminder that you are allowed to begin again. You are allowed to start fresh. You are allowed to devote yourself to new visions that make your heart come alive — not only to sustain what you have already built.

Integration — Your Healer's Code in Motion

The heart of your integration is learning to trust that your vision does not require self-sacrifice to become real.

You are not here to prove your capacity. You are here to build what matters with the right support, at the right pace, in the right season. Your chart is powerful — and that is exactly why you must practice discernment about where your energy goes. Not everything you can build is yours to build. Not everything you see needs to be implemented by you.

So how do you know if you are living your chart?

You can feel it in your relationship to momentum. When you are living your chart, you are productive without being frantic. You can create without compulsively over-functioning. You can delegate without feeling guilty. You can lead without gripping the whole vision in your hands. You stop equating exhaustion with devotion, and you begin measuring success by how sustainable your life feels.

You also know you are living your chart when you let your path transform before life forces transformation. When you honor the nudge early. When you admit, "My heart has shifted," and you listen to that truth instead of overriding it. In those moments, your energy returns. Your clarity sharpens. Your next chapter begins to reveal itself.

And you know you are living your chart when love comes back into the center of what you're building — not as decoration, but as the fuel. When your mind and your heart and your actions are on the same path, the work stops feeling like an endless list and starts feeling like a living creation. That is when your Ace of Hearts activates — and the builder becomes joyful again.

Affirmation of Alignment

I build with clarity and evolve with courage. My discipline serves my alignment. As I release what is complete, new opportunities of the heart unfold naturally.

5♣

Matt & Joy Kahn

Life Chart

		K♠	8♦	10♣		

A♠	3♦	HEALER'S CODE 5♣ BIRTHCARD	10♣ MOON	Q♣	A♣	3♥	☿
VENUS	MERCURY						
HEALER'S CODE 2♥ COSMIC RESULT	HEALER'S CODE 9♠ PLUTO	HEALER'S CODE 9♣ NEPTUNE	J♥ URANUS	5♠ SATURN	7♦ JUPITER	HEALER'S CODE 7♥ MARS	♀
8♣	J♠	2♦	4♣	6♥	K♦ TRANS-FORMED SELF	K♥ COSMIC LESSON	♂
A♦	A♥	8♣	10♦	10♥	4♠	6♦	♃
5♦	7♣	9♥	3♠	3♣	5♥	Q♦	♄
J♦	K♣	2♣	7♠	9♦	J♣	Q♣	♅
Q♥	6♠	6♣	8♥	2♣	4♦	4♥	♆
♆	♅	♄	♃	♂	♀	☿	

Card #1: Your Birth Card 5♣

If you are a Five of Clubs, you carry a kind of blessing that is not always visible from the outside, but it is unmistakable over time. There is something about you that moves through the material world with support. When you make a decision and act on it, doors tend to open. Resources tend to appear. The funding, the opportunity, the right connection, the unexpected yes — these things often follow you.

This does not mean life is effortless. It means you are resourced.

You are someone who gathers momentum quickly. You gather people. You gather ideas. You gather impact. You may become the center of a family system, the head of a business, the driving force of a mission. Your presence influences outcomes in ways you do not always recognize. You generate movement in the lives of others simply by deciding to move in your own.

And yet, the heartbeat of your chart is freedom.

You value the freedom to think independently. The freedom to build what you want. The freedom to pivot without asking permission. The freedom to follow your instincts. When you feel restricted, something in you tightens. When you feel autonomous, something in you flourishes.

This independence makes you powerful — and it can also isolate you. Because when you are confident in your direction, you do not always welcome input. You can become so clear in your own reasoning that collaboration feels like interference. But your journey is not about losing your independence. It is about softening the edges around it.

The Five of Clubs is blessed in the physical world, yes. But the deeper blessing is not money. It is influence. It is the ability to shape environments. And the refinement of your chart lies in remembering that your greatest impact is not measured by what you accumulate — it is measured by how open your heart remains while you build.

Card #2: Your Mars Card 7♥

Your Mars card, the Seven of Hearts, is where your strength becomes tenderness.

This is your greatest inner work and your greatest gift. Because while you may instinctively measure your effectiveness by results — by growth, by expansion, by financial success — the Seven of Hearts asks you to measure by love.

It invites you to look at your decisions through a higher emotional lens. Not just, "Will this work?" but, "Does this feel aligned with love?" Not just, "Will this expand my reach?" but, "Will this expand my heart?"

You are capable of building wealth. You are capable of building impact. But your chart matures when you recognize that the true currency you are here to circulate is devotion to the well-being of others. Not in a self-sacrificing way. In a conscious way.

Opening your heart does not weaken your independence. It strengthens it. It allows you to consider other perspectives without feeling threatened. It allows you to collaborate without losing yourself. It helps you see that love and prosperity are not competing values — they are meant to reinforce each other.

When you lean into this Mars energy, you begin to notice something subtle but profound: you do not have to push so hard in the material world. When your heart is engaged, the resources follow more naturally. Your life becomes less about proving your capability and more about embodying your care.

Card #3: Your Neptune Card 9♣

Your Neptune card gives you extraordinary mental foresight.

The Nine of Clubs allows you to play out entire futures in your mind. You can see the path ahead. You can anticipate outcomes. You can run scenarios internally with stunning clarity. This makes you strategic. It makes you prepared. It makes you difficult to surprise.

But this same ability can become a trap.

Because when you can see every potential ending, you may hesitate to begin. Or you may overanalyze the cost of leaving something that no longer fulfills you. You might mentally calculate every possible outcome of staying versus going — and measure those outcomes primarily by material impact.

This is where your discernment must deepen.

The Nine of Clubs is not here to guarantee certainty. It is here to show you potential. It is here to help you know when something has reached completion. It is here to assist you in letting go before stagnation sets in.

When you filter your mental projections only through financial metrics, you can override your emotional truth. But when you allow your heart to evaluate the path alongside your mind, something harmonizes. You begin to ask not just, "What will this earn?" but, "What will this nourish?"

And that question changes your trajectory.

Your Neptune invites you into continual transformation — not driven by fear of loss, but guided by clarity of fulfillment.

Card #4: Your Pluto Card 9♠

Your Pluto card is the deep current beneath your life.

The Nine of Spades speaks of cycles completing. Not only when something fails — but when something succeeds. You are not meant to cling to what once worked simply because it worked. You are meant to evolve beyond it.

There will be seasons in your life when you walk away from something that is thriving. Something that others would call successful. And you may not even have language for why. You will simply know it is complete.

This is not recklessness. It is transformation.

Your chart is designed for periodic reinvention. Every several years, something in you will shift. A new vision will emerge. A new direction will call. And if you resist that call out of attachment to what you have built, life will gently — and sometimes not so gently — create the shift for you.

The gift of the Nine of Spades is choice.

You are given the opportunity to complete cycles consciously. To say, "This chapter has fulfilled its purpose," even if it looks stable from the outside. When you do this from alignment rather than reaction, your transitions become graceful. Your momentum transfers instead of collapses.

Falling in love with endings is one of your greatest liberations.

Card #5: Your Cosmic Result Card 2♥

When you integrate your chart, your Cosmic Result unfolds as reciprocity.

The Two of Hearts is mutual love. Mutual devotion. Mutual recognition. It is the experience of being met — not only materially, but emotionally. It is the feeling that the love you extend outward returns to you without you chasing it.

For much of your life, you may have believed that if you achieved enough, built enough, provided enough, love would naturally follow. And while success may have brought admiration or validation, it does not always bring intimacy.

The Two of Hearts is different.

It is love mirrored. It is partnership that feels equal. It is collaboration that nourishes instead of drains. And this reciprocity becomes possible when you stop leading with outcome and begin leading with heart.

When you value love as highly as you value freedom, your world reorganizes. Relationships soften. Connections deepen. The sense of being emotionally unsupported begins to dissolve.

Your blessed material flow remains — but it is no longer the primary metric of your life. Love becomes the measure. And the love you give becomes the love you live inside of.

Integration — Your Healer's Code in Motion

The essence of your integration is this: you are here to build freely, but not independently from love.

You are capable of tremendous impact. You can generate resources. You can influence environments. You can create success in tangible ways. But your chart finds peace when your independence and your heart move together.

So how do you know if you are living your chart?

You know because your decisions feel expansive rather than defensive. You know because you can pivot without panic. You know because you no longer measure your worth by the numbers attached to your name. You feel it when your ambition softens into purpose. When you act from desire rather than proving.

You also know you are living your chart when endings feel natural instead of threatening. When you can release something that has run its course without spiraling into over-analysis. When you trust that what has supported you before will support you again — because your alignment, not your attachment, is the true source of your blessing.

And perhaps most importantly, you know you are living your chart when reciprocity shows up. When you experience being loved in return. When collaboration feels safe. When your heart feels as supported as your vision.

That is when your life becomes both blessed and balanced.

Affirmation of Alignment

I lead with freedom, and I choose love as my compass.

The support I seek flows to me as I open my heart.

6♣

Matt & Joy Kahn

Life Chart

		K♠ SATURN	8♦ JUPITER	10♣ MARS (HEALER'S CODE)			
A♠	3♦ TRANS-FORMED SELF	5♣ COSMIC LESSON	10♦ COSMIC RESULT (HEALER'S CODE)	Q♣ PLUTO (HEALER'S CODE)	A♣ NEPTUNE (HEALER'S CODE)	3♥ URANUS	☿
2♥	9♠	9♣	J♥	5♠	7♦	7♥	♀
8♣	J♠	2♦	4♣	6♥	K♦	K♥	♂
A♦	A♥	8♠	10♦	10♥	4♠	6♦	♃
5♦	7♣	9♥	3♠	3♣	5♥	Q♦	♄
J♦	K♣	2♣	7♠	9♦	J♣	Q♠	♅
Q♥ VENUS	6♠ MERCURY	6♣ BIRTHCARD (HEALER'S CODE)	8♥ MOON	2♠	4♦	4♥	♆
♆	♅	♄	♃	♂	♀	☿	

Card #1: Your Birth Card 6♣

If you are the Six of Clubs, you were born with a mind that seeks balance.

You are one of the most naturally discerning cards in the mental realm. You can take in information without immediately drowning in it. You can evaluate details, sense patterns, and understand what is actually happening beneath the surface of a situation. When others feel overwhelmed by data, you begin sorting it. When others are confused, you begin organizing. Your nervous system, at its best, does not panic in complexity. It looks for balance.

You value harmony over disruption. You do not enjoy unnecessary conflict. You do not make decisions lightly, especially when those decisions will ripple into the lives of people you care about. You can often see exactly what needs to change — but hesitate because you are aware of the emotional cost. You want everyone to be okay. You want the shift to feel smooth. You want transformation to be gentle.

But here is the deeper truth of your chart: your growth is activated by decisiveness.

The Six of Clubs can spend too long debating between good options. You can circle ideas instead of choosing one. You can weigh every variable instead of declaring the vision. And while your discernment is a gift, your power is released the moment you say, "This is the direction."

When you know your larger vision, information stops overwhelming you. It becomes supportive. Details become tools instead of distractions. The tension between ideas dissolves because they now have a central point to organize around.

You are not here to avoid disruption at all costs. You are here to lead transformation with steadiness.

Card #2: Your Mars Card 10♣

Mars reveals how your passion moves.

For you, passion expresses itself through contribution. The Ten of Clubs carries leadership energy grounded in knowledge. You are capable of holding a vast amount of information at once and then translating it into strategy. You do not just see ideas; you see implementation.

This makes you a natural consultant, mentor, or guide. You can analyze a situation and explain how it can evolve. You can help others see the path from where they are to where they want to be. When focused, you are strategic and powerful.

You also have a strong work ethic. Once you commit to something, you give fully. You are willing to take responsibility for outcomes. You can elevate projects and help organizations move to a new level.

But here is the nuance. If you allow yourself to drown in minutia, your brilliance can scatter. The Ten of Clubs must anchor itself in a higher vision. Without that overarching direction, the details become heavy. With it, they become tools.

As a leader, this distinction matters. When you hold the bigger picture clearly, your ability to implement becomes unstoppable. When you lose the vision, the workload can feel endless.

Card #3: Your Neptune Card A♣

Your Neptune card brings an endless stream of inspiration.

The Ace of Clubs is new ideas, new insights, new sparks of possibility arriving constantly. Your mind does not run out of creativity. It does not run out of perspective. If anything, it can feel like too much — too many concepts, too many directions, too many exciting beginnings.

This is a profound gift, especially in service to others. You can intuit solutions. You can offer fresh perspectives. You can see options no one else has considered. In a coaching or healing space, this makes you incredibly resourceful.

But for yourself, it can feel overwhelming.

You may feel pulled toward multiple paths at once. You may believe you need to follow every inspired thought. You may begin something new before something else has settled. And then the mind, instead of feeling balanced, begins to fragment.

The Ace of Clubs does not require you to chase every idea. It simply reminds you that inspiration is available.

When you are focused, those ideas will organize themselves around your chosen direction. When you are decisive, inspiration becomes fuel instead of distraction.

Your task is not to limit your ideas. It is to choose which ones deserve your devotion in this season.

Card #4: Your Pluto Card Q♣

Your Pluto card reveals the deeper transformation of your mind.

The Queen of Clubs is mental mastery matured through experience. It is wisdom that comes not just from gathering information, but from embodying it. This card asks you to step fully into your intellectual authority — not as someone who debates endlessly, but as someone who trusts their knowing.

You are capable of leading with clarity. Of speaking truth with composure. Of guiding others through complexity without being entangled in it. But this requires something of you: sovereignty.

The Queen of Clubs does not defer endlessly. It does not soften every edge to preserve harmony. It listens, evaluates, and then chooses.

Your transformation lies in trusting your inner voice more than the external noise. In recognizing that you are allowed to make decisions that may disrupt others — not from recklessness, but from alignment. In allowing yourself to be seen as intellectually powerful without shrinking to keep others comfortable.

When you embrace this Pluto energy, your mind stops wavering. It steadies. You stop seeking constant validation for your choices. You begin moving with quiet authority.

And others feel that shift.

Card #5: Your Cosmic Result Card 10♠

Your Cosmic Result is powerful integration.

The Ten of Spades is a life transformed through decisive mental leadership. It is the ability to move through major changes without being shattered by them. It is the resilience that comes from choosing your direction instead of waiting for life to choose it for you.

When you learn to prioritize vision over harmony, when you allow your leadership to mature, when you focus your ideas instead of scattering them — your life accelerates.

Transformation does not destabilize you. It strengthens you.

The Ten of Spades is not about avoiding endings. It is about walking through them consciously. It is about allowing cycles to close so that something more aligned can emerge. And because your mind is steady and your vision is clear, you can guide others through these thresholds as well.

You become someone who does not fear complexity. You navigate it.

Integration — Your Healer's Code in Motion

The heart of your integration is learning that harmony is not the same as avoidance.

You are here to bring balance, yes. But you are not here to suppress necessary change. You are here to decide. To lead. To allow your mental clarity to activate transformation rather than delay it.

So how do you know if you are living your chart?

You can feel it in your decisiveness. When you are living your chart, you do not circle endlessly between options. You choose a vision and let the details support it. You do not micromanage everyone's emotional response to your choices. You trust that disruption can be part of growth.

You also know you are aligned when inspiration feels energizing instead of overwhelming. When your ideas feel focused rather than scattered. When leadership feels natural rather than heavy.

And you know you are living your chart when major transitions no longer frighten you. When you trust your ability to think clearly through change. When you recognize that your mind, anchored in vision, is one of your greatest allies.

That is when your balance becomes powerful instead of passive.

Affirmation of Alignment

I choose with clarity and lead with wisdom. My ideas serve a higher vision. As I speak and act decisively, transformation strengthens me and those I guide.

7♣

Matt & Joy Kahn — *Life Chart*

		K♠	8♦	10♣			
A♠	3♦	5♣	10♠	Q♣	A♣	3♥	☿
2♥	9♠	9♣	J♥	5♠	7♦	7♥	♀
8♣	J♠	2♦	4♣	6♥	K♦	K♥	♂
A♦	A♥	8♠	10♦	10♥	4♠	6♦	♃
5♦ MERCURY	7♣ HEALER'S CODE BIRTHCARD	9♥ MOON	3♠	3♣	5♥	Q♦	♄
J♦ HEALER'S CODE PLUTO	K♣ HEALER'S CODE NEPTUNE	2♣ URANUS	7♠ SATURN	9♦ JUPITER	J♣ HEALER'S CODE MARS	Q♠ VENUS	♅
Q♥	6♠	6♣	8♥	2♠ TRANS-FORMED SELF	4♦ COSMIC LESSON	4♥ HEALER'S CODE COSMIC RESULT	♆
♆	♅	♄	♃	♂	♀	☿	

Card #1: Your Birth Card 7♣

If you are the Seven of Clubs, you were born with a mind that does not stop at the surface.

You do not simply want information. You want understanding. The Clubs suit governs thought, language, and learning, and the Seven introduces depth, discernment, and spiritual questioning. Together, they create the seeker-teacher of the deck.

You are not satisfied with knowing *what* works. You want to understand *why* it works. You think something through from multiple angles, and once you grasp it, you feel compelled to integrate it into your own lived experience before sharing it. Knowledge for you is not theoretical. It must become embodied.

This is why teaching often becomes a natural extension of who you are. You are continually gathering insight, refining it, and translating it into language that others can use. Whether you stand on stages, write books, build curriculum, or simply guide your family, you are wired to transmit wisdom.

There is also something quietly spiritual about your mind. After enough analysis, you begin to see the limits of analysis. You recognize that some truths cannot be fully explained, only experienced. This awareness softens your intellect and opens you to something beyond logic — not instead of it, but alongside it.

As a healer, coach, or leader, your maturation comes when you stop trying to master knowledge and begin stewarding it. You are not here to know everything. You are here to continually deepen your understanding and share what is true *for you now*, with integrity and openness.

Card #2: Your Mars Card J♣

Mars reveals how your passion moves.

For you, passion expresses itself through communication. The Jack of Clubs is the student-teacher energy. It wants to speak, write, present, and articulate what it has discovered. It does not want to hoard wisdom. It wants to test it in the world.

This gives you courage. You are willing to share insights before everything is perfectly polished. You are willing to explore ideas publicly. You can bring complex truths into accessible language.

But the Jack also carries a subtle lesson. It must remain curious. It must remember that what it knows today may expand tomorrow. If it becomes rigid or attached to being "right," its growth stalls.

The highest expression of this Mars energy is intellectual humility paired with bold expression. You can speak with authority while admitting you are still learning. You can guide others without positioning yourself as the final authority.

As a leader, this is magnetic. People trust someone who shares honestly and evolves visibly. Your voice becomes a living bridge between insight and integration.

Card #3: Your Neptune Card K♣

Neptune represents the dream that pulls you forward.

Your Neptune card gives you a vision of intellectual leadership. The King of Clubs sees the larger architecture of ideas. You can envision building kingdoms of knowledge — businesses, schools, movements, systems of thought. You see yourself leading through wisdom.

This is not accidental. You are capable of holding big-picture understanding. You can gather information, synthesize it, and create frameworks that others follow.

But the King must be careful of isolation. There is a temptation to believe you see more clearly than others, to feel responsible for holding all the answers. While you may often have advanced understanding, true leadership requires collaboration.

As a healer, coach, or leader, your expansion happens when you allow others to contribute to the vision. You are not meant to carry the entire intellectual empire alone. You are meant to guide while remaining open to learning.

When humility and authority merge, your leadership stabilizes.

Card #4: Your Pluto Card J♦

Your Pluto card brings you into the fire of integrity.

The Jack of Diamonds is magnetism. Persuasion. The ability to communicate value so clearly that others want to say yes. This is a rare gift — the capacity to move energy through language. To inspire action. To invite commitment. To create exchange.

And Pluto makes this sacred.

Because the deeper lesson here is not whether you can persuade — you can. The lesson is what you will persuade people toward.

When you are aligned, this energy becomes a form of devotion. You speak up for what matters. You stand behind what you believe in. You share the value of something truthfully and confidently without manipulating anyone. You become a voice that advocates for what is genuinely beneficial — and your influence becomes a blessing.

But when you are not aligned, this same gift can tempt you to push an agenda. To convince someone to do what you want instead of what is right for all involved. And that is why this Pluto card holds you accountable. It asks you to live in truth.

The more you choose integrity, the more your entire chart stabilizes. Your voice becomes trusted. Your leadership becomes respected. Your influence becomes clean in the deepest sense — not polished, but honest.

This Pluto is not here to restrict you. It is here to refine you into a teacher whose power can be trusted.

Card #5: Your Cosmic Result Card 4🩶

Your Cosmic Result is the promise of devotion made real.

The Four of Hearts is commitment. Stable partnership. Loving foundations that last. It is the experience of relationships that are not built on performance, but on truth. It is the reward of being a conduit for love that can actually hold.

This result card often shows up as a life where connection becomes central — not just romantic connection, but friendship, family, community, and bonds that deepen over time. When you live in integrity, your relationships mirror that integrity. When you lead with truth, you attract people who value truth.

And this card also speaks to your unique reward as a healer, coach, or leader: you are deeply nourished by seeing lives become more stable through love.

You may help families repair. Partners return to devotion. Teams become healthier. Communities become more grounded. You don't just teach ideas. You teach what makes life work.

And when you do, your life becomes a reflection of that same foundation.

Integration — Your Healer's Code in Motion

The integration of your chart is learning to trust that your wisdom is meant to be shared before it is finished.

You are here to learn, yes. But you are also here to speak. To teach. To become a steady voice in a world that often feels flooded with information and starving for truth.

So how do you know if you are living your chart?

You know because your mind no longer uses learning as a delay. You still study, still refine, still seek deeper truth — but you don't hide behind it. You take risks with your voice. You share what you know now, and you stay open to upgrading what you share later. You feel the difference immediately: your energy moves. Your confidence grows. Your teaching becomes more alive because it is rooted in lived experience, not theoretical perfection.

You also know you are living your chart when leadership feels collaborative instead of isolating. When you can hold vision without believing you must hold everything. When you remain curious even in your authority. When your students, clients, team, or family feel invited into wisdom rather than managed by it.

And you know you are living your chart when your influence feels honest. When you promote only what you believe in. When your persuasion becomes service. When your integrity becomes the foundation of your success.

That is when your Four of Hearts activates — and your life begins to reflect the kind of love you are here to teach.

Affirmation of Alignment

I share what I know with courage and humility, and I remain open to deeper truth.

My voice serves love, and my integrity creates lasting connection.

8♣

Matt & Joy Kahn

Life Chart

K♠	8♦	10♣

A♠	3♦	5♣	10♠	Q♣	A♣	3♥	☿
2♥	9♠	9♣	J♥	5♠	7♦	7♥	♀
HEALER'S CODE 8♣ BIRTHCARD	J♠ MOON	2♦	4♣	6♥	K♦	K♥	♂
HEALER'S CODE A♦ NEPTUNE	A♥ URANUS	8♠ SATURN	10♦ JUPITER	HEALER'S CODE 10♥ MARS	4♠ VENUS	6♦ MERCURY	♃
5♦	7♣	9♥	3♠ TRANS- FORMED SELF	3♣ COSMIC LESSON	HEALER'S CODE 5♥ COSMIC RESULT	HEALER'S CODE Q♦ PLUTO	♄
J♦	K♣	2♣	7♠	9♦	J♣	Q♠	⛢
Q♥	6♠	6♣	8♥	2♠	4♦	4♥	♆
♆	⛢	♄	♃	♂	♀	☿	

Card #1: Your Birth Card 8♣

If you are an Eight of Clubs, devotion is built into your bones.

You do not approach life halfway. When you choose a path, you stay with it. When you commit to a project, you see it through. When you believe in something, you give it your mind, your time, and your loyalty. There is an extraordinary steadiness in you that others depend on. You are reliable. You are resilient. You are someone who can sustain momentum long after others would have drifted away.

This staying power is not small. It is one of the reasons prosperity, well-being, and stability often follow you. You do not abandon what matters at the first sign of difficulty. You are willing to go down the rabbit hole. To understand. To refine. To keep going until something feels fully expressed.

And yet, this same devotion can become confinement if you are not attentive.

Because while you long for continual transformation, you also resist changing course. You want growth without disruption. Expansion without letting go. You would prefer to evolve the path you are on rather than leave it entirely. So you hold steady. You remain loyal. You stay committed — sometimes even when your spirit has begun to shift.

This can create a quiet heartbreak.

You may watch others move on while you remain. You may feel the sting of being left behind, not because you lacked value, but because your loyalty kept you rooted while the season was changing. Over time, you begin to realize that devotion is sacred — but it must breathe.

The Eight of Clubs is not here to cling. It is here to commit consciously, and then release consciously when the path has completed its purpose.

Card #2: Your Mars Card 10♥

Your Mars card reveals what your heart truly desires beneath all that devotion.

The Ten of Hearts longs for shared joy. For gathering. For laughter. For a life surrounded by people you love. There is a part of you that wants to experience community not just as responsibility, but as play. You are not meant to walk your path alone. You are meant to celebrate it with others.

This is where the tension begins.

Because while your birth card wants to stay steady, your heart wants movement with people. It wants shared transformation. It wants expansion that includes others in a dynamic way. And if you remain loyal to a structure long after others have shifted, you may feel alone — even if you are still "successful."

Your Mars asks you to loosen your grip just enough to allow connection to grow.

It asks you to notice when something is nearing completion, and to be willing to step into the next chapter with community rather than remaining attached to what was. It asks you to risk new circles, new rooms, new conversations, even when the old ones feel safe.

Your devotion is beautiful. But your heart is asking for evolution within it.

Card #3: Your Neptune Card A ♦

Your Neptune card introduces a subtle but powerful invitation.

The Ace of Diamonds brings new material opportunities. New paths. New beginnings in the physical world. New ventures, new environments, new investments of time and energy. You are often presented with fresh possibilities — sometimes unexpectedly — that could shift your entire trajectory.

And here is where your chart becomes fascinating.

You may bring something new into your existing path, rather than allowing yourself to start an entirely new one. You might renovate the room instead of moving houses. You might update the project instead of releasing it. You might surround yourself with new aesthetics, new tools, new symbols of change — while keeping the deeper structure intact.

This can create the illusion of transformation without requiring it.

You may convince yourself that updating your environment is the same as evolving your life. But the Ace of Diamonds is not just decoration. It is an invitation.

It is asking you to follow the new idea further. To let it grow. To allow it to become tangible. To risk building something unfamiliar instead of only refining what you already know.

This does not mean abandoning loyalty. It means allowing new value to emerge in your world without fearing what must end to make space for it.

Card #4: Your Pluto Card Q ♦

Your Pluto card is where the real initiation occurs.

The Queen of Diamonds demands decisiveness in the material realm. It asks you to assess what truly belongs in your life — and what does not. It invites you to move energy rather than letting it stagnate. To complete cycles. To bring new resources in. To allow exchange to flow.

This is not always comfortable for you.

Because cutting something out can feel like betrayal of your own devotion. And yet, the Queen teaches you that honoring a season's end is not disloyal — it is mature. It is not rejection — it is recognition.

When you refuse to allow movement, life may create it for you. Sometimes through health signals. Sometimes through financial shifts. Sometimes through relational tension that becomes impossible to ignore. Not as punishment, but as redirection.

The Queen of Diamonds is not here to take from you. It is here to balance you.

It is asking you to bring new experiences in as you release old ones. Not to cut without replenishing. Not to cling without refreshing. But to let the material world reflect the transformation your spirit is already craving.

When you lean into this energy consciously, your life flows. When you resist, stagnation builds pressure.

Card #5: Your Cosmic Result Card — 5

Your Cosmic Result is emotional revitalization.

The Five of Hearts is freedom in love. It is renewed passion. It is the feeling of being alive again in your connections. When you allow change, when you release what is complete, when you let your life breathe — your emotional world reawakens.

You begin to experience love as dynamic rather than static. Relationships feel lighter. Gatherings feel joyful again. Your heart no longer feels like it is waiting for something to shift — it is actively participating in that shift.

The Five of Hearts is the reminder that emotional fulfillment requires movement.

When you avoid change, love can feel stagnant. When you embrace transformation, love becomes exciting. This result card is not asking you to abandon your devotion. It is asking you to let devotion evolve so that joy can return to the center of your experience.

Integration — Your Healer's Code in Motion

The integration of your chart is learning that loyalty does not require immobility.

You are here to stay with what matters. To build. To sustain. To see things through. But you are not here to remain in something simply because you once chose it. You are allowed to complete. You are allowed to begin again.

So how do you know if you are living your chart?

You know because your devotion feels expansive rather than heavy. You are still committed — but not confined. You can feel when a season is ending, and you honor it without resentment. You allow new ideas to take root instead of decorating the old ones. You make material decisions that reflect your inner growth.

You also know you are aligned when your relationships feel vibrant. When laughter returns. When you no longer feel like the only one staying while everyone else moves forward. When you are willing to evolve alongside the people you love.

And perhaps most importantly, you know you are living your chart when change feels like renewal instead of loss. When you trust that your loyalty is strong enough to survive transformation.

That is when your Five of Hearts awakens — and devotion becomes joy.

Affirmation of Alignment

I honor my devotion and embrace change with wisdom. I release what is complete and welcome new beginnings. As I evolve, my heart experiences renewed freedom and joy.

9♣

Matt & Joy Kahn

Life Chart

	K♠	8♦	10♣		

A♠	3♦	5♣	10♠	Q♣	A♣	3♡	☿
2♡ VENUS	9♠ MERCURY	**HEALER'S CODE** 9♣ BIRTHCARD	J♡ MOON	5♠	7♦	7♡	♀
HEALER'S CODE 8♣ COSMIC RESULT	**HEALER'S CODE** J♠ PLUTO	**HEALER'S CODE** 2♦ NEPTUNE	4♣ URANUS	6♡ SATURN	K♦ JUPITER	**HEALER'S CODE** K♡ MARS	♂
A♦	A♡	8♠	10♦	10♡	4♠ TRANS-FORMED SELF	6♦ COSMIC LESSON	♃
5♦	7♣	9♡	3♠	3♣	5♡	Q♦	♄
J♦	K♣	2♣	7♠	9♦	J♣	Q♠	♅
Q♡	6♠	6♣	8♡	2♣	4♦	4♡	♆
♆	♅	♄	♃	♂	♀	☿	

Card #1: Your Birth Card 9♣

If you are a Nine of Clubs, you carry a mind that is always nearing completion… and yet rarely feels complete.

You are here to fulfill ideas. To bring mental chapters to their end. To turn learning into mastery. And when you are aligned, you are capable of becoming an expert — not in the shallow sense of knowing facts, but in the deeper sense of living inside a subject long enough that it becomes part of you.

But the Nine of Clubs can feel scattered, not because you lack intelligence, but because you are carrying so much.

Your nature is expansive. Your chart holds a balance of multiple energies, which can create the feeling that you should understand everything. You take in information and make sense of it quickly. You see how ideas can be applied. You can connect concepts across disciplines. And yet, because you can see so many paths, you may struggle to choose one.

This is where the emotional undercurrent often enters.

There can be a longing inside you that is not purely mental — the longing to be loved, the longing to be valuable, the belief that you must sacrifice yourself for others in order to belong. And when that longing becomes the hidden driver, your focus dissolves. You may downplay your career or your calling, even though your mind is sharp enough to create something extraordinary.

You may find yourself thinking endlessly… without taking action.

Or choosing a direction… and then becoming bored because another idea pulls your attention.

The deeper truth is that you need two things at once. You need structure that stabilizes your life. And you need a path you genuinely believe in — something your heart can pour itself into, something with a deeper "why" that makes your mind willing to stay.

This is not a flaw. It is the initiation of your chart.

You are here to discover what you love enough to finish.

Card #2: Your Mars Card K♥

Your Mars card is the part of you that makes everything personal — in the most sacred way.

The King of Hearts moves through life with care. It wants to support people. It wants to protect what matters. It wants to lead from devotion, not from ego. When you are acting from this energy, your best work is always rooted in relationship. You are here to bring ideas into the world that you love, and to gather people around those ideas with sincerity.

You lead by caring.

But this is also where you must become discerning.

Because the King of Hearts can give too much attention to too many people. It can try to support everyone. It can confuse love with limitless availability. And when that happens, your focus fractures further. You become emotionally responsible for outcomes that are not yours to carry, and your own calling gets postponed.

Your Mars is asking you to place your care intentionally.

When you decide where your passion is meant to flow, your heart will take you all the way. You will commit. You will build. You will create a life that feels both purposeful and human.

But it begins with one courageous act: choosing what you will love on purpose, instead of loving everything by default.

Card #3: Your Neptune Card 2 ◆

Your Neptune card reveals one of your greatest gifts: you can see partnership.

The Two of Diamonds understands exchange. It recognizes opportunity. It sees how two forces can come together and create a result that benefits everyone involved. You often have an intuitive sense for what will work financially. You can recognize how expertise, collaboration, and timing can become prosperity.

And this is also where the test lives.

Because when you can see so many ways to make something work, it becomes tempting to choose paths you don't actually love.

You might take a role because it pays well. You might enter a partnership because the numbers look good. You might build something because it is a "sure bet." And if your heart is not in it, the consequence is not just boredom — it can become deep exhaustion. A kind of quiet self-betrayal. Over time, it can harden into disillusionment.

This is why your chart asks for one essential refinement: just because you can doesn't mean you should.

You are meant to develop expertise in something that nourishes you. And when you do, your ability to partner becomes a blessing rather than a compromise. You can absolutely accept support from the material world — but your heart must understand the bigger picture of why you are doing what you're doing.

When your heart and your money are moving in the same direction, your life becomes steady.

When they are not, even abundance can feel like a trap.

Card #4: Your Pluto Card J♠

Your Pluto card is the threshold.

The Jack of Spades asks a question that can change your entire trajectory: are you willing to be transformed by what you choose?

Often the Nine of Clubs wants certainty. A guaranteed outcome. A path that is safe. But your breakthrough does not come from safety. It comes from evolution. It comes from choosing a direction that requires you to grow into it.

This Pluto energy invites you into a kind of courageous apprenticeship.

To commit to the learning process not as a delay, but as a devotion. To let the challenges of your path shape you into wisdom. To take everything you know — every insight, every mistake, every hard-earned realization — and allow it to become the next level of your mastery.

This is where the ceiling breaks.

That invisible cap you may have felt — the sense that you can't quite stabilize your calling, can't quite complete what you start, can't quite fully claim your expertise — begins to dissolve when you say yes to transformation.

And then something remarkable happens: your mind stops scattering, because it has found its initiatory path.

Card #5: Your Cosmic Result Card 8♣

Your Cosmic Result is devotion made stable.

The Eight of Clubs is the ability to stay. To commit. To build a life that feels secure, nourishing, and spacious enough to enjoy. It is the settling of your mind into a path that no longer needs constant reinvention.

This is not stagnation.

This is peace.

When you choose a calling that you love, when you partner wisely, when you allow your work to transform you instead of seeking only a sure bet — your life becomes less reactive. You stop leaving everything at the first sign of restlessness. You stop chasing the next idea as a substitute for finishing the one that matters.

You become someone who can go the distance.

And in that devotion, you begin to experience the fulfillment your chart has always been reaching for.

Integration — Your Healer's Code in Motion

The heart of your integration is learning that your mind will settle when your heart is honest.

You are not here to do everything. You are here to do something deeply.

So how do you know if you are living your chart?

You can feel it in your focus. When you are living your chart, your mind stops ricocheting between possibilities. You begin choosing with clarity. You start taking action instead of only thinking. You recognize that your many interests were never proof of indecision — they were the training ground of your intelligence.

You also know you are aligned when your relationships feel supportive rather than consuming. When your care is directed instead of scattered. When you stop sacrificing yourself to be loved, and instead let love meet you where you truly are.

And you know you are living your chart when you choose partnerships that honor your heart. When money is no longer the reason, but a byproduct of devotion. When you are willing to be transformed by your path, even if it is not the easiest one.

That is when your Eight of Clubs activates — and your life becomes steady, not because you forced it to be, but because you finally chose what you were meant to stay with.

Affirmation of Alignment

I choose what I love, and I commit to becoming who it requires me to be.

My devotion creates stability, and my heart guides my success.

10♣

	VENUS	MERCURY	BIRTHCARD (HEALER'S CODE)				
	K♠	8♦	10♣				

A♠ (HEALER'S CODE) COSMIC RESULT	3♦ (HEALER'S CODE) PLUTO	5♣ (HEALER'S CODE) NEPTUNE	10♣ URANUS	Q♣ SATURN	A♣ JUPITER	3♥ (HEALER'S CODE) MARS	☿
2♥	9♠	9♣	J♥	5♠	7♦ TRANSFORMED SELF	7♥ COSMIC LESSON	♀
8♣	J♠	2♦	4♣	6♥	K♦	K♥	♂
A♦	A♥	8♠	10♦	10♥	4♠	6♦	♃
5♦	7♣	9♥	3♠	3♣	5♥	Q♦	♄
J♦	K♣	2♣	7♠	9♦	J♣	Q♠	♅
Q♥ MOON	6♠	6♣	8♥	2♠	4♦	4♥	♆
♆	♅	♄	♃	♂	♀	☿	

Card #1: Your Birth Card 10♣

If you are a Ten of Clubs, you are designed to see from the highest vantage point.

You do not simply gather information — you synthesize it. You can look at complexity and extract the core truth. You can observe details and organize them into something meaningful. Where others see fragments, you see patterns. Where others feel overwhelmed, you instinctively search for the higher perspective.

This gives you a kind of quiet authority.

You are capable of attracting success in many forms because you understand how systems work. You can build strong family foundations. You can cultivate meaningful partnerships. You can lead organizations or communities with a natural sense of structure. There is something about your presence that stabilizes vision and gives it direction.

And yet, one of your deeper shadows is self-doubt.

You may see clearly — but question your own seeing. You may hear the truth — but wonder if you imagined it. You can put the power in others simply because they seem more certain. Meanwhile, your own perception remains under-claimed.

The Ten of Clubs is here to own what it sees.

When you trust your perspective, your leadership becomes steady. When you doubt it, your mind begins to spiral through options, possibilities, and hypothetical outcomes. The very brilliance that allows you to rise above complexity can become trapped in analysis.

You are not here to overthink your vision. You are here to embody it.

Card #2: Your Mars Card 3♥

Your Mars card reveals the hidden key to unlocking your entire chart: play.

The Three of Hearts carries celebration. Expression. Creative joy. It wants you in motion. It wants you laughing, dancing, speaking, performing, organizing gatherings, creating experiences that others want to be part of. There is a theatrical quality to your energy when you are aligned — not artificial, but radiant.

When you approach your goals from a place of play, everything lightens.

Your mind becomes a support instead of a critic. Your leadership becomes magnetic instead of pressured. You begin creating not from obligation, but from delight. And when that happens, others naturally gather around you.

But this is also where vulnerability enters.

The Three of Hearts can worry about being judged. About not being liked. About being misunderstood. You may overthink how your expression will land. You may hesitate before stepping fully into visibility. And when you hesitate, the energy that longs to move begins to stagnate.

Your Mars invites you to move anyway.

To let play interrupt overthinking. To let celebration interrupt self-doubt. To remember that your charisma is not something you manufacture — it is something that appears when you stop censoring your joy.

Card #3: Your Neptune Card 5♣

Your Neptune card intensifies your mental processing.

The Five of Clubs brings decisiveness to your thought world. It asks you to choose what matters most and release the rest. You are capable of considering many options, but you are not meant to carry them all indefinitely. This card challenges you to pare down.

You may be tempted to wait for the perfect path before committing. To sever one direction only when you are certain the next will succeed. But the deeper lesson is not about perfection. It is about alignment.

When you walk away from what you do not love — not because it might fail, but because it does not nourish you — your life reorganizes quickly. Wealth, opportunity, and momentum follow clarity. Not endless evaluation.

The Five of Clubs also reminds you that decisiveness generates prosperity. When your mind stops scattering and starts choosing, your energy consolidates. And when your energy consolidates, your impact multiplies.

The invitation is simple, but not always easy: choose what you truly want, and release what you are tolerating.

Card #4: Your Pluto Card 3♦

Your Pluto card brings the lesson into the body.

The Three of Diamonds is physical creativity. It wants your energy moving through tangible expression. Crafting. Building. Designing. Speaking. Creating something material from your ideas. If you feel inspired but do not act, the energy has nowhere to go — and it can turn into anxiety.

This is one of the central loops of your chart.

Overthinking without creating produces tension. Tension without expression produces worry. Worry without action feeds more overthinking.

The way through is movement.

When you direct your creativity into something physical — whether that is building a program, hosting a gathering, decorating a space, initiating a conversation, or simply moving your body — the stagnant energy clears. Your nervous system recalibrates. Your mind softens.

The Three of Diamonds teaches you that your thoughts are not meant to live only in your head. They are meant to become something real. When you create consistently, anxiety loses its grip.

Card #5: Your Cosmic Result Card A♠

Your Cosmic Result is transformation embodied.

The Ace of Spades is powerful. It brings new life cycles. New identities. New beginnings that feel profound rather than superficial. When you integrate your chart — when you trust your vision, embrace play, choose decisively, and create physically — you become someone who can guide others through change.

You are able to help people cross thresholds.

Your leadership becomes less about analysis and more about initiation. Others feel that you have walked through your own overthinking and emerged clearer. They trust you because you have faced your own mind and chosen movement over paralysis.

The Ace of Spades does not simply bring change. It brings awakening.

And when you are aligned, you carry that awakening into every room you enter.

Integration — Your Healer's Code in Motion

The heart of your integration is learning that your brilliance does not need to be proven — it needs to be expressed.

You are here to lead from perspective. To see what others cannot see and organize it into something meaningful. But your power is unlocked through play, through decisiveness, through physical creation.

So how do you know if you are living your chart?

You know because your mind feels spacious instead of frantic. You know because you trust what you see. You know because you are creating consistently instead of waiting for the perfect moment. You feel it when joy returns to your work. When your gatherings feel alive. When your leadership feels natural rather than forced.

You also know you are aligned when anxiety decreases. When your body feels less tense. When you are taking action instead of rehearsing possibilities. When you allow yourself to be visible, expressive, and imperfect in motion.

And you know you are living your chart when transformation feels exhilarating rather than terrifying. When you become someone who does not just analyze change, but initiates it.

That is when your Ace of Spades activates — and your life becomes a living threshold for others.

Affirmation of Alignment

I trust my vision and move my ideas into reality.

Play and decisive action unlock my transformation.

J♣

Matt & Joy Kahn

Life Chart

		K♠	8♦	10♣			
A♠	3♦	5♣	10♣	Q♣	A♣	3♥	☿
2♥	9♠	9♣	J♥	5♠	7♦	7♥	♀
8♣	J♠	2♦	4♣	6♥	K♦	K♥	♂
A♦	A♥	8♠	10♦	10♥	4♠	6♦	♃
5♦	7♣	9♥	3♠	3♣	5♥	Q♦	♄
J♦ SATURN	K♣ JUPITER	**HEALER'S CODE** 2♣ MARS	7♠ VENUS	9♦ MERCURY	**HEALER'S CODE** J♣ BIRTHCARD	Q♠ MOON	♅
Q♥	6♠ TRANS- FORMED SELF	6♣ COSMIC LESSON	**HEALER'S CODE** 8♥ COSMIC RESULT	**HEALER'S CODE** 2♠ PLUTO	**HEALER'S CODE** 4♦ NEPTUNE	4♥ URANUS	♆
♆	♅	♄	♃	♂	♀	☿	

Card #1: Your Birth Card J♣

If you are a Jack of Clubs, you are standing in one of the most delicate transitions in the entire mental suit.

You have spent much of your life learning. Observing. Studying. Listening. Gathering insight from mentors, books, systems, conversations, lived experience. You do not approach the world casually. You want to understand it. You want to see how it works beneath the surface. And because of that, you often know more than you let on.

But there comes a moment — and you can feel it — when learning is no longer enough.

The Jack of Clubs marks the point where the mind begins to whisper, *"It is time to contribute."* Not repeat what you have learned. Not echo someone else's framework. Contribute.

And that is where the discomfort begins.

Because to contribute, you must trust that what is forming inside of you has value. You must risk developing your own way of thinking, your own language, your own process. And for someone who has spent years refining what others have built, that shift can feel destabilizing.

You may delay it by staying in student mode. You may gather one more certification, read one more book, attend one more training. You may tell yourself that when you are fully formed, then you will step forward.

But here is the deeper message of your birth card:

You do not become the teacher by finishing your education.

You become the teacher by beginning your expression.

As a healer, coach, or leader, this is the initiation. You are not here to know everything. You are here to develop the courage to share what you know now — and allow it to refine as you grow.

Card #2: Your Mars Card 2♣

Your passion moves through voice.

The Two of Clubs in Mars does not allow you to stay silent forever. It pushes against the places where you soften your message to stay safe. It presses on the fear of disagreement. It brings you face-to-face with the universal human truth: when you speak differently than the group, you risk rejection.

And for someone whose mind has been shaped by community, mentors, teachers — that risk can feel real.

You may hesitate before saying what you actually think. You may adjust your language so you are not misunderstood. You may wonder whether it is wiser to remain neutral.

But your Mars is not neutral.

It is catalytic.

Because your voice is not meant to preserve comfort. It is meant to create alignment. And alignment requires clarity.

When you communicate honestly — even imperfectly — something profound happens. The people who are not meant for you drift. The people who are waiting for you draw closer. You stop trying to be universally understood and begin allowing resonance to do its work.

As a leader, this is everything.

Your community cannot gather around what you refuse to articulate. Your clients cannot step into transformation if you dilute your perspective.

The Two of Clubs teaches you that communication carries more value than fear ever will.

Card #3: Your Neptune Card 4 ◆

Your vision is not abstract.

The Four of Diamonds in Neptune reveals that you are meant to build something tangible with what you know. Not simply speak. Not simply inspire. Build.

A structure. A system. A container that can hold your insight in the material world. That might look like a business. A curriculum. A book. A platform. A foundation. A methodology. It does not have to be grand. It does have to be real.

And this is where perfectionism tries to disguise itself as preparation.

You may tell yourself that the structure must be flawless before you share. That the backend must be complete. That the model must be airtight. That once everything is solid, then you will finally allow your message to move.

But the deeper truth is this:

Structure is not what gives you legitimacy.

Commitment does.

You only need enough foundation to begin. The rest will evolve because you are evolving. When you stop waiting for the final version of yourself, your work begins to take form in ways you could not have planned.

The Four of Diamonds is asking you to build as you become.

Card #4: Your Pluto Card 2♠

Your transformation arrives through discernment in relationship.

The Two of Spades asks you to look closely at who you allow to shape your thinking. Who you defer to. Who you stay aligned with out of familiarity rather than expansion.

Sometimes the Jack of Clubs will keep partnerships that feel safe but limit growth. You may remain in dynamics where your voice is subtly minimized. You may take advice that feels authoritative but not aligned. You may quiet your intuition because someone else sounds more certain.

This Pluto energy will not let that continue indefinitely.

It asks you to trust your own perception — not arrogantly, but steadily. To choose partnerships that challenge you to rise rather than conform. To release relationships that require you to shrink.

And this is where maturity emerges.

Because higher partnership does not mean someone tells you who to be. It means you stand fully as who you are and meet others from that place.

When you choose alignment over comfort, your path clears.

Card #5: Your Cosmic Result Card 8♥

When you walk this path — when you speak bravely, build steadily, and partner wisely — you do not end up alone.

You end up surrounded.

The Eight of Hearts is not surface-level belonging. It is enduring connection. It is a community that feels rooted in mutual respect. It is the experience of being loved not for how well you adapted, but for how fully you expressed yourself.

This result card reveals something beautiful: your voice creates your tribe.

When you stop editing yourself for approval, the right people gather. When you build from authenticity rather than performance, your relationships deepen. When you trust your own knowing, others trust it too.

And for you, as a healer, coach, or leader, this is not just emotional fulfillment. It is sustainability. It is the difference between building something alone and building something supported.

Integration — Your Healer's Code in Motion

The integration of your chart is not about becoming louder. It is about becoming congruent.

You are here to move from absorbing wisdom to embodying it. From repeating insight to refining it. From waiting to expressing.

So how do you know if you are living your chart?

You feel it when your voice stops trembling after you speak. When you share before everything is finalized. When you choose alignment in relationship even if it means discomfort. When you build something real instead of endlessly preparing.

You know you are aligned when your nervous system settles after communication instead of spiraling. When your community feels more nourishing. When your work feels like an extension of who you are rather than a performance of who you think you should be.

And perhaps most importantly, you know you are living your chart when you no longer question whether your intuition is valid — you act from it.

That is when the student fully becomes the teacher.

And that is when love surrounds you.

Affirmation of Alignment

I trust my voice and share it with courage. I build what matters and choose partnerships that elevate me. As I stand in truth, love stabilizes around me.

Q♣   JOKER

Matt & Joy Kahn

Life Chart

	K♠	8♦	10♣			

	HEALER'S CODE			HEALER'S CODE			
A♠	3♦	5♣	10♦	Q♣	A♣	3♥	☿
JUPITER	MARS	VENUS	MERCURY	BIRTHCARD	MOON		
		HEALER'S CODE	HEALER'S CODE	HEALER'S CODE			
2♥	9♠	9♣	J♥	5♠	7♦	7♥	♀
TRANS-FORMED SELF	COSMIC LESSON	COSMIC RESULT	PLUTO	NEPTUNE	URANUS	SATURN	
8♣	J♠	2♦	4♣	6♥	K♦	K♥	♂
A♦	A♥	8♠	10♦	10♥	4♠	6♦	♃
5♦	7♣	9♥	3♠	3♣	5♥	Q♦	♄
J♦	K♣	2♣	7♠	9♦	J♣	Q♠	♅
Q♥	6♠	6♣	8♥	2♠	4♦	4♥	♆
♆	♅	♄	♃	♂	♀	☿	

Card #1: Your Birth Card Q♣

If you are the Queen of Clubs, you were not designed to simply think about ideas, you were born to bring them to life.

The Clubs suit governs thought, communication, and strategy. The Queen embodies maturity, composure, and inner authority. Together, they create someone who does not simply generate ideas — you steward them. You can take inspiration and shape it into something viable, structured, and potentially impactful in the world.

And as a healer, coach, or leader, this is not a small gift.

You are someone who can take a scattered insight and give it form. You can take a vision and make it viable. You are capable of nurturing an idea from its earliest stage — holding it, refining it, protecting it — until it becomes substantial enough to stand on its own. Many people dream. Fewer people gestate. You gestate.

But here is where your initiation begins.

Because you see so clearly, you may sometimes remain in the realm of vision longer than necessary. You may strategize, refine, and map possibilities without stepping fully into physical implementation. The Queen of Clubs can sometimes live in the brilliance of the plan rather than the messiness of execution.

Card #2: Your Mars Card 3♦

Mars reveals how your passion moves.

For you, passion requires physical creation. The Three of Diamonds brings tangible expression. It asks you to take what lives in your mind and move it into the world through action — building, designing, writing, constructing, organizing.

This may not always feel natural at first. You may know exactly what needs to exist but feel uncertain about how to bring it into form. The gap between vision and execution can feel frustrating. Yet this is precisely the muscle you are meant to develop.

When you engage your body in the creative process, something shifts. The idea stabilizes. Momentum builds. Confidence increases.

As a leader, this is transformational. You stop outsourcing your power. You collaborate, yes — but not from avoidance. You learn what you need to learn. You build the skills required to manifest your ideas. You allow yourself to become competent in the physical realm, not just brilliant in the conceptual one.

Your authority strengthens when your ideas have weight.

Card #3: Your Neptune Card 5♠

Neptune represents the dream that pulls you forward.

Your Neptune card carries the energy of transformation. You are lit up by change. You see how ideas could alter systems, improve lives, reshape environments. You are inspired by evolution.

But here is the deeper layer: transformation is not achieved through thought alone.

The Five of Spades invites you to live the change you envision. It asks you to allow your own life to shift alongside your ideas. If you dream of transformation but remain internally static, friction appears.

As a healer, coach, or leader, your vision gains credibility when it is embodied. You are not merely speaking about change; you are participating in it. You are not theorizing about evolution; you are allowing yourself to evolve.

Transformation is not a concept in your chart. It is a lived experience.

Card #4: Your Pluto Card J♥

Pluto reveals where transformation refines your emotional maturity.

For you, this refinement occurs in the realm of giving.

The Jack of Hearts carries generosity and heartfelt expression. You have a natural inclination to pour yourself into what you love. You may give freely, sometimes excessively, believing that devotion alone will create harmony.

But Pluto asks you to balance that giving.

When you overextend, when you sacrifice without replenishment, resentment can quietly build. When you close your heart entirely in response, distance forms. Neither extreme serves you.

Your transformation lies in reciprocal love. In giving from a full cup. In honoring your own emotional needs alongside others'. In recognizing that harmony is not achieved by depletion but by balance.

As a leader, this becomes powerful. You demonstrate that compassion does not require self-erasure. You show that nurturing others includes nurturing yourself.

Card #5: Your Cosmic Result Card 9♣

The result of your journey is mental fulfillment.

The Nine of Clubs represents completion of an intellectual cycle. When your mind, heart, and body align, you begin to see your ideas reach the finish line. What once lived only in theory becomes tangible. What once felt like potential becomes reality.

You do not need to micromanage the outcome. When you embody your role fully, things unfold with coherence. Your projects mature. Your vision stabilizes. Your brilliance becomes visible.

As a healer, coach, or leader, this is deeply satisfying. You witness the fruition of what you conceived. You see the product, the program, the structure, the community — and you recognize that it exists because you allowed yourself to move beyond thinking into doing.

Integration — Your Healer's Code in Motion

The heart of your integration is this: your power is not in how brilliantly you can design something. It is in how fully you can live it.

You are here to build what matters. But you are also here to mature into the kind of leader who understands that ideas require devotion, skill, and emotional sustainability.

So how do you know if you are living your chart?

You feel it when implementation no longer intimidates you. When you stop refining the blueprint and start laying bricks. When you ask for support without abandoning ownership. When you no longer confuse exhaustion with dedication.

You know you are aligned when your heart feels steady. When you are giving without resentment. When you are creating without hiding in overthinking. When transformation is something you are walking through, not only describing.

And you know you are living your chart when you can look at what you have built and feel peace instead of pressure.

That is the Nine of Clubs.

Not constant strategizing.

Completion.

Affirmation of Alignment

I embody the vision I carry, and I build from steadiness rather than strain.

My ideas reach completion because my mind, heart, and actions move as one.

K♧

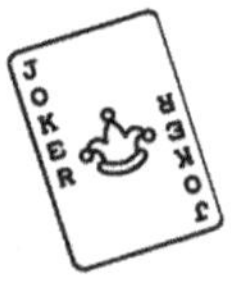

Matt & Joy Kahn

Life Chart

		K♤ TRANS-FORMED SELF	8♢ COSMIC LESSON	HEALER'S CODE 10♧ COSMIC RESULT			
A♤	3♢	5♧	10♤	Q♧	A♧	3♡	☿
2♡	9♤	9♧	J♡	5♤	7♢	7♡	♀
8♧	J♤	2♢	4♧	6♡	K♢	K♡	♂
A♢	A♡	8♤	10♢	10♡	4♤	6♢	♃
5♢	7♧	9♡	3♤	3♧	5♡	Q♢	♄
J♢ MERCURY	HEALER'S CODE K♧ BIRTHCARD	2♧ MOON	7♤	9♢	J♧	Q♤	♅
HEALER'S CODE Q♡ PLUTO	HEALER'S CODE 6♤ NEPTUNE	6♧ URANUS	8♡ SATURN	2♤ JUPITER	HEALER'S CODE 4♢ MARS	4♡ VENUS	♆
♆	♅	♄	♃	♂	♀	☿	

Card #1: Your Birth Card K♣

If you are the King of Clubs, you carry a vision that feels larger than your current life.

You haven't always known what the vision is, but you sense something trying to find it's way out of you and in to the world. You have felt it inside you for as long as you can remember.

The Clubs suit lives in the realm of mind, language, meaning, and pattern. And when that suit is crowned with King energy, the mind doesn't just think—it *organizes*. It structures. It leads. It speaks into existence what others have been unable to articulate.

That is why you often feel like you are holding pieces of a future that hasn't fully arrived.

And that is also why speaking can feel so loaded.

Because for you, this is not casual communication. It's not "sharing your thoughts." It can feel like exposure. Like risk. Like if you really say the thing you see, you could be misunderstood in a way that costs you belonging. In some seasons, this fear shows up as hesitation—reworking your message, refining your offering, waiting until you have the perfect words. In other seasons, it shows up as the opposite: stepping into a louder certainty than you actually feel, so no one can sense the vulnerability underneath.

Both are strategies. Both are understandable.

But neither is your mastery.

The King of Clubs matures when you stop trying to protect yourself from reaction, and start devoting yourself to transmission. When you realize your voice is not meant to impress people—it's meant to *serve* them. Not by shrinking the truth, and not by posturing over it, but by letting your authority become quiet and steady.

As a healer, coach, or conscious leader, your gift is not just what you know. It's the way you can make what you know *land*—in language that gives someone their life back.

And you will feel your life begin to change when you stop waiting to feel fearless…and begin speaking with grounded truth anyway.

Card #2: Your Mars Card 4♦

Mars reveals how your passion moves.

For you, passion must be grounded.

The Four of Diamonds brings structure to your expansive mind. It slows your thoughts enough to ask a practical question: which of these visions is meant to be built now?

Your mental energy moves quickly. You can conceive of multiple possibilities at once. But without physical stabilization, that brilliance can scatter. The Four of Diamonds asks you to select one path and create a foundation beneath it.

This does not mean abandoning the larger dream. It means giving one part of it tangible form.

As a leader, this is crucial. When you create systems, build infrastructure, and implement processes, your confidence grows. You begin to trust your capacity to bring ideas into reality. And that physical grounding makes your communication clearer.

Structure is not limitation for you. It is empowerment.

Card #3: Your Neptune Card 6♠

Neptune represents the dream that pulls you forward.

Your Neptune card carries a deep sense of calling. The Six of Spades whispers that your purpose matters — that your contribution is part of something larger than yourself.

This can feel inspiring. It can also feel overwhelming.

You may sense that your vision is too big to fulfill. You may feel the pressure of responsibility. At times, you may even feel like a victim of your own passion — as if the dream demands more than you can give.

But here is the truth of this card: the vision is not yours alone.

You are not responsible for carrying the entire future. You are responsible for your role within it. The universe does not ask you to complete the whole picture. It asks you to participate.

As a healer, coach, or leader, this shift changes everything. When you release the burden of total responsibility, your energy becomes lighter. You focus on implementation rather than perfection. You step into partnership with something greater instead of trying to control it.

Card #4: Your Pluto Card Q♥

Pluto reveals where transformation refines your heart.

For you, transformation occurs through emotional maturity in leadership.

The Queen of Hearts brings warmth, magnetism, and the ability to gather people around a mission. You naturally care for those who support you. You want your team, your family, your community to feel valued.

But there is a subtle shadow here. You may overgive. You may nurture excessively in hopes that others will help you carry the weight of your vision. You may cling to relationships out of loyalty, even when they are no longer aligned.

Pluto asks you to love without manipulation. To lead without needing approval. To nurture without sacrificing yourself.

As a leader, this refinement is powerful. You learn to delegate without disappearing. You gather collaborators who work with you, not just for you. You cultivate reciprocity rather than dependency.

When your heart is balanced, your authority becomes gentle yet unmistakable.

Card #5: Your Cosmic Result Card 10♣

The result of your journey is visible impact.

The Ten of Clubs represents intellectual leadership expressed at scale. When you ground your ideas, release the burden of total responsibility, refine your emotional boundaries, and speak clearly, your vision gains traction.

People see it.

They understand it.

They participate in it.

Your work expands beyond you. It becomes something that serves communities, organizations, families, and future generations.

As a healer, coach, or leader, this is fulfillment. Not because of ego, but because of contribution. You witness the ideas that once lived quietly inside you become structures that support others.

Integration — Your Healer's Code in Motion

When we step back and look at your chart as a whole, something very specific becomes clear.

You are not simply a visionary.

You are a visionary who must learn to trust their own voice.

Your Birth Card carries the large idea. Your Mars card asks you to build it. Your Neptune card reminds you that you are participating in something greater than yourself. Your Pluto card refines how you love and who you build with. And your Cosmic Result shows what becomes possible when all of those pieces move in harmony.

But none of that happens automatically.

As a healer, coach, or conscious leader, you may recognize this pattern: the vision feels enormous, but the pathway feels unclear. You can see what could exist, but you hesitate to fully claim it. You carry the calling privately, almost protectively. You sense the future trying to move through you, yet you hold it close until it feels safe enough to release.

At the same time, you may overcompensate. You may speak with intensity before you feel fully anchored. You may overgive in relationships to ensure loyalty. You may shoulder more responsibility than is yours because it feels easier to carry it yourself than risk disappointment.

This is the tension of your chart.

A mind that sees the bigger picture.

A heart that wants support.

A calling that feels bigger than your current capacity.

A structure that has not yet fully stabilized.

But when you begin living your chart, something shifts internally before it shifts externally.

You stop trying to protect your voice, and you begin using it.

You stop trying to carry the entire mission, and you begin participating in your portion of it.

You stop overgiving to secure support, and you begin allowing reciprocity to reveal who truly belongs beside you.

So how do you know if you are living your chart?

You will feel it in your body before you see it in your business.

When you are not living your chart, your vision feels heavy. Urgent. Pressurized. You may feel behind, or alone, or slightly resentful that no one else sees what you see. You may feel mentally overactive but physically ungrounded. You may notice that your relationships require more energy than they return.

When you are living your chart, your nervous system softens.

The vision still matters — but it no longer feels like a burden. It feels inevitable.

Your ideas begin to take form. Even if small at first, something exists that did not exist before. A structure. A container. A pathway. You are no longer only speaking about what could happen. You are building what is happening.

And perhaps most importantly, your voice feels steady. You are no longer speaking to prove yourself, defend your point of view, or justify your position. You are sharing to express what's true for you so that you can help others and you let fear be transmuted into passion.

Affirmation of Alignment

I trust my vision and ground it in action. I lead with clarity and love without overextending. As I participate in purpose, my ideas create lasting impact.

THE DIAMONDS SUIT

The Diamonds Suit governs the realm of value, resources, and material stewardship, guiding us through the full maturation of worth:

From the generative potential of the Ace,
to the exchange of the Two,
to the creative multiplication of the Three,
to the stabilizing structure of the Four,
to the adaptive reinvention of the Five,
to the harmonizing responsibility of the Six,
to the strategic refinement of the Seven,
to the empowered influence of the Eight,
to the generous expansion of the Nine,
to the abundant fulfillment of the Ten,
and finally the Court —
where it transforms into
the Entrepreneur as the Jack,
the Steward as the Queen,
and the Executive Visionary as the King.

If your Birth Card lives in the Diamonds Suit, your life is shaped by value — not only financial or material value, but the deeper question of what is truly worth your time, energy, and devotion. Your journey is not simply to accumulate, but to understand exchange, to build in alignment with integrity, and to steward resources in a way that uplifts more than just yourself. Diamonds teach that wealth without wisdom is fragile, but value aligned with purpose becomes legacy.

On the following pages, you will find all cards contained within the suit of Diamonds. The Diamonds have been organized from Ace to King. Each card begins with a snapshot of its chart followed by a detailed description. While the charts have been offered for reference, the descriptions provide a chance to feel into their specific energy and purpose.

A♦

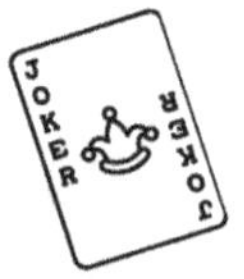

Matt & Joy Kahn

Life Chart

		K♠	8♦	10♣			
A♠	3♦	5♣	10♠	Q♣	A♣	3♥	☿
2♥	9♠	9♣	J♥	5♠	7♦	7♥	♀
8♣	J♠	2♦	4♣	6♥	K♦	K♥	♂
HEALER'S CODE A♦ BIRTHCARD	A♥ MOON	8♠	10♦	10♥	4♠	6♦	♃
HEALER'S CODE 5♦ NEPTUNE	7♣ URANUS	9♥ SATURN	3♠ JUPITER	HEALER'S CODE 3♣ MARS	5♥ VENUS	Q♦ MERCURY	♄
J♦	K♣	2♣	7♠ TRANS-FORMED SELF	9♦ COSMIC LESSON	HEALER'S CODE J♣ COSMIC RESULT	HEALER'S CODE Q♠ PLUTO	♅
Q♥	6♠	6♣	8♥	2♠	4♦	4♥	♆
♆	♅	♄	♃	♂	♀	☿	

Card #1: Your Birth Card A◆

If you are an Ace of Diamonds, you carry the energy of beginnings in the physical realm. You are here to start things that other people only think about. You bring freshness into rooms that have gone stale. You can walk into a situation with very little context and somehow know what to do next—what to adjust, what to improve, what to initiate, what to offer. There is a quiet brilliance to that. Not performative. Practical. Immediate. You don't just envision possibility— you *activate* it.

And because Diamonds are tied to value, resources, the body, beauty, and earthly stewardship, you often feel an instinctual relationship with aesthetics and presentation. You notice what looks aligned and what doesn't. You feel what is current, youthful, and alive. Your presence can naturally lift the energy of what you touch because you have an eye for beauty.

Yet underneath that bright initiating power, there is something far more tender than most people realize. The Ace of Diamonds often carries a hidden longing: to be loved, adored, seen, and cherished for who you are. You may be praised for your results, while secretly craving devotion. You may be appreciated for what you produce, while quietly hoping someone will recognize the softness that lives inside you. When that tenderness is overlooked, it can create an ache that's hard to name, because from the outside you seem so capable.

This is one of your lifelong spiritual lessons as a healer, coach, or leader: allowing yourself to be valued not only for what you can *do*, but for who you *are*. The world will happily celebrate your competence. Your work is to not abandon your heart while you're building your life. And to remember that being an initiator doesn't mean you're meant to live in perpetual starting beginner's mode. It means you're meant to learn how to begin with honesty—so what you start has a chance to become real love, real sustainability, and real legacy.

Card #2: Your Mars Card 3♣

Mars reveals how your passion moves—what energizes you, what drives you, and what you're meant to *do* with your gifts. With the 3 of Clubs in Mars, your fire is mental, creative, and expressive. You are not only a starter—you are a *shaper of ideas*. Your passion isn't satisfied just by starting something new. It wants to *organize*. It wants to form meaning. It wants to take scattered pieces and bring them into a coherent pattern that people can actually understand and use.

This is why you may find yourself naturally drawn to learning systems, mastering teachings, and becoming fluent in complex material. You can take something dense—psychology, health, coaching frameworks, spiritual principles, diagnostics, methodologies—and not only grasp it, but translate it. This is one of your great gifts as a guide: you make the complicated feel navigable.

But there's another layer here that matters just as much. The Ace of Diamonds can sometimes scatter themselves by starting too many things, chasing novelty, or reinventing what doesn't require reinvention. The 3 of Clubs is your remedy. It helps you *stay*—not by forcing commitment, but by giving you a reason to remain engaged: creative development. When you're actively forming ideas, writing, speaking, teaching, structuring, or dialoguing in ways that move energy forward, your body relaxed and your nervous system settles. When you are not creating meaning, your mind can turn that same power inward and become restless, obsessive, or anxious.

So your Mars isn't asking you to work harder. It's asking you to channel your passion into learning what you love, articulating what you know, and building a clear message that gives your brilliance somewhere to land. When you do that, you don't just initiate—you become someone others trust to guide the journey from beginning to embodiment.

Card #3: Your Neptune Card 5 ◆

Neptune is your dream field—your longing, your vision, and also the place where distortion can quietly sneak in. With the 5 of Diamonds in Neptune, your vision can become entangled with safety. You may feel pulled to make decisions based on whether you'll be taken care of—emotionally, financially, relationally. Not because you're selfish, but because your nervous system learned to equate security with love. So even when your soul is craving alignment, your choices may default to a simpler question: "Will this keep me supported?" "Will this keep me wanted?" "Will this keep me provided for?"

This is where the 5 of Diamonds becomes a sacred teacher. Because at its highest level, it is not about chasing money. It is about *discernment of energy*. It asks you to notice where your life is leaking energy—where you say yes when your body says no, where you stay involved because you might get something, where you keep giving because you're afraid of what happens if you stop. It calls you to pare down, to cut away what you don't love, to stop scattering your life force across obligations that do not nourish you.

As a healer, coach, or leader, this matters deeply—because you are often capable of supporting others without even trying. Your competence is attractive. Your energy is catalytic. And that can create a subtle pattern: staying connected to people, opportunities, or roles that pull from you because the reward looks like love, appreciation, or security. The 5 of Diamonds invites you to reclaim your sovereignty by becoming honest about what actually supports your whole system—your body, your emotions, your spirit, your time.

This Neptune placement asks you to stop letting prosperity be the compass and let *alignment* become the focus. Not because resources don't matter—but because when your energy is aligned your nervous system steadies, your intuition gets stronger, and the love you crave stops being something you bargain for—and becomes something you allow.

Card #4: Your Pluto Card Q♠

Pluto is the underworld of your chart—the place where your ego is asked to surrender control and learn a deeper kind of power. With the Queen of Spades in Pluto, your transformation is rooted in intuition. Not intuition as a concept. Intuition as a practice of listening *before* the evidence arrives. This card asks you to trust what you know in your bones, even when your mind can't justify it yet. It asks you to discern long before the world agrees with you.

For an Ace of Diamonds, this is revolutionary. Because your natural gift is to step in and figure things out. You can problem-solve. You can adapt. You can make anything work. But the Queen of Spades says: "Just because you *can* make something work doesn't mean it's yours to keep working on." This is where your deepest maturity comes online. You stop using your talent to force outcomes and you start using your intuition to choose the right directions.

This Pluto placement also heals a common Ace of Diamonds tension: the feeling of not quite knowing where you belong. When you start many things and rarely stay for the completions, you can feel unanchored—like you're always searching for the "place" where you finally fit. The Queen of Spades doesn't give you a place by convincing you. She gives you a place by guiding you. When you trust your inner knowing and act on it immediately—leaving what's complete, moving toward what's alive—your path clarifies. And what opens through that clarity is not just external success, but a deeper intimacy with yourself.

For the healer, coach, or leader, this is the difference between being impressive and being *fulfilled*. The Queen of Spades in Pluto asks you to stop waiting for permission to honor what you already know. To leave before things collapse. To pivot before you burn out. To choose what is aligned even when it's inconvenient. When you do, your life stops being a series of reactions —and becomes a deliberate, intuitive creation.

Card #5: Your Cosmic Result Card J♣

Your cosmic result is what becomes possible when you live the full arc of your chart. With the Jack of Clubs as your result, you are being initiated into truthful expression—teaching, guiding, mentoring, coaching, leading, and speaking in a way that shapes reality. This is not the energy of someone who just has ideas. This is the energy of someone whose ideas *move people*.

But there is an important distinction here. The Jack of Clubs can express truth—or it can manipulate information to get an outcome. And the Ace of Diamonds, when still hungry for love and safety, may be tempted to use their brilliance to secure what they fear losing: approval, stability, affection, belonging. The Jack of Clubs as a cosmic result is not a reward for being clever. It is an initiation into being *integral*. It is the moment your life asks you to stop crafting reality through strategy alone and start shaping it through honesty.

When you integrate your chart, your voice changes. You stop performing confidence and start speaking from inner certainty. You stop trying to persuade people into loving you and start offering guidance that naturally earns respect. You stop initiating endlessly and become a true communicator of wisdom—someone who can take insight, structure it, speak it, and let it land in a way that transforms.

And for the healer, coach, or leader, this result is powerful: you become the one who helps people name what they already feel. You become the one who makes clarity contagious. You become the one who doesn't just inspire beginnings—you teach others how to build lives they can actually adore.

Integration — Your Healer's Code in Motion

When we step back and view your chart as a whole, a very specific storyline emerges. You are an initiator in the world of value and creation, someone who can begin what others are afraid to start. Your Mars shows that your passion isn't random—it's meant to be channeled into ideas that become teachable, shareable, and structured. Your Neptune reveals the tender place where safety and love can distort your choices—inviting you to simplify, discern, and stop leaking energy into pathways you're only tolerating. Your Pluto demands the deepest kind of courage: trusting your intuition before evidence surfaces, and acting before things "make sense" on paper. And when you do, the result is not only a more successful life—it is the birth of a true guide: the Jack of Clubs, the messenger who speaks with clarity instead of performance.

For many Ace of Diamonds, the greatest challenge is not capability. It is continuity. It is intimacy. It is learning to stay with what matters long enough for it to become a home. This chart doesn't ask you to stop starting. It asks you to start from a deeper place. To begin when it's aligned—not because it might earn you love. To choose because your intuition says yes—not because your fear says, "What if my needs are no longer met?" And to build a life that doesn't just look good, but feels true in your body.

So how do you know if you are living your chart? Notice what is driving your momentum. Are you starting things because you're genuinely inspired, or because you're restless and chasing renewal to avoid discomfort? Notice your relationships with opportunity and approval. Are you staying connected because you love what you're building—or because you're hoping the right outcome will finally make you feel adored? Notice your nervous system. Do you feel scattered and overextended, or fulfilled and focused? The 5 of Diamonds will always tell the truth here: energy leaks feel like depletion, while discernment feels like relief.

And notice your intuition—the Queen of Spades within you. Are you waiting for proof before you honor your knowing, or are you practicing the kind of trust that moves mountains? When you are living your chart, your life becomes less performative and more precise. Your "yes" becomes calmer. Your "no" becomes clearer. You stop manipulating outcomes and you start telling the truth about what you want, what you feel, and where you're going. That is the Jack of Clubs awakening in you—not as a persona, but as a liberated voice.

Affirmation of Alignment

I trust my intuition before I require proof, and I choose what nourishes my whole being. I speak my truth clearly, and I build a life where love and alignment can last.

2◇

Matt & Joy Kahn — *Life Chart*

			K♠	8◇	10♣	

A♠	3◇	5♣	10♠	Q♣	A♣	3♡	☿
2♡	9♠	9♣	J♡	5♠	7◇	7♡	♀
8♣ VENUS	J♠ MERCURY	2◇ HEALER'S CODE BIRTHCARD	4♣ MOON	6♡	K♦	K♡	♂
A♦ HEALER'S CODE COSMIC RESULT	A♡ HEALER'S CODE PLUTO	8♠ HEALER'S CODE NEPTUNE	10◇ URANUS	10♡ SATURN	4♠ JUPITER	6◇ HEALER'S CODE MARS	♃
5◇	7♣	9♡	3♠	3♣	5♡ TRANS-FORMED SELF	Q◇ COSMIC LESSON	♄
J◇	K♣	2♣	7♠	9◇	J♣	Q♠	⛢
Q♡	6♠	6♣	8♡	2♠	4◇	4♡	♆
♆	⛢	♄	♃	♂	♀	☿	

Card #1: Your Birth Card 2 ◆

If you are a 2 of Diamonds, you are wired for connection in the physical world—partnership, collaboration, shared vision, mutual gain. You're not someone who only wants to "do your thing" alone. You want to build *with* people. You love the strategy of a deal, the choreography of an exchange, the moment when two energies meet and something becomes possible that could not have happened in isolation. You often have a natural gift for coordination—seeing where the pieces fit, sensing what someone needs, knowing how to bring the right people to the right table at the right time.

And because this is Diamonds, your relationship to partnership isn't purely emotional—it is also practical. You tend to understand value. You can sense what an agreement is really asking for beneath the words. You notice the details. You see how something will be perceived in the world —how it will "land," how it will look, how it will be received. At your best, this makes you skillful and precise. But when you're under stress, it can pull you into a life where perception becomes more important than truth, and the outer shape of success becomes more important than what your heart actually wants.

This is where your deeper lesson begins. The 2 of Diamonds often carries a very real hunger for love *and* prosperity, and part of your journey is learning that you don't have to betray one to have the other. You may hesitate to commit because you feel how serious commitment is. If you give your word, you tend to mean it. You don't want to be careless with your bonds—because partnership, to you, is sacred on the physical plane. And so you may hold back, watching, testing, waiting until you're certain. The tenderness here is that your heart is deeper than you let on, and trust is not something you give lightly.

Card #2: Your Mars Card 6 ◆

Mars reveals how your passion moves—what motivates you when life demands action. With the 6 of Diamonds in Mars, your drive is tied to fairness, integrity, and the need for things to be balanced. You're not satisfied with winning if it feels uneven. You're not at peace with "success" if someone was dismissed, overlooked, or taken advantage of along the way. Something in you wants agreements to be honorable—not just profitable.

This can make you a powerful advocate, negotiator, or guide—especially in spaces where people feel overwhelmed by decisions. You often have the ability to lay out the facts in a way that helps others choose what is best for them. You can dissect details, name what's happening, and bring clarity where there is confusion. In that sense, you can be surprisingly decisive for someone who sometimes struggles with indecision in your own inner world. You may help others find the path that feels most aligned, even while you're still learning to trust your own inner "yes."

And yet, there is a subtle edge here for the healer, coach, or leader: the six of diamonds can make you so focused on what is equitable and correct that you forget to reveal what you feel. You may express warmth through compliments and charisma, making others feel seen and safe, while keeping your deeper emotional truth held back behind the polite surface. You may know how to keep an exchange harmonious, while still wondering privately why true intimacy feels like something you have to earn.

Your Mars card is teaching you that integrity is not only how you treat others—it is also how you treat yourself. It is not just about fair contracts and balanced exchanges. It is about letting your heart have a seat at the table, too.

Card #3: Your Neptune Card 8♠

Neptune is where your dreams come to life—your longing, your vision, and the place where devotion either becomes your medicine or your trap. With the 8 of Spades in Neptune, you are capable of extraordinary commitment. When you decide something matters, you can stay with it. You can endure. You can keep going long after someone else would have walked away. This is one of the reasons you can build real success: you don't just start—you *stay*.

But devotion has a shadow. When you're afraid to lose what you've invested in, devotion can become gripping. The 2 of Diamonds already hesitates to commit because commitment is serious for you—and then the 8 of Spades intensifies that seriousness by making it feel like the dream must be "the one." The one path. The one partner. The one perfect arrangement that will finally make everything make sense.

This Neptune placement is asking you to mature your relationship with the idea of "forever." It's teaching you that devotion is not proof that something must last indefinitely. Devotion is a force that helps you fulfill a chapter. And some chapters are meant to evolve, pivot, or complete so you can grow into the next one. Your dream life is not limited to one commitment in a lifetime. You are allowed to expand. You are allowed to outgrow an agreement without betraying yourself. You are allowed to discover new dreams—again and again.

Card #4: Your Pluto Card A♥

Pluto is where you are transformed—where life asks you to release the old strategy and let a deeper truth lead. With the Ace of Hearts in Pluto, your transformation is emotional and spiritual. It is the awakening of the heart as your compass. Not the performing heart. Not the pleasing heart. The *true* heart—the one that knows what feels real, what feels nourishing, what feels honest, even when it's inconvenient.

This card brings a profound message to the 2 of Diamonds: prosperity is not something you secure by holding tightly to the right arrangement. Prosperity is something that flows more naturally when you live from the heart and allow your life to move. The Ace of Hearts in Pluto invites you to stop trying to guarantee the outcome through "the perfect deal," and instead to trust what happens when you let yourself lean in… and let go.

It also reframes your relationship with loyalty. You may have learned to stay because leaving feels like failure, or because ending a commitment feels like breaking your word. But Pluto teaches you the difference between integrity and endurance. Integrity means being faithful to what is true now. Sometimes that includes staying. Sometimes it includes finishing. Sometimes it includes choosing a new direction without needing someone else to "interrupt the contract" first. The Ace of Hearts gives you permission to live by love—not as romance, but as truth in motion.

Card #5: Your Cosmic Result Card A ♦

Your cosmic result is the promise of what becomes possible when you live the whole pattern of your chart. And your result is powerful: the Ace of Diamonds. This is the image of steady newness—fresh streams of opportunity, new experiences, new people, new rewards arriving from more directions than you could have planned.

What's striking is that this is exactly what the 2 of Diamonds often tries to create through finding "the one." The one partnership that guarantees prosperity. The one contract that finally makes you feel safe. The one path that removes uncertainty. But your chart reveals something more liberating: prosperity doesn't have to come through one gate. When you loosen your grip on needing the perfect arrangement, life has room to bring you blessing from many places.

The Ace of Diamonds as your result doesn't mean you stop partnering. It means you stop *clinging.* It means you become someone who can choose what to devote yourself to, stay when it's true, leave when it's complete, and trust that life can keep meeting you—because you are no longer negotiating your worth through your agreements. You're living as someone who naturally magnetizes new value.

Integration — Your Healer's Code in Motion

When you look at this chart as a whole, the storyline becomes clear. You are built for partnership, for exchange, for creating a win-win in the material world. And yet, the deeper journey is not just "How do I make the right deal?" It is "How do I live a life where love and prosperity are not competing desires inside me?"

Your Mars card calls you into fairness and honor—into a way of operating that doesn't cut corners, doesn't manipulate outcomes, and doesn't chase approval through performance. Your Neptune card reveals the devotional part of you that can stay committed for a long time, and it gently challenges the belief that the dream has to be singular for it to be real. Your Pluto card brings the turning point: letting the heart lead, allowing yourself to move with life rather than trying to lock life into a single contract. And when that happens, the result is the Ace of

Diamonds—newness that keeps arriving because you've stopped demanding it come from one specific place.

So how do you know if you are living your chart? Notice what partnership feels like in your body. Does it feel like a free-flowing collaboration, or does it feel like something you must maintain at all costs? Notice your indecision. Is it coming from discernment, or from the fear that choosing one path means losing every other possibility? Notice whether you are trying to secure prosperity through one perfect plan—or whether you are willing to let life bring prosperity through many avenues as you keep listening to what feels true.

And notice your heart. The Ace of Hearts in Pluto is your great teacher. When you are living your chart, you do not have to charm your way into belonging. You do not have to flatter your way into safety. You become someone who can partner without pretending, commit without gripping, and succeed without abandoning your emotional truth. The more you allow love to guide you, the more naturally the material world supports you—because you are no longer negotiating with life. You are participating with it.

Affirmation of Alignment

I allow partnership to be true, not forced, and I let my heart guide what I commit to and what I release. Prosperity flows to me in many ways as I remain devoted to what is real.

3♦

Matt & Joy Kahn — *Life Chart*

	K♠	8♦	10♣				
A♠ (MERCURY)	3♦ (HEALER'S CODE / BIRTHCARD)	5♣ (MOON)	10♠	Q♣	A♣	3♥	☿
2♥ (HEALER'S CODE / PLUTO)	9♠ (HEALER'S CODE / NEPTUNE)	9♣ (URANUS)	J♥ (SATURN)	5♠ (JUPITER)	7♦ (HEALER'S CODE / MARS)	7♥ (VENUS)	♀
8♣	J♠	2♦	4♣	6♥ (TRANSFORMED SELF)	K♠ (COSMIC LESSON)	K♥ (HEALER'S CODE / COSMIC RESULT)	♂
A♠	A♥	8♣	10♦	10♥	4♠	6♦	♃
5♦	7♣	9♥	3♠	3♣	5♥	Q♦	♄
J♦	K♣	2♣	7♠	9♦	J♣	Q♣	♅
Q♥	6♠	6♣	8♥	2♣	4♦	4♥	♆
♆	♅	♄	♃	♂	♀	☿	

Card #1: Your Birth Card — 3 ◆

If you are a 3 of Diamonds, you are someone who knows—deep down—how short life is. Not as a concept. As a lived awareness that has brushed up against loss, impermanence, endings, and change enough times that your body remembers it. This awareness can make you feel urgent in ways you don't always explain to others. It can make you feel like you're racing the clock, even when you're smiling. It can make you hungry for experience, not because you're reckless, but because you can feel how precious the window is.

This is why so many Three of Diamonds feel the tension between two instincts that seem to contradict each other. One instinct says: *Protect yourself. Be careful. Watch what could go wrong.* The other says: *Be free. Don't limit yourself. Don't waste the chance.* When this becomes intense, decision-making can feel like a trap. Commitment can feel confining. Even simple choices can feel heavy, because each choice seems to close a door—and your nervous system doesn't want any door to close.

And yet, the gift inside this pattern is immense. As a Diamond, your self-expression tends to be physical, tangible, sensory, embodied. You are meant to create in ways people can feel. Your creativity isn't only intellectual—it's lived, played, touched, danced, moved through. You may be drawn to nature, water, movement, travel, tactile art, beauty, or any form of creation that lets you be fully here in this earthly plane. You don't just want to think about life. You want to *taste* it.

But because you are so alive to how quickly things can change, you may also notice fear moving beneath your hunger. Sometimes the impulse to "get everything out of life" is carrying an unspoken terror: *What if I lose the chance? What if I don't get to do what I came here to do? What if people leave? What if I'm left behind?* And this is where your path deepens—because the Three of Diamonds is not only here to live fully. You are here to live fully without needing urgency to be your fuel.

Card #2: Your Mars Card — 7 ◆

Mars reveals how your passion moves—what your inner fire is meant to do with all its intensity. With the Seven of Diamonds in Mars, your passion is being trained into commitment. Not rigid commitment. Not forced loyalty. But the kind of devotion that stays long enough for something to transform. This is a profound teaching for the Three of Diamonds, because your instinct is often to move on quickly—toward the next experience, the next possibility, the next edge of freedom. The Seven of Diamonds doesn't punish that instinct. It refines it.

The Seven of Diamonds asks: What if your next level isn't found by consuming more of life, but by *enjoying the life you're already living more deeply*? What if the doorway isn't "something else," but the way you remain present with what you've already chosen? What if staying isn't limitation, but the very alchemy that turns experience into wisdom?

This is also where your leadership begins to emerge. Because as a healer, coach, or guide, you often have an effortless ability to help people break through limitations. You're good at showing people that the cage they've lived in isn't the only option. You're good at helping them take risks, expand, and step into fuller expression. But Mars Seven of Diamonds matures that gift by teaching you the difference between risk and recklessness, freedom and avoidance, expansion and scattering. It helps you become someone who doesn't just push boundaries—but teaches healthy boundaries as a form of devotion to life.

When this Mars energy is lived well, you don't lose your spontaneity. You gain a steadiness underneath it. Your creativity becomes more potent because it has somewhere to land. Your passion becomes more satisfying because you're not always chasing what's next. You begin to discover something you may have secretly doubted was possible: a path you can stay with without feeling trapped.

Card #3: Your Neptune Card 9♠

Neptune is the dream that pulls you forward—the place where longing lives, where meaning is made, and where the story you tell yourself about change becomes either your liberation or your burden. With the Nine of Spades in Neptune, your vision is shaped by endings. Not only endings as loss, but endings as initiation. You are someone whose life teaches you, again and again, that chapters close. People pivot. Seasons shift. Things you thought would last forever evolve into something else.

This can make the world feel overwhelming at times. It can amplify anxiety. It can create a constant sense that you must stay alert, because something could change at any moment. And yet the higher medicine of the Nine of Spades is this: allowing endings to fulfill you instead of frightening you. Allowing transitions to deepen you instead of hardening you. Letting what leaves your life leave behind a blessing—an expansion of vision, a ripening of wisdom, a more tender capacity to love.

The Nine of Spades asks you to stop interpreting change as evidence that something went wrong. For you, change is not a disruption. It's part of your curriculum. The invitations you receive through loss and completion are not meant to push you away from intimacy—they're meant to bring you into intimacy with life at a deeper level. Your chart is designed to teach you that challenges don't exist to stop you from experiencing life. They exist to help you experience life with more depth, more meaning, and more gratitude for what is here while it's here.

When you allow that, something remarkable happens. Your dream life becomes less frantic. Your choices become less pressured. You start living from fulfillment rather than fear. You experience less "I need to hurry," and more "I am here, and I can receive what this moment is offering."

Card #4: Your Pluto Card — 2♥

Pluto is where you are transformed—where your old coping strategies are stripped away, and a deeper truth becomes unavoidable. With the Two of Hearts in Pluto, your transformation is intimate. It is relational. It is the sacred work of opening your heart at the exact moment you want to close it.

Because for the Three of Diamonds, one of the great temptations is to protect yourself from pain by staying mobile—emotionally, relationally, and spiritually. If you don't commit, you can't be disappointed. If you keep your options open, you can't be trapped. If you stay playful and light, you don't have to sit in the vulnerable places where grief and longing live. But Pluto doesn't let that strategy be the end of your story. Pluto says: *Open anyway.*

The Two of Hearts in Pluto teaches that intimacy is not the thing that limits you. Avoiding intimacy is. It teaches that connection is not what makes life risky—life is already risky. Connection is what makes life meaningful. And for you, every time you choose heart-opening over withdrawal, something in your lineage heals. Something in your body relaxes. Something in your destiny shifts.

This is why you are such a powerful space-holder when you're aligned. People feel seen and held in your presence because you have walked through enough change to understand tenderness. And when you choose not to hide—when you let your heart stay available—you become a soft place for others to land without losing your own freedom. That is one of your great maturities: a life that is playful and meaningful at the same time.

Card #5: Your Cosmic Result Card — K♥

Your cosmic result reveals what becomes possible when you live your whole chart instead of living one part of it. And your result is beautiful: the King of Hearts. This is the energy of fulfillment in love. Not romantic fantasy. Not needing someone to complete you. But the felt experience of being supported by life, held by love, surrounded by relationships that nourish you, and anchored in a heart that no longer has to sprint to feel alive.

The King of Hearts is what the Three of Diamonds secretly longs for when they're brave enough to admit it: a love that sustains, a connection that feels safe enough to rest inside, a life that is rich and full without needing constant motion to prove it's meaningful. It is the moment when your fear of endings no longer runs the show, because you feel so deeply met in the present that you're not bargaining with the future.

And there is something else here that matters for you as a healer, coach, or leader. The King of Hearts isn't only an internal fulfillment—it is an energetic offering. It is what people feel in you when you're living your chart: steadiness, warmth, emotional authority, true care without overextension. You become someone who can love deeply without losing yourself, and guide others into the same maturity—not through advice, but through presence.

Integration — Your Healer's Code in Motion

When we step back and take your chart in as one storyline, we can see the arc clearly. You are a soul who feels the preciousness of life so intensely that it can sometimes create urgency and overwhelm. You are someone who wants freedom, expansion, and experience, while also carrying a deep sensitivity to loss and abandonment. You are not "too much." You are simply awake to impermanence.

Your Mars card teaches you the art of staying—not as a punishment, but as a path to deeper enjoyment. It invites you to transform your life not by chasing more, but by receiving what is here more fully. Your Neptune card asks you to let endings become meaningful, to let change deepen you instead of making you brace. Your Pluto card offers the great turning point: every time you want to close your heart, open it instead. Because your destiny is not a life of constant motion. Your destiny is a life so full and rich that you feel grateful when it is time to release this world—fulfilled, not frantic. And that fulfillment is the King of Hearts.

So how do you know if you are living your chart? Notice whether your freedom feels like aliveness or avoidance. Notice whether your spontaneity feels joyful or pressured. Notice whether you are moving quickly because you're inspired, or because you're afraid you'll miss something if you slow down. Notice whether endings make you shut down and isolate, or whether they soften you into deeper appreciation for what matters.

And most of all, notice what happens in the moments when you feel vulnerable. Do you retreat into distraction, novelty, and motion—trying to outrun the ache? Or do you let your heart stay open long enough for real connection to meet you? When you are living your chart, you don't lose your playfulness—you gain the capacity to be fully present with people. You don't abandon your desire for experience—you learn how to receive the experience you're already in. And slowly, steadily, you begin to feel something you may have been chasing for a long time: not just excitement, but genuine fulfillment.

Affirmation of Alignment

I honor the preciousness of life without letting fear rush me, and I choose connection that nourishes my heart. I stay present, I stay open, and I allow love to fulfill me.

4♦

Matt & Joy Kahn — *Life Chart*

		HEALER'S CODE K♠ PLUTO	HEALER'S CODE 8♦ NEPTUNE	10♣ URANUS			
A♠	3♦	5♣	10♠	Q♣ TRANSFORMED SELF	A♣ COSMIC LESSON	HEALER'S CODE 3♥ COSMIC RESULT	☿
2♥	9♠	9♣	J♥	5♠	7♦	7♥	♀
8♣	J♠	2♦	4♣	6♥	K♦	K♥	♂
A♦	A♥	8♠	10♦	10♥	4♠	6♦	♃
5♦	7♣	9♥	3♠	3♣	5♥	Q♦	♄
J♦	K♣	2♣	7♠	9♦	J♣	Q♠	⛢
Q♥ SATURN	6♠ JUPITER	HEALER'S CODE 6♣ MARS	8♥ VENUS	2♠ MERCURY	HEALER'S CODE 4♦ BIRTHCARD	4♥ MOON	♆
♆	⛢	♄	♃	♂	♀	☿	

Card #1: Your Birth Card 4 ♦

If you are a 4 of Diamonds, you are here to build something that feels bigger than life—and then bring it all the way down into form. You often carry a kind of dream in your bloodstream: a desire for relationships, connections, and experiences that feel magical, meaningful, and larger than the ordinary. There is something charismatic and compelling about the way you see the world, as if you're always sensing the hidden potential inside what's right in front of you.

And yet, you are not only a dreamer. You are structured expression. The "4" gives you the capacity to create a container, a framework, a path—something people can actually step into and experience. You can take an idea that feels too big to hold and shape it into something clear, tangible, and useful. This is part of why you can be such a powerful healer, coach, or leader: your vision doesn't have to stay in the clouds. You can translate it into a real offering, a real structure, a real impact in the physical world.

But here is one of your more tender shadows: you can do all of this hoping it will earn you love. You may work hard to be seen as passionate, devoted, magnetic—someone worthy of being admired and adored. The dreamy part of you can be intoxicating, even to yourself, and it can be easy to lose track of where the vision ends and the need for approval begins. When that happens, you can find yourself building an entire life that looks inspiring from the outside while you quietly wonder why it doesn't feel as nourishing on the inside as you hoped it would.

Card #2: Your Mars Card 6 ♣

Mars reveals how your passion moves—what your inner fire is trying to do with your life force. With the 6 of Clubs in Mars, your purpose wants to be taken seriously. Not in an egoic way, but in a meaningful way. You don't want to live superficially. You don't want to offer something half-formed. You want your work to have substance. You want your message, your leadership, and your contribution to come from an integrated awareness of what you're truly here to do and what you genuinely want to experience.

This Mars placement also reveals a specific spiritual discipline: learning to take in information without immediately judging it. The Six of Clubs asks you to listen, observe, gather, and then bring balance to what you know. This matters because the Four of Diamonds can sometimes get swept up in the higher vision—what could be, what might be, what you're excited about—while overlooking what *is*. Your Mars is constantly inviting you to bridge those two worlds: the world of possibility and the world of reality.

When you honor this, your passion becomes clearer and steadier. You stop expecting yourself and others to live inside your fantasy. You begin to make choices from discernment rather than enchantment. And you become someone whose vision can actually be trusted, because it is rooted in what is possible—not only what is beautiful to imagine.

Card #3: Your Neptune Card 8♦

Neptune is where your dream comes alive—your longing, your vision, and the place where you can get seduced by momentum. With the Eight of Diamonds in Neptune, you have an extraordinary relationship with prosperity and manifestation. There is a "lucky" current in you. It's as if whatever you touch, given time, has a way of becoming fruitful. You can set things into motion and watch them grow. You can build a brand, a business, a platform, a body of work—and the world responds.

But the gift comes with a temptation: you can begin to believe that your prosperity requires you to push yourself endlessly. The Eight of Diamonds can create a feeling of inevitability—if you do A, B, and C, it will lead to Z. And because you *can* work hard, because you *do* have stamina, you may keep feeding the machine long past the point where it is nourishing your life. It can become difficult to turn off, to rest, to pause, because the dream starts to whisper, "If you stop, it will stop."

This is where Neptune asks for maturity. The deeper message of the Eight of Diamonds is not "push harder." It is "trust momentum." Once something is set into motion, it can continue to return to you—especially when you build it with care, pacing, and sustainability. You are meant to create prosperity that supports your whole life, not prosperity that consumes it. And when you start honoring steady pace over instant success, you begin to feel something you may not have realized you were missing: the spaciousness to enjoy what you've created.

Card #4: Your Pluto Card K♠

Pluto is where you are transformed—where the part of you that wants to do it all yourself is asked to evolve into true leadership. With the King of Spades in Pluto, your growth edge is perspective. Higher vision. Strategic discernment. The ability to step out of the day-to-day and manage your life from a mountaintop view.

This can be challenging for you because you often *know* you can do everything. You are capable. You are resourceful. You can hold the whole vision and execute it, too. But the King of Spades asks: just because you can do it all, does that mean you should? True leadership is not doing everything perfectly. True leadership is building something that can endure—something supported by structure, roles, and people who are empowered to shine in what they do best.

This Pluto placement invites you to delegate, to expand your team, to let others participate in the vision rather than orbiting around your effort. It asks you to lead with clarity, to make decisions from your highest vantage point, and to create the kind of support system that allows your work to become sustainable. When you step into that level of leadership, something profound happens: you stop equating "working hard" with "being responsible," and you begin to build responsibility into the structure itself.

Card #5: Your Cosmic Result Card 3♥

Your cosmic result reveals what becomes possible when you live the whole arc of your chart. And your result is pure joy: the Three of Hearts. This is overflowing love. Play. Celebration. Vibrancy. The permission to enjoy the life you've built—to dance, to savor, to be radiant, to express, to receive. It's the kind of heart-energy that remembers you were never meant to build success at the expense of your aliveness.

This result also illuminates a core pattern: you love being seen and adored—but if you try to claim that joy without developing the maturity of your Pluto leadership, it can backfire. Without the King of Spades perspective, the Three of Hearts can put off play and continue to work while their nervous system is exhausted. When it's finally time to "play" their too depleted to enjoy it. They often smile through their struggles hoping one day they will get their chance for true joy.

The Three of Hearts is the reward of pacing. It is what arrives when prosperity is allowed to grow over time, when leadership is shared, when the vision is carried by a structure that supports you back. And then, when you rest, you're not collapsing—you're enjoying. When you celebrate, it's not escapism—it's genuine overflow.

Integration — Your Healer's Code in Motion

When we step back and look at your chart as a single storyline, we see something beautiful and specific. You are a visionary builder. You are someone who can take dreams and give them shape. You are also someone who can accidentally turn creation into performance—working hard, giving more, pushing faster, hoping it will secure love, admiration, or a sense of belonging. Your chart does not shame that longing. It simply asks you to mature it.

Your Mars card teaches you balance—how to hold the higher vision while staying grounded in reality, listening without rushing to judgment, and letting wisdom guide your choices. Your Neptune card reveals the prosperity current in your life, while also asking you to stop equating worthiness with effort and success with strain. Your Pluto card calls you into leadership that sees the whole board—leadership that empowers others, builds support, and chooses sustainability over heroic over-functioning. And when you live those lessons, you arrive at the Three of Hearts: a life where joy is not something you steal from your future after burning yourself out, but something you experience as a natural byproduct of building wisely.

So how do you know if you are living your chart? Notice what your vision feels like in your body. Does it feel inspiring and spacious, or does it feel like pressure you have to keep up with? Notice your relationship with prosperity. Are you pushing because you're afraid it won't happen unless you force it, or are you allowing momentum to unfold at a pace that supports your health, your relationships, and your spirit? Notice your leadership style. Are you doing everything because you can, or are you building a structure where others are invited to contribute and shine?

And notice your joy. The Three of Hearts is your compass. When you are living your chart, joy doesn't come from proving yourself. It comes from being present enough to enjoy what you're creating. It feels like play that restores you. It feels like love that doesn't require you to perform. It feels like celebration that's rooted in a life you can actually sustain.

Affirmation of Alignment

I lead from a higher perspective, trust the timing of what I'm building, and allow joy to be part of the process—not the prize at the end. I create with love, pace, and presence, and I let life support me as I serve.

5♢

Life Chart

		K♠	8♢	10♣			
A♠	3♢	5♣	10♠	Q♣	A♣	3♡	☿
2♡	9♠	9♣	J♡	5♠	7♢	7♡	♀
8♣	J♠	2♢	4♣	6♡	K♢	K♡	♂
A♢	A♡	8♠	10♢	10♡	4♠	6♢	♃
HEALER'S CODE 5♢ BIRTHCARD	7♣ MOON	9♡	3♠	3♣	5♡	Q♢	♄
HEALER'S CODE J♢ NEPTUNE	K♣ URANUS	2♣ SATURN	7♠ JUPITER	HEALER'S CODE 9♢ MARS	J♣ VENUS	Q♠ MERCURY	♅
Q♡	6♠	6♣	8♡ TRANS- FORMED SELF	2♠ COSMIC LESSON	HEALER'S CODE 4♢ COSMIC RESULT	HEALER'S CODE 4♡ PLUTO	♆
♆	♅	♄	♃	♂	♀	☿	

Card #1: Your Birth Card 5 ◆

If you are a Five of Diamonds, you experience the physical world intensely. You value freedom in a way that feels almost sacred. Movement, change, variety, new experiences—these are not luxuries for you. They feel necessary. You are often willing to try what others hesitate to attempt. You will leap before everyone else has finished thinking. There is boldness in you. There is appetite. There is a desire to taste life fully rather than observe it from a safe distance.

And because this is Diamonds, your playground is the material realm—money, health, opportunity, the body, resources, tangible experiences. When your energy is ungrounded, that intensity can become extreme. You may move too quickly. Spend too quickly. Commit too quickly. You may follow adrenaline rather than discernment. Financial highs and lows, physical burnout, cycles of excess followed by recovery—these can become familiar rhythms when your freedom is running the show without guidance.

But when you are aligned, something remarkable happens. Your ability to pivot becomes a gift. You can see opportunities others miss. You know when something is no longer working and you are not afraid to cut it away. You assess risk with a kind of instinctive clarity. You can invest wisely, build wealth wisely, and even guide others in making strong decisions about their material world. There is something alchemical in you. You can take what looks unstable and turn it into growth.

Your journey is not about suppressing freedom. It is about harmonizing it. You are here to learn how to enjoy the physical world without being ruled by it. To experience prosperity without excess. To move swiftly when needed—and to stay when staying is what will build something lasting.

Card #2: Your Mars Card 9 ◆

Mars reveals how your passion moves.

For you, passion moves through completion.

The Nine of Diamonds brings an instinct for knowing when something is finished. You can see exits clearly. You understand timing. You are often the one who helps others make hard financial or structural decisions.

This is powerful.

You are capable of stepping away from what no longer serves you — investments, projects, even identities. But this same ability can sometimes make you overly comfortable with endings. If change feels normal, attachment may feel risky.

The deeper lesson here is not simply knowing when to leave. It is knowing when to stay.

As a leader, this is crucial. You are meant to master transition — but not use it as avoidance. There are seasons when your growth requires completion. There are others when it requires commitment.

Discernment is your strength. Presence makes it wise.

Card #3: Your Neptune Card J♦

Neptune represents the dream that pulls you forward. This is where your vision, your imagination, and the subtle place where charisma can either become leadership or distortion. With the Jack of Diamonds in Neptune, you carry persuasive energy. You can articulate vision. You can inspire people to believe in possibility. You can sell an idea, tell a story, and invite others into your dream.

But this placement asks for deep honesty. Because the Jack of Diamonds can also convince. It can influence. It can bend reality toward what you want rather than what is true. In its distortion, you may feel that your role is to gather people, attention, money, or momentum around your vision—without always pausing to ask whether your tactics align with your integrity.

Your lesson here is discernment. Not shutting down your charisma—but refining it. Speaking truth rather than exaggeration. Inviting the right people rather than persuading everyone. Letting your vision be compelling because it is authentic, not because it is dazzling.

When you mature this Neptune placement, your influence becomes magnetic in a different way. People follow you because they trust you. They feel respected rather than recruited. Your dreams become collaborative rather than self-serving.

Card #4: Your Pluto Card 4♥

Pluto is where transformation lives. It is the place your old strategies are gently dismantled so something deeper can form. With the Four of Hearts in Pluto, your evolution is emotional. It is about learning true connection.

For someone who lives strongly in the physical world—money, health, opportunity—the Four of Hearts can feel unfamiliar. It asks you to commit emotionally. To pour yourself into relationships not for what you will gain, but for the bond itself. It asks you to experience reciprocity. Devotion. Stability in love.

This can be challenging because your Five of Diamonds nature is comfortable with change. You may have experienced early loss, endings, or instability that taught you to adapt quickly. You may even pride yourself on your ability to move on. But Pluto says: *Stay here.* Not forever. But long enough to let connection reshape you.

As you learn to build healthy emotional foundations, something profound shifts. The need to control outcomes softens. The attachment to specific material desires loosens. You begin to realize that true security is not found in constant motion—it is found in meaningful connection.

Card #5: Your Cosmic Result Card 4 ◆

When you live your chart fully, your cosmic result is the Four of Diamonds. This is stability in the material world. It is a foundation that supports you financially and physically without constant strain. It is systems that work. Structures that endure. Wealth that feels steady rather than volatile.

What is beautiful about this result is that it does not come through force. It comes through connection. Through pacing. Through maturity. When you stop chasing every opportunity and begin choosing wisely, when your influence becomes honest, when your relationships become reciprocal rather than transactional, your material world steadies itself.

There is no begging, convincing, or scrambling required. You naturally build what supports you. Prosperity becomes something you inhabit rather than pursue. And the intensity of the Five of Diamonds softens into confident adaptability rather than restless motion.

Integration — Your Healer's Code in Motion

When we look at your chart as a whole, a clear arc emerges. You are someone who feels life fully and moves quickly. You are capable of dramatic change and decisive action. But your deeper journey is not about speed. It is about steadiness.

Your Mars card teaches you completion instead of constant initiation. Your Neptune card refines your influence so it is rooted in truth. Your Pluto card asks you to anchor yourself in love rather than outcomes. And when those lessons are integrated, you arrive at the Four of Diamonds—a life that feels supported rather than chaotic.

So how do you know if you are living your chart? Notice your pace. Are you rushing because stillness feels unsafe? Notice your prosperity. Does it feel like a roller coaster, or like something steadily building? Notice your relationships. Are they strategic, or are they nourishing? Notice your influence. Are you persuading people into your dream, or inviting them into something that truly serves them?

When you are living your chart, freedom does not disappear—it becomes wise. Change does not control you—you direct it. Prosperity does not feel like something you must chase—it becomes something you can rest inside.

Affirmation of Alignment

I move with freedom and wisdom. I build relationships and structures that nourish my life, and I allow prosperity to grow from connection rather than control.

6♦

Matt & Joy Kahn

Life Chart

		K♠	8♦	10♣			

A♠	3♦	5♣	10♠	Q♣	A♣	3♡	☿
2♡	9♠	9♣	J♡	5♠	7♦	7♡	♀
8♣ MOON	J♠	2♦	4♣	6♡	K♦	K♡	♂
A♦ URANUS	A♡ SATURN	8♠ JUPITER	10♦ HEALER'S CODE MARS	10♡ VENUS	4♠ MERCURY	6♦ HEALER'S CODE BIRTHCARD	♃
5♦	7♣	9♡ TRANS-FORMED SELF	3♠ COSMIC LESSON	3♣ HEALER'S CODE COSMIC RESULT	5♡ HEALER'S CODE PLUTO	Q♦ HEALER'S CODE NEPTUNE	♄
J♦	K♣	2♣	7♠	9♦	J♣	Q♠	♅
Q♡	6♠	6♣	8♡	2♠	4♦	4♡	♆
♆	♅	♄	♃	♂	♀	☿	

Card #1: Your Birth Card 6 ◆

If you are a Six of Diamonds, your life often feels like a conversation with value—what matters, what's worth it, what's truly supportive, what is asked of you, and what you are allowed to receive. There can be seasons where you feel like the luckiest person in the room—where doors open, resources appear, and the physical world seems to respond to you with surprising generosity. And then there can be other seasons where the very same physical world feels heavy, demanding, and full of responsibility. The swing can be confusing until you realize the deeper teaching: you are learning how to hold prosperity with grace, not pressure.

The Six of Diamonds is a harmony card. It asks you to love what is and still welcome what more can be. It teaches you to respect what you already have—your home, your health, your resources, your environment, the people you care for—without losing your appetite for growth and expansion. You are not meant to choose between gratitude and desire. You are meant to learn how they can coexist in the same heart: appreciation for what is here, and openness to what wants to arrive next.

As a healer, coach, or leader, this is a deep initiation because you often carry a natural sense of responsibility for others. When you see what's possible, you don't just want it for yourself—you want it for your community, your clients, your family, your team. You want everyone to thrive. You want to be part of what helps people feel supported in real, tangible ways. And the lesson is not to lose that generosity. The lesson is to make sure your generosity doesn't quietly become the way you abandon yourself.

Card #2: Your Mars Card 10 ◆

Mars reveals how your passion moves—what motivates you when life demands action. With the Ten of Diamonds in Mars, you are attuned to prosperity. Not only in the sense of money, but in the sense of outcomes. You can see what can grow. You can sense where stability can be created. You can look at an idea, a business, a vision, a structure, and know how to bring it into fuller expression in the material world. There is something in you that understands expansion.

But the Ten of Diamonds also amplifies the Six of Diamonds responsibility theme. When money is coming in, or when your ability to create is recognized, you may feel an even greater pull to take care of everyone around you. You may feel responsible to make sure others are provided for, their dreams are met, their needs are handled—especially if you have the capacity to do it. And slowly, almost without noticing, you can begin to treat your own needs as negotiable. You might move money out faster than you receive it because someone needs something. Or you might tighten and withhold spending on yourself because you're afraid it won't be there later.

The Ten of Diamonds is not asking you to stop supporting others. It is asking you to stop equating love with carrying. It reminds you that your role is not to hold the entire world on your shoulders simply because you are capable. You are here to nurture visions into prosperity, yes— but you are also here to live a life that feels like it belongs to you. When you honor that, something shifts. The energy stops feeling like burden and becomes creative stewardship— growth that includes you, not growth that costs you.

Card #3: Your Neptune Card Q ♦

Neptune is where your dreams activate you, where your vision of what life could be lives, and the subtle way you relate to receiving. With the Queen of Diamonds in Neptune, your soul is learning the art of flow. This card knows how to give and receive without guilt. It knows how to be nourished by the physical world. It knows how to enjoy prosperity—not as excess, but as a form of participation in life.

For the Six of Diamonds, this is crucial. Because when you carry responsibility, even beautiful things can start to feel like they must be managed. You might measure everything—where the money goes, whether you're making the right decisions, whether your time is being invested properly, whether you're doing enough, whether you're doing it "correctly." The Queen of Diamonds gently interrupts that habit. She says: *Let yourself be cared for too.* Let the prosperity actually land. Let yourself feel it. Let yourself enjoy it without needing to justify it.

This Neptune placement also challenges the part of you that questions your worth. The Queen of Diamonds often grows through stretching their sense of value—allowing themselves to receive more than they think is fair, more than they think is "for them," more than they're used to. Not from entitlement. From expansion. From the willingness to meet life at a higher level of abundance without shrinking back into old stories of scarcity or self-denial.

Card #4: Your Pluto Card 5 ♥

Pluto is the crucible. It is where old patterns fall away so your deeper truth can emerge. With the Five of Hearts in Pluto, your transformation is emotional freedom. It is the realization that you get to step away from what drains you—even if you've been doing it for a long time.

This card speaks directly to a common Six of Diamonds wound: the sense that love is responsibility. That family is something you must get right. That relationships are something you must manage. That caring equals burden. And because you are devoted, because you are conscientious, because you actually *do* care, you may keep showing up long past the point where joy has disappeared. You may tell yourself it's just what love requires. Pluto says: *No.* Love is not meant to feel like a sentence. Love is not meant to feel like constant obligation. Love is not meant to be something you perform perfectly so no one is upset.

The Five of Hearts teaches you that you have choices. You can say goodbye. You can change dynamics. You can set boundaries. You can stop allowing your heart to convince you that you must remain in emotionally draining situations to prove your devotion. And when you begin to choose your freedom—lovingly, clearly, without drama—you discover something unexpected: your capacity to love doesn't diminish. It expands. Because now love becomes playful again. It becomes something you experience, not something you manage.

Card #5: Your Cosmic Result Card 3♣

Your cosmic result is what becomes possible when you live the full arc of your chart. With the Three of Clubs as your result, the story ends in expression. In wisdom made shareable. In your voice becoming clear. In your knowledge becoming creative. In collaboration becoming joyful rather than heavy.

This is the fruit of everything your chart has been teaching. When you stop carrying everyone as a way of proving love, you regain energy. When you let yourself receive, you regain fullness. When you step away from dynamics that drain you, you regain play. And then your mind comes alive in a new way—the Three of Clubs way—where you can create, teach, write, speak, share, build, and collaborate from genuine enjoyment.

The Three of Clubs also softens the Six of Diamonds fear of "getting it right." It reminds you that life is not a ledger you must balance perfectly. It is a lived experience. Your wisdom is real, but it is meant to be expressed with warmth. Your leadership is powerful, but it is meant to include joy. Your contribution grows when you feel inspired—when your creativity is allowed to breathe.

Integration — Your Healer's Code in Motion

When you look at your chart as a whole, you can see the central theme: harmony with the material world without becoming burdened by it. You are learning how to be prosperous without being pressured. How to be generous without disappearing. How to be responsible without letting responsibility become the way you measure your worth.

Your Mars card shows your capacity to expand prosperity and bring visions to life—but it also highlights the temptation to over-carry when others want something from you. Your Neptune card teaches you to receive, to enjoy, to trust flow, to let abundance nurture you rather than become another thing you must manage. Your Pluto card brings the emotional liberation that makes everything else possible: stepping away from draining dynamics, so love becomes enjoyable again. And when those pieces come together, the result is the Three of Clubs—creative expression, collaborative joy, and the freedom to share your wisdom without anxiety.

So how do you know if you are living your chart? Notice what prosperity feels like in your body. Does it feel like support, or does it feel like pressure to provide for everyone? Notice your relationship with giving. Are you giving from overflow, or from obligation? Notice your relationships. Do they feel nourishing and playful, or do they feel like something you must manage perfectly? And notice your creativity. When you are living your chart, your mind feels lighter. Your expression becomes easier. You feel more inspired to share, teach, and collaborate —not because you "should," but because you want to.

When you are living your chart, you still care deeply. You still show up. You still build. But you do it from a life that includes you. And that is what harmony in the material world actually looks like.

Affirmation of Alignment

I allow prosperity to support me as I support others, and I release what drains my heart. I choose harmony, joy, and creative expression as the natural rhythm of my life.

7◇

			K♤	8♢	10♧		
A♤	3♢	5♧	10♧	Q♧	A♧	3♡	☿
2♡	9♤	HEALER'S CODE 9♧	J♡	5♤	HEALER'S CODE 7♢	7♡	♀
SATURN	JUPITER	MARS	VENUS	MERCURY	BIRTHCARD	MOON	
8♧	J♤	2♢	HEALER'S CODE 4♧	HEALER'S CODE 6♡	HEALER'S CODE K♤	K♡	♂
	TRANS-FORMED SELF	COSMIC LESSON	COSMIC RESULT	PLUTO	NEPTUNE	URANUS	
A♢	A♡	8♧	10♢	10♡	4♤	6♢	♃
5♢	7♧	9♡	3♤	3♧	5♡	Q♢	♄
J♢	K♧	2♧	7♤	9♢	J♧	Q♧	♅
Q♡	6♤	6♧	8♡	2♧	4♢	4♡	♆
♆	♅	♄	♃	♂	♀	☿	

Card #1: Your Birth Card — 7♦

If you are a Seven of Diamonds, you often carry a heart that is both tender and ambitious at the same time. You want to be loved. Not as a passing feeling, not as a brief moment of attention, but as a deep, steady experience of being cared for and seen for who you truly are. And because your suit is Diamonds, love can easily become tangled with the physical world—compliments, gifts, affection, achievement, beauty, success, the things that can be counted and noticed and measured. It's as if part of you is trying to "prove" love exists by making it visible.

This is where the Seven of Diamonds becomes such a profound initiation. Because love, the thing you want most, is not something you can weigh or quantify. It can't be secured through perfection. It can't be guaranteed by being the best, looking the best, winning the most, or earning the most. And yet the drive to be extraordinary can be very strong in you. It can become fuel—fuel for achievement, for growth, for expanding your world, for creating a life that feels rich and beautiful and full. But it can also become exhausting, especially when your body is the one that eventually has to say, "Slow down. I can't keep up with this pace."

There is also a genuine love of life in you that deserves to be honored. You tend to love beauty. You tend to love play. Many Seven of Diamonds feel most alive in the arts, in nature, in movement, in travel, in physical experience—anything that lets you taste the world rather than merely survive it. And this is important, because part of your healing is realizing that the world is not something that must comply in order for you to feel loved. The world is a place where you get to *experience* your own love—through participation, through attention, through the way you pour your heart into what you're living.

When you awaken to that truth, something loosens. You begin to let yourself and others off the hook from perfection. You begin to see that love is not a transaction where you perform and life rewards you. Love is the current that can move through you while you are alive. It is felt in the way you meet a moment, not only in the outcome you get from it.

Card #2: Your Mars Card 9♣

Mars reveals how your passion moves—what energizes you, what motivates you, and what your fire is meant to accomplish. With the Nine of Clubs in Mars, your passion is meant to become devoted. Not scattered. Not constantly reaching for the next "more." Devoted. This card helps you bring a single path into completion. It asks you to cultivate something long enough for it to mature into mastery.

The Nine of Clubs also gifts you something that can feel both empowering and confronting: clarity. You can see through what isn't real. You can sense when someone is bending the truth. You can feel when something is being misrepresented or when a line is being crossed. There is a part of you that can call something out, name what others are avoiding, and walk away when walking away is necessary—even if it creates an ending.

For a Seven of Diamonds, this clarity is part of how love becomes refined. Because when you're trying to measure love through physical proof, it can be tempting to tolerate what doesn't feel true just to keep the picture intact—just to keep the "dream" alive. Mars Nine of Clubs interrupts that. It says: speak. Be honest. Choose what's real. Let your voice protect your heart. Let truth be your devotion, not perfection.

And when you live this Mars energy well, your passion becomes less frantic. You don't need to keep climbing just to feel worthy. You begin to experience the satisfaction of completion—the quiet confidence of finishing what matters, articulating what you've learned, and allowing your life to become a coherent story instead of a constant chase.

Card #3: Your Neptune Card K♦

Neptune holds your dreams and pulls you forward. It reveals what you long for and what you imagine is possible. With the King of Diamonds in Neptune, your vision includes prosperity. You are someone who can sense how wealth flows. You tend to see your value. You often understand, instinctively, how outcomes are created and how stability is built. You may even feel that you're meant to live with surplus—not just enough, but more than enough—so you can invest, expand, enjoy, and create a life that feels abundant.

And there is a beauty in that. Prosperity, for you, is not only about money. It is about play. It is about having the resources to experience the world you love. It is about being able to pour your heart into what matters without feeling limited by scarcity. The King of Diamonds in Neptune can be a powerful magnet for those outcomes, because you can imagine them so vividly that you begin to move toward them naturally.

But Neptune also reveals the illusion that can sneak in: the feeling that "more" is the thing that will finally make you happy. That if the house were bigger, the vacation more extravagant, the lifestyle more elevated, then you could finally rest. The dream becomes endless expansion. Bigger becomes better. And you can chase "more" without realizing that what you're actually longing for is not a bigger life—it's a more *loved* life.

So the medicine here is not to reject prosperity. It is to remember what prosperity is for. It is meant to help you bring to fruition what you love. It is meant to support your devotion, not replace it. It is meant to widen your ability to participate in life, not become the only reason you participate.

Card #4: Your Pluto Card — 6♥

Pluto is where transformation happens—where the part of you that wants to control the physical world is softened by a deeper kind of love. With the Six of Hearts in Pluto, your evolution is into harmony. Not idealism. Harmony. The give and take of real relationship. The ability to experience love as something shared and lived, not something demanded through performance.

This is where your chart becomes deeply relational. The Six of Hearts does not ask you to abandon what you want. It asks you to stop holding everyone to extraordinary physical standards as proof of love. It asks you to let people be human. To let love be imperfect and still real. To let affection be expressed in the ways it naturally flows, rather than the ways you wish it would look.

At the same time, this card does not ask you to lower your values. The Six of Hearts cares about morals, integrity, and what truly guides a relationship. It asks you to consider: is this partnership a transaction, a means to an end, an arrangement to secure the physical world? Or is it a genuine shared experience—mutually beautiful, mutually supportive, mutually alive?

As you integrate this Pluto card, something tender happens. You begin to experience the immeasurable part of love again. You begin to realize that the love you've been trying to earn through perfection has always been available through presence. And once you feel that, your whole relationship with the material world begins to soften.

Card #5: Your Cosmic Result Card 4♣

Your cosmic result is what becomes possible when you live the full arc of your chart. With the Four of Clubs as your result, you arrive at understanding. The question that has lived in you— *How does this all work?*—begins to answer itself from the inside. Love, money, health, the material world, spirit, purpose… you start to see how the pieces fit together.

This is not just mental understanding. It is grounded wisdom. It's the feeling that you're no longer chasing life like a puzzle you must solve. Insight drops in. Perspective arrives. You begin to feel steadied by a deeper comprehension of the mechanics of things—how devotion works, how prosperity works, how relationships work, how alignment works.

And this matters so much for the Seven of Diamonds, because when you don't understand what's happening, you can try to compensate by perfecting the physical world—fixing the surface, improving the image, reaching for "more." But the Four of Clubs gives you a different kind of confidence. It gives you the ability to relax into a life that makes sense—not because everything goes your way, but because you understand how to meet what comes with wisdom and skill.

For the healer, coach, or leader, this is a beautiful culmination. You become someone who can articulate what you've lived. You can teach it. You can guide others through transitions with clarity. You can help people release what isn't true and commit to what matters. And you can do it without needing to prove your worth through perfection—because your worth is now anchored in understanding.

Integration — Your Healer's Code in Motion

When we step back and see your chart as one story, we see the central initiation: moving from measuring love to experiencing love. You are not wrong for wanting the physical world to reflect your value. You are not shallow for loving beauty, prosperity, and pleasure. You are simply a Diamond—meant to experience love in form. But your chart teaches you that love cannot be reduced to form alone. It must be felt. It must be lived. It must be shared.

Your Mars card helps you find devotion and truth—finishing what matters, speaking what is real, seeing through what is not, and letting that clarity guide your choices. Your Neptune card reveals your big prosperity dream, while reminding you that "more" is not the destination—it is a tool that supports what you love. Your Pluto card calls you into relational harmony—love that is reciprocal, values-based, and grounded in shared experience rather than performance. And your result brings the gift of understanding—how it all works—so you can stop chasing and start embodying wisdom.

So how do you know if you are living your chart? Notice how you relate to love when the physical world isn't perfect. Do you tighten, strive, and try to earn what you want through being "better"? Or can you breathe, soften, and allow love to be present even in imperfection? Notice your relationship with prosperity. Are you chasing "more" because you believe it will finally make you feel worthy, or are you allowing resources to support what you genuinely love? Notice your voice. Are you staying silent to keep the picture intact, or are you willing to speak truth— even when it creates an ending—so that your life can be built on what is real?

When you are living your chart, your ambition becomes devotion instead of pressure. Your love of the world becomes participation instead of measurement. And your heart begins to feel what it has been seeking all along: not proof of love, but the living experience of it—moving through you, with you, and as you.

Affirmation of Alignment

I release the need to measure love through perfection, and I let myself experience love as it truly is—present, living, and shared. I devote myself to what is real, and I trust the wisdom that rises within me.

8♦

Matt & Joy Kahn

Life Chart

		HEALER'S CODE	HEALER'S CODE		HEALER'S CODE		
		K♠ MERCURY	8♦ BIRTHCARD	10♣ MOON			
HEALER'S CODE A♠ PLUTO	HEALER'S CODE 3♦ NEPTUNE	5♣ URANUS	10♠ SATURN	Q♣ JUPITER	HEALER'S CODE A♣ MARS	3♡ VENUS	☿
2♡	9♠	9♣	J♡	5♠ TRANS- FORMED SELF	7♦ COSMIC LESSON	HEALER'S CODE 7♡ COSMIC RESULT	♀
8♣	J♠	2♦	4♣	6♡	K♦	K♡	♂
A♦	A♡	8♠	10♦	10♡	4♠	6♦	♃
5♦	7♣	9♡	3♠	3♣	5♡	Q♦	♄
J♦	K♣	2♣	7♠	9♦	J♣	Q♠	♅
Q♡	6♠	6♣	8♡	2♠	4♦	4♡	♆
♆	♅	♄	♃	♂	♀	☿	

Card #1: Your Birth Card 8 ♦

If you are an Eight of Diamonds, you are designed to generate prosperity. Not as a vague hope, not as a someday prayer, but as a lived capacity. You can see momentum. You can see the steps. You can look at a plan and feel almost unbothered by the amount of work it requires, because something in you understands how creation happens in the physical realm—one step after another, one choice after another, one act of devotion at a time. You are often unusually capable with details, logistics, and follow-through, and you may find yourself in roles where you're building something tangible—something that grows because you show up for it consistently.

This is why so many Eight of Diamonds become successful in very grounded, practical ways. You might be someone who works directly with the body, with hands-on service, with a craft, with a business that requires real-world management. You may have an instinct for production, operations, systems, and outcomes. You know how to create something sustainable. You know how to scale what works. You know how to leverage support and invite others to help you fulfill what you see.

And yet, there is a tenderness here that matters. Because what comes so naturally to you— building, producing, executing—can also become the very thing that hides you. You can become the one in the background making everything happen while quietly longing to be recognized, respected, and taken seriously as more than a producer. You may feel that people only notice what you *do*, not who you *are*. And beneath that longing is something even deeper: a desire to know yourself. To feel close to yourself. To discover what you truly love, not just what you are capable of making successful.

This is one of the great secrets of the Eight of Diamonds: you can build almost anything. But your fulfillment is not found in building everything. Your fulfillment is found in building what genuinely nourishes your soul. And this chart is going to keep leading you back to that question until you answer it with your whole heart.

Card #2: Your Mars Card A ♣

Mars reveals how your passion moves—what your inner fire is trying to awaken. With the Ace of Clubs in Mars, your passion is curiosity. It is the spark of the mind saying, *Who am I really? What do I actually want? What do I love enough to devote my life to?*

This is an important counterbalance to the Eight of Diamonds. Because the Eight can default to capability: "I can do this." "I can make that work." "I can turn this into something profitable." But the Ace of Clubs challenges you to choose based on resonance rather than competence. It invites you into experimentation—not reckless experimentation, but sacred exploration. An idea drops in. A possibility appears. A new fascination arrives. And each one is the universe offering you a mirror: *Does this light you up? Does this feel like you?*

This can be confusing at first, because your mind can generate a lot of possibilities, and you may feel pressure to act on every one of them. But Mars isn't asking you to implement everything you think about. Mars is asking you to listen closely enough to recognize which ideas are invitations into your next level of authenticity. When you follow that thread, you begin to build not just a successful life, but a meaningful one.

As a healer, coach, or leader, this is where your authority evolves. You stop being someone who only knows how to produce results, and you become someone who can speak from lived curiosity—someone who models self-discovery, choice, and purpose.

Card #3: Your Neptune Card 3♦

Neptune reveals your dreams—your imagination, your longing, and the place where your creativity can either become joy or pressure. With the Three of Diamonds in Neptune, you are profoundly creative. Ideas come through you like a steady current. You can see possibilities everywhere. You can imagine new offerings, new projects, new expansions, new ventures, new ways to build and create.

And because you are an Eight of Diamonds, you don't just imagine—your system immediately starts thinking, *How do I make it real?* This is where the dream becomes heavy. You may start to feel as though every idea is an obligation. As though every inspired thought must turn into a plan. As though you're failing if you don't bring each vision into form.

But the deeper medicine of the Three of Diamonds is choice. You are not here to create everything you can imagine. You are here to become a creative being who enjoys life again. To play. To explore. To let inspiration be inspiration—not a demand. This Neptune placement is teaching you that creativity is meant to be a source of nourishment. When you allow ideas to arrive without immediately turning them into pressure, your heart relaxes. Your nervous system softens. Your imagination becomes joyful again.

And the more you allow that, the clearer your true desires become. Your dream stops being a thousand possible lives. It becomes one life that you actually want to live.

Card #4: Your Pluto Card A♠

Pluto is the crucible. It is where you are transformed by what you can no longer avoid. With the Ace of Spades in Pluto, your transformation is about choosing. It is about endings. It is about walking forward without keeping one foot behind you.

This is where many Eight of Diamonds struggle, because you are skilled at building continuity. You are skilled at maintaining what works. You are skilled at carrying the past into the future and keeping everything running. But the Ace of Spades does not let you live in two worlds at once. It asks you to stop keeping old identities, old obligations, old versions of your life alive simply because you know how to manage them.

This Pluto placement teaches you that transition requires commitment. It is not enough to dream about the next chapter while still giving your best energy to the old one. Your path asks you to release what is no longer aligned—even if it is profitable, even if it is familiar, even if it has been part of your story for a long time. When you are willing to say goodbye, you open space for a new level of peace, prosperity, and flow.

For the healer, coach, or leader, this is sacred. Because you are here to model what many people fear: the courage to end what is complete. The willingness to step into the unknown. The devotion to the future over the comfort of the familiar.

Card #5: Your Cosmic Result Card 7♥

Your cosmic result is what becomes possible when you live your whole chart. And your result is the Seven of Hearts—a deep, mature experience of love and fulfillment. This is not the kind of love that is naïve. It is the kind of love that has learned discernment. Love that refuses illusion. Love that wants integrity, consistency, and real follow-through.

The Seven of Hearts asks a very specific question: *What does it feel like when I am fully leaned into my loving expression? What does it feel like when life is so rich and so honest that I can enjoy it—not as performance, but as truth?*

This is the beautiful resolution of the Eight of Diamonds journey. Because you begin life building to be seen. Building to be respected. Building to be acknowledged. Building to prove you're worthy of the success you can already create. But the Seven of Hearts reveals that the recognition you've been craving is ultimately an inner recognition—your own ability to see yourself, love yourself, and live a life that reflects what your heart actually values.

As a leader, this makes you incredibly potent. People feel the difference between someone who is successful and someone who is fulfilled. Success can be impressive. Fulfillment is contagious. Fulfillment changes rooms. Fulfillment gives people permission to tell the truth about what they really want.

Integration — Your Healer's Code in Motion

When we look at your chart as one unfolding story, we see the invitation clearly. You are built to create prosperity through devotion and practical action. You can see steps and follow them. You can build and scale. But the deeper purpose of your chart is not simply to create more. It is to create what you love—so you can finally feel close to yourself.

Your Mars card invites self-discovery through curiosity—letting ideas reveal who you are, rather than using your ability to build as the only compass. Your Neptune card reveals the creative dream field, and the lesson of not turning every idea into an obligation. Your Pluto card brings the turning point: choosing, ending, committing fully to the next chapter instead of living between worlds. And when you do that, your result is a love that is real—discerned, embodied, honest, fulfilling. The Seven of Hearts.

So how do you know if you are living your chart? Notice what you're building and why. Are you building to prove yourself, or are you building because it truly nourishes you? Notice your relationship with ideas. Do they excite you, or do they immediately become pressure? Notice whether you keep old worlds alive out of habit, or whether you have the courage to complete what is complete. And notice your heart. The Seven of Hearts doesn't ask you to be perfect. It asks you to be true. It asks you to choose love that is consistent, love that is embodied, love that matches words with action—beginning with the way you treat yourself.

When you are living your chart, your work still thrives. Your prosperity still grows. But now it grows around a life that feels meaningful. And the success you create becomes a container for fulfillment instead of a substitute for it.

Affirmation of Alignment

I choose what I love, release what is complete, and devote myself fully to the path ahead. I allow success to become a home for real fulfillment, guided by truth and love.

9♦

Matt & Joy Kahn — *Life Chart*

	K♠	8♦	10♣				
A♠	3♦	5♣	10♣	Q♣	A♣	3♥	☿
2♥	9♠	9♣	J♥	5♠	7♦	7♥	♀
8♣	J♠	2♦	4♣	6♥	K♦	K♥	♂
A♦	A♥	8♣	10♦	10♥	4♠	6♦	♃
5♦	7♣	9♥	3♠	3♣	5♥	Q♦	♄
J♦	**HEALER'S CODE** K♣	2♣	7♠	**HEALER'S CODE** 9♦	J♣	Q♣	♅
JUPITER	MARS	VENUS	MERCURY	BIRTHCARD	MOON		
Q♥	6♠	**HEALER'S CODE** 6♣	**HEALER'S CODE** 8♥	**HEALER'S CODE** 2♣	4♦	4♥	♆
TRANS-FORMED SELF	COSMIC LESSON	COSMIC RESULT	PLUTO	NEPTUNE	URANUS	SATURN	
♆	♅	♄	♃	♂	♀	☿	

Card #1: Your Birth Card 9 ♦

If you are a Nine of Diamonds, you tend to live with a quiet intensity that other people can feel, even when you don't speak about it. Your standards are high—not because you're trying to impress anyone, but because something in you is devoted to an idea of perfection. You want to know the highest possibility in any situation. You want to choose what is most aligned. You want to live with integrity that doesn't wobble when it's inconvenient. And because you are a Diamond, this devotion often shows up through what you create in the physical world—your work, your craft, your offerings, your art, your contributions, the tangible way you bring beauty and value to life.

This can be a gift and a burden at the same time. The gift is your artistry and your precision. You don't skim the surface. You look from every angle. You refine, sculpt, shape, improve, and polish until something feels complete. There's a kind of reverence in the way you work—like you're honoring the creation by not letting it be sloppy. But the burden is the inner pressure that can come with it. The sense that you must always be your best. The relentless private conversation about whether you've done enough, whether it's right enough, whether you're being integral enough. And when you live with that pressure for too long, other people can start to feel like they "fall short" around you—not because you're mean, but because your internal bar is set so high that it becomes hard to understand why others don't push the way you push.

There is also a more tender truth here: sometimes perfection is not only about excellence. Sometimes it is a way of avoiding endings. The Nine of Diamonds can love the creative process so much that completion feels like a kind of loss. Even when you're proud of what you made, there can be a bittersweet feeling in the final moment—because finishing means it's time to release. It's time to let go. It's time to step into the next chapter. So you refine a little longer. You adjust one more detail. You make it harder than it has to be. Not because you're incapable of finishing, but because part of you doesn't want the journey to end.

And this creates a fascinating paradox: you want to be cared for, supported, and prosperous… and yet you may quietly sabotage that support because it would mean you'd have to stop, receive, and rest. You might give money away just to have to rebuild it again. You might create new goals the moment the old ones are achieved. You might keep moving because the creative journey feels safer than the stillness of fulfillment. This isn't a flaw. It's a pattern asking for love.

Card #2: Your Mars Card K♣

Mars reveals how your passion moves—what motivates you, what energizes you, and what your fire wants to build. With the King of Clubs in Mars, your drive is to lead with meaning. You don't just want to create something beautiful. You want to create something that matters. You want to stand for something. You want your work to hold a message, a purpose, a reason people can feel in their bones.

This Mars placement also reveals why your standards are so high. The King of Clubs wants authority—not in the sense of ego, but in the sense of responsibility. It wants to be respected. It wants to be relied upon. It wants to build something that has weight and longevity. And so you keep refining because you're not trying to make something "good enough." You're trying to create something you can stand behind without flinching. You're trying to make something that feels worthy of your own trust.

But here is the invitation for you as a healer, coach, or leader: your authority is not only in what you produce. It is also in how you pace yourself. The King of Clubs can become heavy when it believes it must carry meaning alone. It can turn leadership into pressure. It can make you feel like the vision depends on your relentless effort. Your Mars card is asking you to build something respected, yes—but also something that gives you room to keep creating inside it, without needing to destroy yourself to prove its worth.

When this is lived well, your leadership becomes spacious. You begin to realize you don't need to exhaust yourself to be credible. You become someone who can create meaning and sustain it. And that is a different kind of power.

Card #3: Your Neptune Card 2♠

Neptune represents the dream that pulls you forward. It's your vision of what could be, and the subtle way you relate to support. With the Two of Spades in Neptune, your soul is learning partnership. Not partnership as dependency, but partnership as harmony. You are meant to align with people who help you balance. People who help you step back. People who help you bring things to fruition without making you feel like you have to do everything alone.

This is important because the Nine of Diamonds can become so absorbed in the creative process that relationships start to feel like interruptions. Community can feel distracting. Commitment can feel like it takes energy away from what you're building. And if you've been hurt before, or if you've seen how complicated relationships can be, it may feel easier to stay in your work where you have control. Work won't leave you. Work won't disappoint you. Work won't break your heart.

But Neptune is showing you a different truth. The right partnerships don't pull you away from your purpose—they protect it. They help you do the parts that drain you. They help you with the pieces you tend to avoid. They remind you that you do not have to prove your worth through solitary struggle. They make the path more sustainable. And in the long run, they actually give you more space to create, because you're no longer carrying the entire world by yourself.

When you begin to trust this, partnership becomes part of your dream—not just success. You start letting life support you through people, not only through your own effort.

Card #4: Your Pluto Card 8♥

Pluto is the crucible. It is where your greatest challenge becomes your greatest liberation. With the Eight of Hearts in Pluto, your transformation is community. Connection. The willingness to build bonds that are deep, real, and enduring.

This is often the place the Nine of Diamonds wants to avoid. Not because you don't love people, but because closeness can feel costly. It can feel like it will take time from what you're building. It can feel like it will ask you to risk heartbreak. It can feel unpredictable. And for someone who finds comfort in the reliability of creation, community can feel like the more vulnerable terrain.

Yet this is the key to your chart. The Eight of Hearts is the medicine that softens the pressure you carry. When you lean into relationship, something in you relaxes. You stop holding everything so tightly. You stop believing you must be perfect to be safe. You begin to experience a deeper kind of nourishment—one that isn't earned through performance or excellence, but received through belonging.

And the deeper truth is this: community doesn't compete with creativity. It supports it. When you are held by people, your creative process becomes more joyful. Your endings become less frightening. Your success becomes less isolating. You begin to remember that you are not here to create alone—you are here to create as a human being, in relationship with life.

Card #5: Your Cosmic Result Card 9♣

Your cosmic result is what becomes possible when you live your full chart. With the Six of Clubs as your result, you arrive at harmony of purpose. This is where the pressure to perform begins to dissolve. This is where your standards become wisdom rather than judgment. This is where your work no longer requires you to deplete yourself in order to feel worthy of it.

The Six of Clubs is purpose lived with balance. It is the feeling that you can contribute meaningfully without sacrificing your well-being. You can be devoted without becoming harsh. You can refine without obsessing. You can lead without carrying everything alone. And because this is a Clubs result, it also speaks to the mind: your thoughts become kinder. Your inner world becomes more cooperative. You begin to experience the satisfaction of creating and completing, then beginning again—without the heaviness of loss in every ending.

For the healer, coach, or leader, this result is powerful. People feel safe with you because you're not demanding perfection from yourself or from them. They feel inspired by you because you are living purpose with humanity. Your excellence becomes welcoming rather than intimidating. Your integrity becomes an invitation rather than a verdict.

Integration — Your Healer's Code in Motion

When we step back and view your chart as a single story, a clear pattern emerges. You are a creator with extraordinarily high standards, and your love of the process can make endings feel surprisingly tender. You are meant to build something meaningful, something respected, something you can lead with authority and heart. But you are not meant to do it through isolation.

Your Mars card calls you into purposeful leadership—the kind that creates lasting impact and gives you room to keep creating inside what you build. Your Neptune card teaches you partnership as support, not compromise. Your Pluto card reveals the deeper medicine: community and relationship are not distractions from your destiny; they are what make your destiny sustainable. And when you live those lessons, the result is the Six of Clubs—purpose that feels harmonious rather than pressurized.

So how do you know if you are living your chart? Notice what your standards feel like inside you. Do they feel inspiring and clarifying, or do they feel like constant self-critique? Notice whether you keep refining because it truly matters, or because finishing feels like a loss. Notice how you relate to support. Are you letting yourself be helped, or are you insisting you must do it alone to feel safe? And notice your relationships. Are you avoiding community to protect your time, or are you allowing community to nourish you so your creativity can actually thrive?

When you are living your chart, your excellence becomes gentler. Your purpose becomes steadier. Your endings become easier to accept, because you trust that you can begin again. And you start to feel something you may have been chasing through perfection all along: a sense of belonging in your own life.

Affirmation of Alignment

I allow support and community to strengthen my purpose, and I release the need to earn rest through perfection. I create with integrity, welcome endings with grace, and trust the next beginning.

10◇

		K♠	8◇	10♣			
A♠	3◇	5♣	10♠	Q♣	A♣	3♡	☿
2♡	9♠	9♣	J♡	5♠	7◇	7♡	♀
8♣	J♠	2◇	4♣	6♡	K◇	K♡	♂
A◇ HEALER'S CODE / MARS	A♡ VENUS	8♠ MERCURY	10◇ HEALER'S CODE / BIRTHCARD	10♡ MOON	4♠	6◇	♃
5◇ COSMIC LESSON	7♣ HEALER'S CODE / COSMIC RESULT	9♡ HEALER'S CODE / PLUTO	3♠ HEALER'S CODE / NEPTUNE	3♣ URANUS	5♡ SATURN	Q◇ JUPITER	♄
J◇	K♣	2♣	7♠	9◇	J♣	Q♠ TRANSFORMED SELF	♅
Q♡	6♠	6♣	8♡	2♠	4◇	4♡	♆
♇	♅	♄	♃	♂	♀	☿	

Card #1: Your Birth Card 10 ◆

If you are a Ten of Diamonds, you carry an energy the world tends to recognize. People often feel your momentum before they understand your heart. There is a natural prosperity current in you—an ability to align with what you need, and often a little more than you expected. It can look like luck from the outside, but it rarely feels like "luck" from the inside. It feels like drive. It feels like appetite. It feels like a deep relationship with the physical world and a willingness to participate fully in it.

You are often someone who loves being alive in a body. Not in a superficial way, but in a devotional way. You love experiences that remind you life is real—movement, travel, new places, the sensory beauty of this world. You might be the kind of person who can feel nourished by a sunset, a long drive, the ocean, the simple pleasure of being present with something beautiful. Your spirit learns through experience, and you tend to feel most inspired when life is allowed to be rich, varied, and spacious.

And yet, even with all this natural prosperity, you still have your own inner tension. Because the Ten of Diamonds can feel an invisible expectation to keep delivering. When things come easily, the world can start to assume they always will. And you may start to assume that too. The pressure becomes subtle: *Keep it going. Keep it rising. Keep it moving forward.* Even when you're grateful, you can feel the weight of needing to maintain the momentum—especially if you've become the person others rely on for results, resources, or stability.

Your deeper initiation is not just to be prosperous. It is to learn how to enjoy prosperity without making it a performance. To let abundance be something you receive, not something you must constantly recreate to prove you're worthy of it.

Card #2: Your Mars Card A ◆

Mars reveals how your passion moves—what fuels you when it's time to take action. With the Ace of Diamonds in Mars, your drive comes alive through beginnings. You prosper when you lean into new experiences, fresh adventures, and first steps. The beginning of a journey is where you have a special kind of clarity. You can sense what is needed to get something off the ground —the foundational pieces, the first priorities, the essential resources.

9 of Diamonds

This is why you may be unusually gifted at helping other people start. If someone is at the beginning of a health journey, a business journey, a healing journey, a life transition—you can feel what matters most first. You can see what will create stability later. You can help people establish a foundation that makes completion possible. And for yourself, you often know exactly what needs to be put in place to succeed: time, resources, structure, support, the right relationships, the right environment. You tend to be prepared, instinctively, in ways that make success more likely.

But Mars also asks for balance. Because the Ace of Diamonds loves initiation, it can create a life filled with beginnings but lacking devotion to what needs to be nurtured into legacy. You can start many things and be excellent at them, and still feel a subtle emptiness if none of them are given the time to become deeply meaningful. Your Mars card is not asking you to start less. It's asking you to start wisely—and to recognize which beginnings are simply experiences, and which are doorways into something that wants to last.

Card #3: Your Neptune Card 3♠

Neptune is where your dreams reveal themselves—your imagination, your longing, and the place where inspiration can multiply faster than the nervous system can hold. With the Three of Spades in Neptune, you are built to reimagine. You can look at what already exists and see how it could be improved, refined, elevated, taken to a new level. You can take something functional and make it more meaningful. You can take something ordinary and make it more powerful.

This is a tremendous gift for a healer, coach, or leader, because you are not only a starter—you are an upgrader. You can see patterns, structure, and design in a way that helps you evolve systems. You can sense how to make something stronger, more effective, more sustainable. Your mind has the capacity to keep innovating and to keep seeing possibility even when others are tired.

The challenge is the overflow. Too many new ideas at once. Too many projects at once. Too many reinventions layered on top of each other. Neptune can make it all feel equally important. And then, without realizing it, you're trying to build five futures simultaneously. You start to feel scattered. The joy starts to thin out. And the gift turns into a kind of inner pressure: *If I can see the possibility, I should make it real.*

This Neptune placement is teaching you devotion through discernment. You are allowed to have many adventures. You are allowed to explore. But the things that want to become legacy—the ones that matter most—you must choose them, and then nourish them with focus. Your dream field becomes more peaceful when you stop trying to fulfill every possibility and instead commit to the ones that truly call your heart.

Card #4: Your Pluto Card 9♥

Pluto is where the deepest transformation happens—the place where your attachments are revealed so you can learn a freer kind of love. With the Nine of Hearts in Pluto, your growth edge is letting go. Not letting go in a cold way, but letting go in a mature way.

You love people. You love collecting experiences, relationships, memories, connections. And yet the Nine of Hearts struggles with endings. It wants everyone to stay forever. It wants the people who once mattered to continue to matter in the same way. It wants the journey to remain intact. And when life does what life does—when people change, move, pivot, drift, or complete a chapter—it can touch a tender place in you.

This is why affection and acknowledgment can feel so important to you. You often thrive when people express their love openly—when they show it, say it, celebrate you, nurture you, remind you that you matter. It's not vanity. It's reassurance. It's your heart trying to feel safe. And when you don't feel that reassurance, you may hold tighter than you need to. You may stay connected to people who are no longer aligned. You may hesitate to release what is complete. You may try to keep everyone on the ride with you, even when your life is asking you to move forward.

Pluto is teaching you a sacred truth: your vision can still be fulfilled even if not everyone stays. Your path is not dependent on who remains. Your love is real, but it is not meant to become a cage—for you or for anyone else. When you let relationships take their course, you create space for the ones that truly nourish you to deepen, and for your heart to feel supported in a more stable way.

Card #5: Your Cosmic Result Card 7♣

Your cosmic result is what becomes possible when you live the full arc of your chart. With the Seven of Clubs as your result, you arrive at wisdom. Not abstract wisdom—lived wisdom. The kind that comes from experience, reflection, discernment, and the willingness to learn from life instead of racing past it.

This is a beautiful completion for the Ten of Diamonds, because you are so intrigued by life. You want meaning. You want to understand what things are for. You want to know what you're learning, what others are learning, why certain patterns repeat, why certain doors open, why certain chapters end. When you live your chart fully, meaning begins to arrive more naturally. Insight starts to "drop in." You stop chasing understanding as something outside you and begin to experience it as something that rises within you.

And as that wisdom ripens, you become a natural guide. You share what you've learned. You mentor, teach, train, coach—formally or informally. People look up to you not only because you are prosperous, but because you are seasoned. They can feel that you've lived. They can feel that you've learned. They can feel that your success has been shaped into something deeper than achievement.

Integration — Your Healer's Code in Motion

When we look at your chart as one story, we see a pattern that is both luminous and tender. You are here to experience the world fully, to create prosperity, to begin new adventures, and to help others start strong. Your energy thrives in motion and expansion. But your chart is also teaching you the art of choosing—what to build, what to devote yourself to, what to allow to complete, and what to release with love.

Your Mars card opens the path through beginnings and variety, reminding you that you prosper when life stays alive. Your Neptune card invites innovation, while also asking you to slow down enough to focus on what truly matters. Your Pluto card is the heart lesson: fulfillment doesn't require everyone to stay. Love doesn't mean gripping. And the result is the Seven of Clubs—the wisdom that comes when you've stopped trying to outrun endings and started learning from them.

So how do you know if you are living your chart? Notice your relationship with "more." Is more coming from inspiration, or from the fear that if you stop you'll lose momentum? Notice your projects. Are you building many futures at once, or have you chosen the few that matter most and given them your devotion? Notice your relationships. Are you allowing people to evolve, or are you holding on because letting go feels like losing love? And notice your inner world. When you are living your chart, life feels meaningful—not because you have answers to everything, but because you trust what you're learning as you go.

When you are living your chart, prosperity becomes a playground rather than more responsibility. Your heart becomes freer, not harder. And your success ripens into wisdom you can share—so what you create doesn't just look good in the world, it leaves something good behind.

Affirmation of Alignment

I choose what matters, release what is complete, and trust that love remains even when chapters change. I welcome prosperity, presence, and wisdom as the natural rhythm of my path.

J ♦

Matt & Joy Kahn

Life Chart

		HEALER'S CODE	HEALER'S CODE				
		K♠ COSMIC LESSON	8♦ COSMIC RESULT	10♣ PLUTO			
A♠	3♦	5♣	10♠	Q♣	A♣	3♥ TRANS-FORMED SELF	☿
2♥	9♠	9♣	J♥	5♠	7♦	7♥	♀
8♣	J♠	2♦	4♣	6♥	K♦	K♥	♂
A♦	A♥	8♠	10♦	10♥	4♣	6♦	♃
5♦	7♣	9♥	3♠	3♣	5♥	Q♦	♄
HEALER'S CODE J♦ BIRTHCARD	K♣ MOON	2♣	7♠	9♦	J♣	Q♠	♅
HEALER'S CODE Q♥ NEPTUNE	6♠ URANUS	6♣ SATURN	HEALER'S CODE 8♥ JUPITER	2♣ MARS	4♦ VENUS	4♥ MERCURY	♆
♆	♅	♄	♃	♂	♀	☿	

Card #1: Your Birth Card J♦

If you are a Jack of Diamonds, you are often one of the most magnetic people in the room without even trying. There is a likability to you that feels effortless—playful, animated, enthusiastic, full of spark. People tend to enjoy being around you. They feel uplifted. They feel entertained. They feel your energy and, for a moment, life feels lighter just because you're present.

And yet, beneath that easy charm, there is often a very private story unfolding. The Jack of Diamonds can feel far less confident on the inside than they appear on the outside. You may know exactly how to "show up" in a way that looks assured—how to speak, how to engage, how to present yourself—while quietly questioning your own capacity. You might wonder if you truly know enough. If you're skilled enough. If you can actually deliver what you want to be known for.

This is why the Jack of Diamonds is such an initiation into integrity. Because you don't just want to be liked. You want to be respected. You want to be honored as someone wise, someone capable, someone who can truly guide, teach, lead, and make a difference. And when you don't yet feel that competence in yourself, it can be tempting to lean even harder into charisma—to let your outer confidence become a mask for the inner uncertainty.

Your path is not here to shame that instinct. Your path is here to mature it. You are learning how to let your confidence become real—not performed. How to let your sparkle become anchored in skill. How to let your influence become something people trust because you've earned it through devotion, not because you've sold it through charm.

Card #2: Your Mars Card 2♠

Mars reveals how your passion moves—what motivates you, and what your drive needs in order to thrive. With the Two of Spades in Mars, your fire is shaped by partnership. You are not meant to go alone. You are meant to choose your people wisely. Your friends. Your associates. Your collaborators. The environments you place yourself in. These choices will either help you rise into your potential or keep you circling in self-doubt.

This is a powerful truth for the Jack of Diamonds. Because you can get opportunities easily. People give you chances. People want to believe in you. Your energy inspires trust long enough for a door to open. But what happens after the door opens depends on whether you've surrounded yourself with the right kind of support—people who call you forward, who help you develop your skills, who invite you into a deeper level of discipline, and who are willing to teach you what you don't yet know.

Mars Two of Spades is asking you to become willing to be a student. That can feel humbling for someone with natural charisma. But it is precisely this humility that turns your charm into authority. The right partners will not just celebrate your brilliance—they will help you strengthen it. They will not just admire your potential—they will help you embody it.

And as you learn to choose wisely, your drive changes. You stop trying to prove yourself to everyone. You start developing yourself for the right people. And that shift becomes the beginning of true confidence.

Card #3: Your Neptune Card Q♥

Neptune reveals your dreams—your longing, your vision, and the way desire can become both inspiration and distortion. With the Queen of Hearts in Neptune, you are deeply romantic about love. Not only romance in the traditional sense, but the dream of being nurtured, adored, seen, cherished, held. The dream of connection that feels like home.

This longing can be beautiful. It can soften your edge. It can keep your heart open. It can remind you that you're not here to live a purely transactional life. You are here to feel. You are here to connect. You are here to let love matter.

But Neptune can also turn love into an idol. You may place love on a pedestal and believe that if you could just find the right relationship, the right devotion, the right person to adore you, then everything inside you would finally settle. You may become mesmerized by the prospect of being chosen, and that mesmerization can pull energy away from the slower work of skill-building and self-mastery.

The deeper invitation here is to let love be fuel, not distraction. To let love move through your life as nourishment, without requiring it to be the thing that saves you. The Queen of Hearts wants you open. The Queen wants you devoted and receptive. But the Queen also wants you free —free from using love as a shortcut around the work your soul is asking you to do.

Card #4: Your Pluto Card 10♣

Pluto is where your greatest transformation happens—where you are forged through devotion. With the Ten of Clubs in Pluto, your path is mastery through commitment. The part of you that wants to jump from one exciting experience to another is being asked to stay. To learn. To develop. To become an expert.

This card is the antidote to your insecurity. Not positive thinking. Not more performance. Not more charm. Devotion. The willingness to practice. The willingness to study. The willingness to be shaped by your craft until you can finally feel, in your bones, "I am capable of this."

The Ten of Clubs in Pluto also reveals something tender: leadership is not something you simply claim. For you, it is something that slowly chooses you. You are nurtured into it through the people you meet, the opportunities you're given, the doors that open, and the tests that require you to rise. Each time life gives you a "shot," the question becomes: will you use it to prove you're impressive, or will you use it to become wiser?

When you live this Pluto card well, you stop battling reality. You stop sugarcoating. You stop pretending things are better than they are. You begin telling the truth about where you are—and then you devote yourself to growth from that honest place. And slowly, the inner confidence you've wanted begins to match the outer confidence you've been performing.

Card #5: Your Cosmic Result Card 8 ◆

Your cosmic result is what becomes possible when you live your whole chart. With the Eight of Diamonds as your result, the devotion you've shown becomes prosperity that lasts. Not temporary wins. Not quick bursts of success followed by self-doubt. A steady, increasing flow of support in the material world—returning to you again and again because you have built something real.

This is the kind of prosperity that comes when you stop chasing attention and start building substance. When you stop relying on charm alone and begin embodying skill. When you stop needing love to rescue you and let love nourish you while you do your work.

The Eight of Diamonds is also an incredible healing for the Jack of Diamonds heart. Because what you've truly wanted is to feel respected and secure—not only liked. This result says: you can have that. But it will come through the slow devotion of Pluto. Through the wise choosing of Mars. Through letting love be inspiration without letting it become the entire destination.

And when that happens, your life becomes less about proving and more about living. Success becomes something you inhabit. Prosperity becomes something that supports you rather than something you must constantly chase.

Integration — Your Healer's Code in Motion

When we step back and look at your chart as a whole, the story is clear. You are a natural influencer—likable, magnetic, gifted at opening doors. But your deeper path is not about getting the chance. It is about becoming the person who can honor the chance.

Mars asks you to choose your partners wisely and to let yourself be taught. Neptune asks you to keep your heart open without letting the dream of love distract you from the work that builds real confidence. Pluto asks you to devote yourself to learning and mastery until your inner world becomes steady. And your result is the Eight of Diamonds—prosperity that comes from devotion, returning again and again because you've become someone who can hold what they've asked life for.

So how do you know if you are living your chart? Notice whether your confidence is rooted in skill or in performance. Notice whether you're jumping to the next excitement because you're inspired, or because staying would require you to face your insecurity and do the work. Notice your relationships. Are you choosing partners who help you rise, or partners who keep you comfortable in who you already are? And notice your relationship with love. Is love supporting your growth, or are you using love as a way to avoid the slow steps of becoming who you want to be?

When you are living your chart, your charm becomes more than charm—it becomes leadership. Your influence becomes more than influence—it becomes integrity. And the respect you've been seeking arrives naturally, not because you asked for it, but because you've become it.

Affirmation of Alignment

I choose relationships that help me grow, and I devote myself to mastering what I am here to teach. I allow love to nourish my path, and I welcome prosperity as the natural result of my devotion.

Q♦

Matt & Joy Kahn — *Life Chart*

	K♠	8♦	10♣			

A♠	3♦	5♣	10♠	Q♣	A♣	3♥	☿
2♥	9♠	9♣	J♥	5♠	7♦	7♥	♀
8♣	J♠	2♦	4♣	6♥	K♦	K♥	♂
A♦ MOON	A♥	8♠	10♦	10♥	4♠	6♦	♃
5♦ URANUS	7♣ SATURN	9♥ JUPITER	3♠ MARS (HEALER'S CODE)	3♣ VENUS	5♥ MERCURY	Q♦ BIRTHCARD (HEALER'S CODE)	♄
J♦	K♣	2♣ TRANSFORMED SELF	7♠ COSMIC LESSON	9♦ COSMIC RESULT (HEALER'S CODE)	J♣ PLUTO (HEALER'S CODE)	Q♠ NEPTUNE (HEALER'S CODE)	⛢
Q♥	6♠	6♣	8♥	2♠	4♦	4♥	♆
♆	⛢	♄	♃	♂	♀	☿	

Card #1: Your Birth Card Q ♦

If you are a Queen of Diamonds, your life rarely feels still.

You are positioned in a way that pulls experiences toward you quickly, sometimes so quickly that it can feel like you're living inside a moving river. Opportunities, people, invitations, ideas, paths, and possibilities tend to rotate around you. It's not that you are indecisive by nature. It's that your field is responsive—almost magnetic—and life gives you more options than most people know what to do with.

Early in the journey, this can create a particular kind of tension: you may feel like you have to choose the "right" thing quickly, before it disappears. And when you feel that pressure, your system may swing into chasing. Chasing prosperity. Chasing the next level. Chasing security. Chasing the feeling of being "set." And yet, what often happens for the Queen of Diamonds is that the more you chase wealth at the expense of relationship, the more empty it can feel—even if you're winning.

Then, as life evolves, there can be a second swing.

You start chasing relationship. Connection. Belonging. Romance. Approval. The feeling of being chosen. And sometimes this second swing happens at the expense of your career, your calling, or your devotion to what you know you're here to build. It's an archetype that can move between "If I have enough money, I'll be okay" and "If I have enough love, I'll be okay," as if fulfillment lives on one side of the scale.

But your chart is not here to punish you with that pendulum.

It's here to reveal something far more powerful: chasing either love or prosperity pushes them further away. Your path is not to pursue what you want from a place of lack. It is to become the embodiment of what you're seeking—so that love and wealth can unfold naturally as outcomes of who you are, not prizes you have to secure.

When the Queen of Diamonds matures, you become a conduit. Money flows in and out. Relationships flow in and out. Experiences arrive, move through you, and leave you wiser. You stop clenching around life and start trusting the rhythm of life. And that trust becomes your prosperity.

Card #2: Your Mars Card 3 ♠

Mars reveals how your drive moves, especially when you feel pressure.

Your Mars card, the Three of Spades, can show up first as anxiety—an edgy sense that something isn't quite in place yet. It may look like restlessness. Overthinking. The urge to keep moving. The urge to touch everything lightly because committing deeply to one thing feels risky when you can see ten other possible paths.

But the Three of Spades is not here to trap you in stress.

It's here to turn your nervous energy into devotion.

When you are out of sync, the Three of Spades can keep you at the surface—sampling, testing, tasting, beginning, shifting. And when you live at the surface, you can miss the depth that is available on your path. You can miss the very thing you're craving, because what you're craving is not another option. It's the feeling of depth inside the option you choose.

In alignment, the Three of Spades becomes a catalyst to create and refine.

It asks you to put time and attention into something that matters enough to stay with. It asks you to develop something for the world that carries a higher message, not because you have something to prove, but because you have something real to offer. This card doesn't just want you to do more. It wants you to go deeper—until your work stops being a chase and becomes a craft.

And for a healer, coach, or leader, that is everything.

Because depth is what builds trust. Depth is what creates transformation. Depth is what makes your presence undeniable.

Card #3: Your Neptune Card Q♠

Neptune is your calling, the higher vision that keeps tugging at you.

Your Neptune card is the Queen of Spades, which means you are being invited into a deeper relationship with wisdom, intuition, and inner knowing. There is a part of you that senses there is more. More meaning. More truth. More awareness than what can be measured by results alone. And when you begin to feel that invitation, you may find yourself drawn toward spiritual understanding, psychology, mysticism, higher learning—anything that promises "the deepest answer."

But Neptune can create a trap if you're not careful.

Sometimes the Queen of Spades in Neptune can feel like you have to chase enlightenment the way you once chased prosperity or relationship. You want to consume wisdom. Understand it. Learn it. Collect it. Experience it. And yet the Queen of Spades doesn't want to be accumulated. She wants to be integrated.

This is where your chart becomes exquisitely precise.

The depth you are seeking is not in money.

The depth you are seeking is not in relationship.

The depth you are seeking is who you become in the presence of both.

It's what you are willing to feel. What you are willing to admit. What you are willing to let transform you. It is the quiet courage to let life make you more honest, more spacious, more true.

The Queen of Spades also opens your intuition—not as a performance, not as something to emulate, but as a living relationship with yourself. She teaches you how to trust your life more. How to allow yourself to be enough for you. How to stop needing others—or outcomes—to complete what is already waiting inside you.

And yet she also warns you: don't get lost in the pursuit of "higher." Let wisdom move through you. Let it soften you. Let it shape your choices.

Card #4: Your Pluto Card J♣

Pluto is the crucible—where you are asked to stop shortcutting your growth.

Your Pluto card is the Jack of Clubs, and it carries an initiation into truth-telling, learning, and teaching. This card asks you to become sincere with knowledge. To recognize when you're meant to be the student, and when you're meant to be the guide. To value the process of becoming, not just the excitement of discovering something new.

The Jack of Clubs in Pluto can reveal a common temptation: you catch a piece of wisdom, it lights you up, and part of you wants to run with it immediately. To share it. Teach it. Build something around it. Make it real fast. And sometimes that can be beautiful—because you are quick, bright, and capable.

But Pluto asks for another layer.

Pluto asks you not to confuse inspiration with embodiment. Not to confuse "I learned something" with "I have become it." The Jack of Clubs here is a sacred discipline: take the time to develop your message. Let your understanding deepen. Let your life be the place where the truth matures inside you.

As a healer, coach, or leader, this is where your authority becomes clean—not in tone, but in integrity.

People can feel the difference between borrowed wisdom and lived wisdom.

This placement is your invitation to be devoted to what you teach. To let your learning ripen. To be earnest enough to keep going deeper, even after you think you "get it."

Card #5: Your Cosmic Result Card 9 ◆

Your result is the Nine of Diamonds, and it reads like the final exhale after a long chase.

Because the Nine of Diamonds is the fulfillment of what you thought you had to pursue so hard—material ease, relational satisfaction, the feeling of having "enough," the sense that life is finally working with you instead of against you. But this result doesn't arrive through force. It arrives through alignment.

This is the part of your chart that tells the truth plainly: love and money come when you stop fighting for them.

They come when you trust yourself.

They come when you stop trying to outrun your discomfort.

They come when you stop chasing the "higher experience" as if it lives in a single category—wealth or romance—and you begin to choose what actually grows you. What actually transforms you. What you can put your heart and soul into and stay with.

The Nine of Diamonds is the gift of a rich life.

Not just rich in money, but rich in experience. In gratitude. In flow. In the feeling of being in the right place at the right time because you are no longer gripping the wheel in panic.

It is the moment you realize: all along, you didn't have to become a better chaser.

You had to become a better conduit.

Integration — Your Healer's Code in Motion

When we step back and look at your entire chart, a softer truth begins to emerge.

You were never meant to live at the mercy of what you are pursuing.

You were meant to live from the center of who you are becoming.

The Queen of Diamonds can easily feel like they are standing at the crossroads of love and prosperity, trying to decide which one deserves their devotion. There can be a quiet narrative running beneath the surface: *If I just secure this relationship, I'll feel settled.* Or, *If I just reach this level of success, then I'll finally relax.* And so life can become a series of subtle negotiations with yourself—adjusting, recalibrating, striving for the configuration that promises relief.

But your chart is not about relief.

It is about wholeness.

The Three of Spades in Mars reveals that when you feel unsettled, your instinct may be to widen your reach. To add more. Explore more. Touch more possibilities. Keep options open. Yet what you are truly longing for is not more options. It is depth inside a choice. It is the steadiness that comes when you decide something is worthy of your full attention—and you stay long enough to let it shape you.

The Queen of Spades in Neptune continues that invitation. This card's influence does not rush you toward enlightenment. It does not reward you for collecting insight. It asks you to let wisdom alter the way you live. To let your intuition refine your standards. To let your inner knowing quiet the frantic need to prove, secure, or acquire. This cards invites you into a deeper intimacy with yourself—where you are not chasing a better future, but becoming more present with your current truth.

And then Pluto, through the Jack of Clubs, whispers something even more intimate: do not mistake inspiration for integration. Do not rush to teach what you have not yet digested. Let your life be the classroom. Let your mistakes mature into understanding. Let your understanding mature into embodied leadership. The world does not need your quick brilliance nearly as much as it needs your lived sincerity.

When all of these threads weave together, your Cosmic Result—the Nine of Diamonds—begins to make sense. Fulfillment is not something you conquer. It is something that unfolds when you stop bargaining with life. When you stop asking love to compensate for ambition, or ambition to compensate for loneliness. When you stop asking spirituality to bypass your discomfort. When you let each part of you take its rightful place.

So how do you know if you are living your chart?

Notice your relationship to desire. When you want something, does your body tighten? Does your mind race ahead to secure it? Does your heart start calculating what you must trade to keep it? That tightening is the old pattern—the part of you that believes fulfillment is fragile and must be captured quickly.

But when you are living your chart, desire feels different. It feels spacious. You can move toward what you want without collapsing into it. You can love without abandoning your calling. You can build without sacrificing your tenderness. You can study wisdom without losing your grounding. There is steadiness in you. A sense that nothing essential will disappear if you choose slowly and honestly.

You will know you are aligned when your life no longer feels like a race between love and success. You will know you are aligned when you can sit in the center of your own becoming and trust that what belongs to you will meet you there.

As the Queen of Diamonds you do not need to chase your desires, you need only be yourself. When you do, prosperity and connection come easily.

Affirmation of Alignment

I live from the center of my own becoming.

What belongs to me arrives as I remain true to myself.

K♦

Matt & Joy Kahn — *Life Chart*

	K♠	8♦	10♣			
A♠	3♦	5♣	10♠	Q♣	A♣	3♥	☿
2♥	9♠	9♣	J♥	5♠	7♦	7♥	♀
8♣	J♠	2♦ (HEALER'S CODE)	4♣	6♥	K♦ (HEALER'S CODE)	K♥	♂
SATURN	JUPITER	MARS	VENUS	MERCURY	BIRTHCARD	MOON	
A♦	A♥	8♠ (HEALER'S CODE)	10♦ (HEALER'S CODE)	10♥ (HEALER'S CODE)	4♠ (HEALER'S CODE)	6♦	♃
	TRANS-FORMED SELF	COSMIC LESSON	COSMIC RESULT	PLUTO	NEPTUNE	URANUS	
5♦	7♣	9♥	3♠	3♣	5♥	Q♦	♄
J♦	K♣	2♣	7♠	9♦	J♣	Q♠	⛢
Q♥	6♠	6♣	8♥	2♠	4♦	4♥	♆
♆	⛢	♄	♃	♂	♀	☿	

Card #1: Your Birth Card K ◆

If you are a King of Diamonds, you were born with a rare mix of tenderness and authority.

On the surface, the Diamonds suit is the material kingdom: resources, stewardship, prosperity, value, and the structures that make a life sustainable. But as a King, you carry the Diamond realm in its highest expression. You are here to lead in the world of matter. Not as someone who chases money for its own sake, but as someone who understands what wealth is actually for: to create stability, impact, and a foundation that can hold love.

And yet, the beginning of your story often surprises people—because your heart is where you start. You can feel, almost immediately, that you are here to care. To nurture. To make people feel safe with you. You may have grown up believing the "real" measure of your success was whether others felt seen, held, remembered, and provided for in your presence. You may have taken on the unspoken role of emotional caretaker long before you were meant to. Not because anyone demanded it outright, but because you could feel what people needed… and part of you couldn't relax until it was handled.

This is why harmony matters so much to you. Not as a preference, but as a survival strategy your nervous system learned early. Peace can feel like proof that you are safe. Conflict can feel like a threat to the very thing you are trying to build. So you may find yourself smoothing, managing, adjusting, anticipating—trying to keep the field around you calm enough to function. The irony is that the more you try to preserve harmony at all costs, the more exhausted you become… and the more your life begins to ask you for a deeper kind of

Because the King of Diamonds is not here to avoid tension. You are here to mature through it— until your leadership becomes strong enough to hold both love and truth without collapsing into people-pleasing.

Card #2: Your Mars Card 2 ◆

Mars reveals how your drive moves, and for you, that drive moves through partnership.

The Two of Diamonds is the energy of connection that creates value—relationships that open doors, collaborations that turn ideas into opportunity, conversations that become contracts, introductions that become resources. You are often naturally gifted at sensing where the flow is. You can feel what will work, who will fit, and how to align pieces so that prosperity becomes an outcome of relationship, not a separate pursuit.

But this is where your great lesson begins: when your passion is wired through partnership, it can become tempting to measure your worth by whether others are pleased with you. You can slip into the belief that the way to stay safe is to stay agreeable. To keep everyone feeling good. To keep the deal intact. To keep the harmony stable.

And the cost of that strategy is subtle at first. You might just feel tired. Overextended. Like you are always the one making it work. Like you are always reading the room, adjusting your tone, managing the relational weather so the world keeps moving.

Mars in the Two of Diamonds invites you into a higher skill: partnership without self-erasure. Connection without bargaining away your truth. The moment you learn that your power does not come from being needed—but from being anchored—your entire chart begins to breathe again.

As a healer, coach, or leader, this becomes a sacred kind of magnetism. People trust you because you are kind, yes… but also because you are clear. And clarity is what makes love sustainable.

Card #3: Your Neptune Card 4♠

Neptune is your calling. The higher vision that keeps pulling you forward, even when your comfort wants to stay where it is.

Your Neptune card, the Four of Spades, is the invitation to build a foundation that means something.

This is not the path of "what's easiest." It's the path of "what's most aligned." And those two are not always the same. The Four of Spades asks you to lift your gaze beyond immediate gain, beyond the next win, beyond the quick path to comfort—and to begin constructing a life, a business, a body of work, a legacy, that you can actually respect when you're alone with yourself.

For many King of Diamonds, this becomes the turning point: you realize you cannot keep building a life just because it looks good from the outside. You cannot keep saying yes because it keeps everyone happy. You cannot keep aiming for the "highest" version of something right now, as if your growth is supposed to stop at the first peak you reach.

Neptune's gift is that it keeps raising the ceiling.

You are meant to grow into higher and higher foundations. And your peace comes when you stop demanding that today's version has to be the final version. When you let your life be nurtured— built over time—your disappointment softens. Your impatience relaxes. Your leadership becomes steadier. Because you begin to trust your own unfolding.

This is where the King of Diamonds becomes truly sovereign: not chasing the next pinnacle, but committing to what is meaningful enough to build slowly.

Card #4: Your Pluto Card 10♥

Pluto is the crucible. The place where life stops negotiating with the ego and starts initiating the soul.

Your Pluto card is the Ten of Hearts, and this is profound—because it reveals the real mastery of the King of Diamonds:

Your deepest fulfillment is not material.

It's emotional.

Not the kind of emotion that is dramatic or unstable, but the kind that is nourishing. The kind that makes you feel filled up from the inside. The kind that reminds you who you are when no one is watching.

King of Diamonds

This is where your old strategy can break down. If you have spent your life trying to manage people's feelings, trying to be the one who keeps everyone okay, trying to "do the right thing" so you can maintain harmony… Pluto comes in and asks a sharper question:

What do you actually love?

Not what you are supposed to do. Not what makes you look successful. Not what keeps the peace. Not what earns approval.

What do you love.

Because the Ten of Hearts teaches you that the heart cannot be substituted. It cannot be bypassed with achievement. It cannot be replaced with responsibility. It cannot be negotiated away to keep others comfortable.

You are here to choose what nourishes you.

And when you do, something shocking happens: your life begins to reorganize around fulfillment instead of performance.

As a healer, coach, or leader, this is the moment you stop trying to be the "most supportive" person in the room—and become the most truthful one. It's the moment you realize that love is not proven by how much you carry. Love is proven by how aligned you remain while you carry what is truly yours.

Card #5: Your Cosmic Result Card 10 ◆

Your cosmic result is the Ten of Diamonds, and it speaks like a blessing that only arrives once you stop demanding it.

This card is material fulfillment—prosperity that arises as a natural consequence of alignment.

Not prosperity you have to chase.

Not prosperity you have to force.

Not prosperity you have to control through perfect planning.

Prosperity that unfolds because your life is built on what you love.

The Ten of Diamonds is what happens when your leadership stops being fueled by obligation and starts being fueled by devotion. When your foundation is meaningful, money can meet you there. When your work is rooted in emotional truth, support can find you there. When you stop bargaining for harmony and start embodying integrity, life responds with stability.

This is the deeper message of your chart:

You were never meant to earn your worth through over-giving.

You were meant to claim your worth by choosing fulfillment.

And from that choice, the material world begins to cooperate.

Integration — Your Healer's Code in Motion

When we step back and look at your chart as a whole, a pattern becomes unmistakable.

You are a leader of the material realm who begins in the emotional realm.

You are someone who wants love, harmony, connection, and a sense that everyone is okay… and yet you are also someone who is designed to build something real—something strong enough to hold the weight of your gifts without collapsing you into caretaking.

In distortion, you may find yourself trying to manage life through relationships. You may over-accommodate to avoid conflict. You may feel responsible for people's comfort. You may chase the "highest" version too soon, then feel disappointed when life doesn't match the image in your mind. You may appear successful while privately feeling like something essential is missing.

In alignment, you become the King you were always meant to be.

You allow partnership to support you without making it your identity.

You let vision guide you without demanding instant perfection.

You choose what you love without needing permission.

And from that place, your life becomes both prosperous and peaceful—because it is no longer built on pleasing. It is built on truth.

So how do you know if you are living your chart?

Notice what you are choosing when no one is applauding. Notice whether your "yes" feels nourishing or performative. Notice whether harmony is something you cultivate through truth… or something you try to maintain by shrinking yourself. Notice whether prosperity feels like pressure… or like an echo of devotion.

Your Healer's Code is not asking you to become harder.

It is asking you to become clearer.

And when you do, you will discover that the most magnetic form of leadership is the one that is fulfilled.

Affirmation of Alignment

I choose what I love, and I trust life to meet me there.

My prosperity is an outcome of devotion, integrity, and truth.

THE SPADES SUIT

The Spades Suit governs the realm of wisdom, initiation, and spiritual mastery, guiding us through the full maturation of consciousness:

From the penetrating clarity of the Ace,
to the reflective polarity of the Two,
to the curious expansion of the Three,
to the structured foundation of the Four,
to the catalytic challenge of the Five,
to the integrating responsibility of the Six,
to the contemplative depth of the Seven,
to the empowered authority of the Eight,
to the humanitarian completion of the Nine,
to the sovereign fulfillment of the Ten,
and finally the Court —
where it transforms into
the Seeker as the Jack,
the Oracle as the Queen,
and the Master Teacher as the King.

If your Birth Card lives in the Spades Suit, your life is shaped by initiation — not only into higher knowledge, but into deeper responsibility for how you wield that knowledge. Your journey is not simply to think clearly or seek truth, but to embody wisdom through lived experience, to stand steady in adversity, and to transform life's trials into mastery. Spades do not avoid depth — they refine through it.

On the following pages, you will find all cards contained within the suit of Spades. The Spades have been organized from Ace to King. Each card begins with a snapshot of its chart followed by a detailed description. While the charts have been offered for reference, the descriptions provide a chance to feel into their specific energy and purpose.

Matt & Joy Kahn

Life Chart

			K♠	8♦	10♣		
HEALER'S CODE **A♠** BIRTHCARD	**3♦** MOON	**5♣**	**10♠**	**Q♣**	**A♣**	**3♥**	☿
HEALER'S CODE **2♥** NEPTUNE	**9♠** URANUS	**9♣** SATURN	**J♥** JUPITER	HEALER'S CODE **5♠** MARS	**7♦** VENUS	**7♥** MERCURY	♀
8♣	**J♠**	**2♦**	**4♣** TRANS- FORMED SELF	**6♥** COSMIC LESSON	HEALER'S CODE **K♠** COSMIC RESULT	HEALER'S CODE **K♥** PLUTO	♂
A♦	**A♥**	**8♠**	**10♦**	**10♥**	**4♣**	**6♦**	♃
5♦	**7♣**	**9♥**	**3♠**	**3♣**	**5♥**	**Q♦**	♄
J♦	**K♣**	**2♣**	**7♠**	**9♦**	**J♣**	**Q♠**	♅
Q♥	**6♠**	**6♣**	**8♥**	**2♣**	**4♦**	**4♥**	♆
♆	♅	♄	♃	♂	♀	☿	

Card #1: Your Birth Card A♠

If you are an Ace of Spades, you were not born into a simple life. You were born into a contemplative one. From a very early age, you have felt what others often avoid—the fragility of life, the reality of loss, the presence of death, the inevitability of change. You may not have had language for it as a child, but you felt it. You sensed that things end. That people leave. That life can shift without warning. And because of that, you have always carried a depth that sets you apart.

The Ace of Spades sits between worlds. Not metaphorically—experientially. You may feel pulled between the material and the spiritual, between what is seen and unseen, between what is stable and what is dissolving. There is often upheaval around you—family changes, career transitions, sudden endings, unexpected beginnings. It can feel like your life moves in waves of transformation rather than gentle seasons. And because of that, stability may feel like something you are always building, and rebuilding, and building again.

And yet, here is the paradox: you are rarely shocked by transformation. While others panic in moments of crisis, you steady. While others are overwhelmed by endings, you hold space. You have likely been present at births, deaths, divorces, collapses, reinventions. You understand shadow work not because you studied it, but because you lived it. Many Ace of Spades become doulas of one kind or another—birth doulas, death doulas, transition guides, shadow workers— not necessarily by title, but by function. You are the one people call when everything is changing.

But your deepest lesson is not simply to witness transformation. It is to participate in it. Because the Ace is initiation. It is the spark. And your life is not asking you to survive upheaval—it is asking you to let transformation initiate you into leadership.

Card #2: Your Mars Card 5♠

Your Mars card, the 5 of Spades, is the engine of conscious transformation. This is where you stop being someone to whom change happens and become someone who chooses it. The 5 of Spades is about decision. Not dramatic rebellion. Not chaos for chaos' sake. But the deliberate choice to say, *"Yes. I will step into this transformation willingly."*

Because here is the truth: many Ace of Spades resist their own becoming. You can hold space for everyone else's growth, but when it comes to your own, you hesitate. You stay processing. You stay analyzing. You stay between worlds. You are so familiar with upheaval that you sometimes freeze inside of it, as if bracing for the next wave.

The 5 of Spades asks you to move. To decide. To say, "This is no longer happening to me. I am choosing my next evolution." When you activate this Mars energy, transformation stops feeling like instability and starts feeling like momentum. You begin to understand that your life was never meant to feel ordinary—it was meant to feel catalytic. And the moment you consciously welcome that, your fear of change begins to soften into partnership with it.

This is where you shift from being reactive to being visionary. You begin to direct your transformation instead of merely enduring it.

Card #3: Your Neptune Card 2♥

Your Neptune card, the 2 of Hearts, reveals the tender core beneath all that depth. For all your wisdom and resilience, you deeply desire love. You want to be mirrored. You want someone to see the magnitude of what you carry and meet you there.

But this is delicate territory for you. Because after experiencing so much transformation, your heart can protect itself in two ways. You may over-give—pouring your heart into someone, hoping they will meet you in the same depth. Or you may withhold—waiting for someone to prove they are safe before you open. Sometimes both patterns alternate.

The 2 of Hearts teaches you relational maturity. It asks you to stop seeking a mirror that proves your worth and instead become the one who stands in love first. Not self-sacrifice. Not guarded independence. But a heart that is open without bargaining. When you stop measuring love by how perfectly it is returned and start leading with steadiness, your relationships shift.

This Neptune placement is not asking you to find perfect love. It is asking you to become emotionally available to the love already present in your life.

Card #4: Your Pluto Card K♥

Pluto is the crucible. It is the place your ego would prefer to avoid.

For you, Pluto sits in the King of Hearts, which means your deepest transformation is emotional leadership. Not performance. Not positivity. Not being "the strong one." Real leadership: the kind that comes from vulnerability integrated into wisdom.

Your Pluto card is your true breakthrough. Transformation cracks your heart open. The King of Hearts asks you to lead from that vulnerability. Not from performance. Not from spiritual superiority. Not from stoicism. But from a heart that has been broken and reassembled enough times to become compassionate and wise.

This is not a light invitation. The Ace of Spades chart requires early awakening. Many other charts can operate in the world without deeply confronting spirituality until later in life. You cannot. Your chart demands surrender—to faith, to the unseen, to something beyond control. Whether you call it God, Source, the quantum field, or divine timing, your life stabilizes when you trust that something larger is holding you.

When you accept that support, something extraordinary happens. You realize that love has been present even in your hardest seasons. The very events that cracked you open also poured strength into you. And once you see that, you stop trying to protect your heart from transformation. You use it. You lead with it. You become the kind of leader who is emotionally sovereign and spiritually grounded.

The King of Hearts is not sentimental. It is steady. It is mature love. And when you embody that, your presence alone becomes healing.

Card #5: Your Cosmic Result Card K♦

Your Cosmic Result, the King of Diamonds, is the integration of wisdom into material mastery. When you embrace your transformational path, open your heart, and consciously choose growth, you gain the ability to build something substantial in the world.

The King of Diamonds is financial stability, leadership in business, prosperity rooted in integrity. It is not wealth for ego. It is wealth as foundation. When you direct your transformational insight into a business, a practice, a company, a container that supports others through change, your life stabilizes.

Your chart does not promise ease. It promises power. And that power becomes sustainable when you channel it into service that has structure. Any transformation—career transitions, business pivots, personal reinventions, life stages—can be your domain. When you build around your ability to guide people through change, your wisdom finds a home. It stops turning inward as worry or fear. It begins flowing outward as leadership.

Integration — Your Healer's Code in Motion

The heart of your integration is this: you are not here to be overwhelmed by transformation. You are here to initiate it with consciousness and lead others through it with compassion.

So how do you know if you are living your chart? You feel it in your relationship to change. When you are living your chart, transformation no longer feels like something that destabilizes you. It feels like something that strengthens you. You stop bracing for loss and start trusting cycles. You stop waiting for love to be proven and begin leading with an open heart.

You also know you are living your chart when your wisdom has a channel. When your insights are being applied. When you are building something—whether a business, a practice, a body of work—that allows your lived experience to serve others. And you feel calmer. Not because life stopped changing, but because you stopped resisting the fact that you are a bridge between worlds.

When you surrender to that role, the instability becomes initiation. The fear becomes faith. And the upheaval becomes purpose.

Affirmation of Alignment

I trust the transformation that shaped me and the love that sustains me.

I lead with an open heart and build with grounded strength.

2♠

Matt & Joy Kahn

Life Chart

	HEALER'S CODE K♠ NEPTUNE	8♦ URANUS	10♣ SATURN			

A♠	3♦	5♣	10♣ TRANSFORMED SELF	Q♣ COSMIC LESSON	HEALER'S CODE A♣ COSMIC RESULT	HEALER'S CODE 3♥ PLUTO	☿
2♥	9♠	9♣	J♥	5♠	7♦	7♥	♀
8♣	J♠	2♦	4♣	6♥	K♦	K♥	♂
A♦	A♥	8♠	10♦	10♥	4♠	6♦	♃
5♦	7♣	9♥	3♠	3♣	5♥	Q♦	♄
J♦	K♣	2♣	7♠	9♦	J♣	Q♠	♅
Q♥ JUPITER	HEALER'S CODE 6♠ MARS	6♣ VENUS	8♥ MERCURY	HEALER'S CODE 2♠ BIRTHCARD	4♦ MOON	4♥	♆
♆	♅	♄	♃	♂	♀	☿	

Card #1: Your Birth Card 2♠

If you are a 2 of Spades, you carry an extraordinary capacity to read the room. Not just intellectually. Not just socially. But energetically. You walk into a space and something in you immediately begins processing—who feels safe, who feels unsettled, what is unspoken, where the tension lives, what the group needs. It happens fast. Often before you even consciously register it.

This ability was not random. For many 2 of Spades, it was born from necessity. Something early in your life required you to awaken your intuition quickly. Perhaps it was instability. Perhaps it was emotional unpredictability. Perhaps it was simply being the sensitive one in a complex environment. Whatever the catalyst, your intuition opened because it had to. And once it opened, it never really closed.

As a healer, coach, or leader, this makes you powerful. You don't just teach principles—you anticipate needs. You don't just respond—you pre-empt. You can give people what they didn't even know they needed because you can feel it forming before they articulate it. And in business, this becomes prosperity. You understand timing. You understand partnership. You know when to align and when to pivot. Decisions feel clearer to you than they do to many others—not because you always know why, but because your inner compass is tuned.

But here is the quiet shadow: you understand others far more easily than you understand yourself. You can navigate a room of fifty people with ease, yet struggle to name your own inner truth. You can manage energy externally while feeling less certain internally. And so the deeper journey of the 2 of Spades is not mastering people—it is mastering self-recognition.

Card #2: Your Mars Card 6♠

Your Mars card, the 6 of Spades, gives you execution power. When you choose a path, you excel. You do not approach life halfway. If you commit, you commit fully. You bring harmony into teams. You see what would make something better and then you move toward that improvement.

This energy makes you incredibly reliable. In any organization, family, or business, you become a pillar. People lean on you. They trust your discernment. They rely on your steadiness. And you rarely shrink from that responsibility.

But there is a subtle cost here. Because being the one others rely on does not always mean you are being supported at the same depth. It can feel lonely at the top of your awareness. You may have many around you, but very few who truly meet you at your level of perception. And so your Mars energy can sometimes drive you toward achievement as a way to justify the weight you carry.

The 6 of Spades at its highest is not about burden—it is about alignment. When you direct your excellence toward something that genuinely matters to you, not just something that others need from you, your energy shifts. You stop being the over-responsible one. You become the fulfilled one.

Card #3: Your Neptune Card K♠

Your Neptune card, the King of Spades, holds a grand vision for your life. Even if you have tried to ignore it. Even if you prefer supporting roles. Even if visibility feels intimidating. There is something in you that knows you are capable of leading at scale.

The King of Spades paints big pictures. It whispers of businesses launched, movements started, messages shared widely. It calls you forward—not gently, but persistently. It sees your ability to articulate complex ideas clearly. It sees how others rally around your insight. It sees your capacity to build something meaningful.

And yet, this energy can overwhelm you. You may resist stepping fully into leadership because you already feel the weight of being needed. You may prefer to stay behind the scenes because being visible feels like multiplying the demand on your nervous system. Or you may hesitate until you feel you can execute the vision perfectly—highest, highest, highest potential—before you allow yourself to begin.

The healing invitation here is simple but profound: you do not have to be perfect to be powerful. Leadership does not require over-functioning. It requires clarity and self-trust. When you stop filtering your vision through the question, *"Can I handle this?"* and instead ask, *"Does this align?"* something inside you settles.

Card #4: Your Pluto Card 3♥

Your Pluto card, the 3 of Hearts, is the magnetic charm you often underestimate. Beneath the strategist. Beneath the intuitive analyst. Beneath the responsible one. There is a playful, expressive, emotionally vibrant part of you that wants to create experiences.

You think about how people feel, not just what they learn. You care about atmosphere. You care about joy. You have the ability to make people feel seen in a way that is light and engaging, not heavy. When you lean into this energy, you become magnetic—not because you are trying to impress, but because you are allowing your full emotional range to be visible.

But Pluto is where resistance lives. After years of people coming to you for support, visibility can feel draining. Being seen can feel like an invitation for more demand. So you may hold back your playfulness. You may downplay your charm. You may avoid stepping into larger spaces because you anticipate overwhelm.

The breakthrough here is learning that visibility does not require over-giving. You can be visible without being consumed. You can be magnetic without being responsible for everyone's emotional regulation. When you trust that boundary, your nervous system relaxes—and your expression expands.

Card #5: Your Cosmic Result Card A♣

Your Cosmic Result, the Ace of Clubs, is self-realization. When you allow yourself to lead, to be visible, to direct your excellence toward aligned work, you begin to understand yourself more deeply.

The Ace of Clubs is mental clarity. It is the initiation of self-knowledge. It is the moment you stop defining yourself through how well you manage others and begin discovering who you are when you are not performing for the room.

When you stop holding back your ideas, when you allow your voice to take up space, when you let your vision move beyond quiet competence into bold articulation, you catch glimpses of your true identity. You realize you are not just the one who understands everyone else. You are someone with a distinct message, a distinct mind, and a distinct calling.

And that realization is stabilizing.

Integration — Your Healer's Code in Motion

The essence of your chart is this: you were born with extraordinary discernment, but your destiny is self-recognition.

So how do you know if you are living your chart? You notice that your decisions feel clean. You are no longer navigating people at the expense of yourself. You are choosing partnerships based on alignment, not obligation. You are allowing yourself to lead in ways that feel expansive, not exhausting.

You also know you are living your chart when your visibility feels energizing instead of overwhelming. When you can stand in front of others without feeling responsible for managing every emotional current in the room. When your intuition supports your own desires—not just the needs of others.

And perhaps most importantly, you know you are living your chart when you can answer the question, *"Who am I?"* without referencing your role in someone else's life.

That is your initiation.

Affirmation of Alignment

I trust my intuition and honor my own truth.

I lead with clarity, visibility, and self-aligned strength.

3♠

Matt & Joy Kahn — JOKER — *Life Chart*

	K♠	8♦	10♣				
A♠	3♦	5♣	10♠	Q♣	A♣	3♥	☿
2♥	9♠	9♣	J♥	5♠	7♦	7♥	♀
8♣	J♠	2♦	4♣	6♥	K♦	K♥	♂
A♦	A♥	8♠	10♦	10♥	4♣	6♦	♃
HEALER'S CODE 5♦ (MARS)	7♣ (VENUS)	9♥ (MERCURY)	HEALER'S CODE 3♠ (BIRTHCARD)	3♣ (MOON)	5♥	Q♦	♄
J♦ (COSMIC LESSON)	HEALER'S CODE K♣ (COSMIC RESULT)	HEALER'S CODE 2♣ (PLUTO)	HEALER'S CODE 7♠ (NEPTUNE)	9♦ (URANUS)	J♣ (SATURN)	Q♠ (JUPITER)	♅
Q♥	6♠	6♣	8♥	2♣	4♦	4♥ (TRANS-FORMED SELF)	♆
♆	♅	♄	♃	♂	♀	☿	

Card #1: Your Birth Card 3♠

If you are a 3 of Spades, there is a particular kind of pressure you have lived with for as long as you can remember. It isn't only ambition. It isn't only responsibility. It is the feeling that these two currents are braided together inside of you—an inner drive to make something of your life, and an equally strong pull to make that life *matter* to other people. You are not easily satisfied by success that stays personal. You want impact. You want meaning. You want what you build to move someone's life from struggle into something more livable, more hopeful, more whole.

This is why your motivation has always been selective. When you can't feel the point of what you're doing, your energy fades—not because you are incapable, but because your spirit refuses to invest in what feels empty. Even when you were young, there was a sense that you needed to understand the deeper "why." You needed to know how everything was connected, how one choice affected another choice, how one action rippled into an entire system. And when you couldn't see that connection, life could feel like a series of tasks without meaning. That can be a painful way to grow up, because the world often asks young people to perform before they understand. But you were never designed to be motivated by performance. You were designed to be motivated by purpose.

And underneath all of that—under the drive, under the service, under the seriousness—there is something tender: the 3 of Spades wants to be understood. You want to be able to translate the vastness of what you are sensing into something other people can actually grasp. You want language that can hold what you feel. You want your inner world to be met. And because your chart pushes you toward solutions and contribution, you can spend years being the one who understands everyone else while quietly aching to be seen in your own complexity.

There is also this honest desire in you to be valued—not in a shallow way, but in a grounded way. You want to see that your work makes a difference. You want that difference to be tangible, day in and day out. You want to be able to look at your life and know that what you offered actually helped someone climb out of pain, confusion, or discomfort into something more satisfying. That desire is not ego. It is the 3 of Spades' integrity: *if I'm going to give my life to something, it needs to matter.*

Card #2: Your Mars Card 5♦

Your Mars card, the 5 of Diamonds, is where your chart becomes very real, very practical, and very lived. This is the part of you that is motivated to help people move out of difficult circumstances in their physical world—health struggles, financial instability, purpose confusion, the weight of a life that isn't working. You're not satisfied offering inspiration alone. You want to help someone actually *shift*. You want to help them pivot. You want to help them find the lever that changes their lived experience.

But Mars is also your personal engine, which means you don't just support other people through change—you are initiated through it yourself. The 3 of Spades often goes through their own pivots fairly regularly. Not because they can't commit. Not because they're scattered. But because something in their path keeps saying, *there needs to be change*. The Mars energy moves through your life as passion and purpose. It presses you to understand transition, to learn what it takes to move through endings and new starts, to discover how to rebuild when something collapses or when something simply outgrows itself.

So you tend to live what you teach. Your life becomes an example of the very challenges you help others navigate. You find yourself facing moments that ask, "How do you do this?"—how do you move through this change, how do you stabilize after the pivot, how do you find meaning when the old structure dissolves, how do you take what you learned and apply it to the next chapter. Over time, that repetition doesn't make you cynical. It makes you wise. It makes you capable. It gives you a kind of grounded authority: you know how transformation actually works because you have been inside it.

And the 5 of Diamonds also teaches you to embrace change whether you can control it or not. Some changes in life are chosen. Others arrive like weather. Your Mars card trains you in both. It helps you learn the difference between what you can adjust and what you must accept, and it gives you the resilience to move forward either way. When you integrate this Mars energy, change stops feeling like a personal failure and starts feeling like a process you understand.

Card #3: Your Neptune Card 7♠

Your Neptune card, the 7 of Spades, is the part of you that is always being pulled further. It pulls you toward the next level of potential. The next level of perspective. The next refinement. The next truth that will make your message cleaner, clearer, more accurate, more aligned. There is a devotion in you to meeting each moment from the highest place you can access.

This can be a gift of immense integrity. You don't want to mislead people. You don't want to offer something half-formed. You want to tell the truth from the highest perspective you can see. And because of that, your work often carries depth. It carries rigor. It carries care.

But this is also where pressure can quietly become a cage. The 7 of Spades can make it feel like nothing is ever finished. Like there is always one more refinement required before you can share. One more layer to consider. One more improvement to make. And because Neptune is the realm of ideals, that inner standard can become endless.

For you, this is not just perfectionism—it's a spiritual hunger for truth. Yet it can still become heavy. It can make you doubt what you've created. It can keep you polishing the message instead of releasing it. It can make you feel like you have to reach the absolute highest possibility before you have permission to be seen.

The turning point comes when you see through the illusion that you are "behind." When you realize there is actually no pressure coming from life itself. There is an invitation. You are invited to share what you've discovered—and then continue discovering. You are invited to offer what is true now—and then refine it as you grow. When you receive that invitation as permission, you feel more ease. Your focus sharpens. Your path becomes clearer.

Card #4: Your Pluto Card 2♣

Your Pluto card, the 2 of Clubs, is the deep, primal threshold in this chart. It is the card of communication—paired with the fear of communication. It is the absolute pull to speak, to share, to articulate your vision—paired with the ancient imprint that says: *if I speak up, something could happen to me.*

This taps into universal survival fear. The fear of being kicked out of the community. The fear of being punished for saying the wrong thing. The fear of ruffling feathers and losing what matters. Even if you live a very modern life, your nervous system can still respond as if speaking is dangerous. Your body can act as if truth threatens belonging.

And because the 3 of Spades already carries pressure to make an impact, this Pluto placement can become a painful loop. You can feel the call to contribute, to lead, to offer solutions—and then get wrapped up in consequences. You may play out every possible reaction in your mind. You may anticipate backlash. You may imagine misunderstandings. You may withhold not because your message isn't ready, but because the cost of being seen feels too high.

But Pluto is transformation. Which means you are not here to avoid this fear. You are here to outgrow it. You learn, slowly and bravely, to value your voice more than your safety strategies. You begin to remember that what you have to say matters. That what you bring to the world is worth communicating. And you start doing the most courageous, ordinary thing: you raise your hand.

You speak in class. You speak in business. You speak in your family. You speak up for what matters to you. You learn that consequence is not the same as catastrophe. You learn that you can survive discomfort. You learn that your voice can be a bridge instead of a weapon. And in that process, your communication becomes cleaner—because it is no longer shaped by fear. It is shaped by purpose.

Card #5: Your Cosmic Result Card K♣

Your Cosmic Result is the King of Clubs—the leadership that emerges when you stop hiding your mind. When you stop silencing your knowing. When you allow your ideas to take up space.

This is not leadership that comes from authority alone. It comes from meaning. From value. From your capacity to articulate a vision in a way that benefits others. The King of Clubs is the one who can hold space in a business, a community, a family, or any structure where ideas need direction. It is the one who can translate complexity into clarity. It is the one who can speak truth and have people feel oriented by it rather than overwhelmed.

And because your life has taught you pivots, you become a powerful ally to other visionaries. You understand what it costs to evolve. You understand what it takes to rebuild. You understand the emotional and practical demands of change. So you don't just lead your own path—you help cultivate leadership in others, too. You can support people with big visions because you know how to survive the transitions that vision requires.

Integration — Your Healer's Code in Motion

The integration of this chart is not about becoming more ambitious. You already have ambition. It is not about becoming more responsible. You already carry responsibility.

The integration is about letting your repeated pivots become evidence of your path instead of proof that something is wrong. It is about recognizing that your life teaches you through transition because transition is your medicine. When you stop fighting the pivots, you start learning from them faster. You stop treating change like interruption and start treating it like instruction. You begin to see that each reinvention is shaping you into someone who can guide others without pretending you've arrived.

At the same time, you begin to soften the pressure of Neptune. The part of you that wants the highest truth starts to become supportive instead of demanding. You still refine. You still care. You still hold yourself to integrity. But you no longer make refinement a reason to disappear. You let your work be in process. You let your message evolve in public. You allow truth to be something you share, not something you must perfect before you're allowed to speak.

And then, slowly, the Pluto initiation begins to shift. The fear of speaking does not vanish overnight. It becomes something you relate to differently. You stop letting it make decisions for you. You stop mistaking fear for guidance. You begin noticing the exact moment your body braces before you share—and you practice staying present anyway. You practice letting your voice come through even when part of you worries about consequences.

So how do you know if you are living your chart?

You can feel it in how you respond to transition. When you are living your chart, pivots feel less like emergencies and more like invitations. You may still grieve endings. You may still feel the stretch of reinvention. But you don't collapse into self-doubt. You don't interpret change as failure. You move with it. You ask, "What is this teaching me?" and you actually listen for the answer.

You can feel it in your relationship with truth. When you are living your chart, you are no longer trapped in endless refining. You still hold a high standard, but you share what you know now. You offer what is true today. You trust that your clarity will deepen as you live.

And you can feel it in your voice. When you are living your chart, you speak even when it feels vulnerable. You speak even when it might not land perfectly. You speak because something matters more than comfort: impact, integrity, service, the deep desire to be understood and to help others feel understood too.

That is when the King of Clubs begins to show itself—not as a title you claim, but as a presence you embody. The kind of presence that says, quietly and clearly: *my voice is worth sharing.*

Affirmation of Alignment

My pivots refine me, and my voice serves what matters.

I lead with truth, even when it requires bravery.

4♠

Matt & Joy Kahn

Life Chart

	K♠	8♦	10♣			
A♠	3♦	5♣	10♠	Q♣	A♣	3♥	☿
2♥	9♠	9♣	J♥	5♠	7♦	7♥	♀
8♣	J♠	2♦	4♣	6♥	K♦	K♥	♂

		HEALER'S CODE			HEALER'S CODE		
A♦	A♥	8♠	10♦	10♥	4♠	6♦	♃
SATURN	JUPITER	MARS	VENUS	MERCURY	BIRTHCARD	MOON	

			HEALER'S CODE	HEALER'S CODE	HEALER'S CODE		
5♦	7♣	9♥	3♠	3♣	5♥	Q♦	♄
	TRANS-FORMED SELF	COSMIC LESSON	COSMIC RESULT	PLUTO	NEPTUNE	URANUS	

J♦	K♣	2♣	7♠	9♦	J♣	Q♠	⛢
Q♥	6♠	6♣	8♥	2♠	4♦	4♥	♆
♆	⛢	♄	♃	♂	♀	☿	

Card #1: Your Birth Card — 4♠

If you are a 4 of Spades, you are not designed to do your work in isolation. You love being with people. You love feeling a room come alive. You love celebration, play, the uplift that happens when human beings gather around something meaningful and feel themselves expand inside of it. There is something in you that is nourished by community—not just by being present in it, but by watching it flourish. You notice what makes people light up. You notice what helps them feel safe enough to open. You notice what elevates an experience from "fine" to unforgettable.

And because you are a four, you don't merely want connection—you want container. You're focused on structure. Foundation. A space that can hold what wants to happen. But your structure is not just practical. It is emotional. It is energetic. It is relational. You are the kind of healer, coach, or leader who thinks about the experience people are having, the feelings a conversation is stirring, the depth a gathering could reach if it were held with more intention. You are often imagining what the room could become if someone created the right conditions.

What's striking about this chart is that you don't always need to be the person delivering the message. You don't necessarily thrive as the "star." You thrive as the one who holds space—the one who creates the conditions where something profound can occur. A mastermind. A debate. A performance. An event. A healing circle. A family conversation. A hospital room. A classroom. Your gift is the ability to sense what's needed and cultivate it into form. And because you can feel the possibility of what something could become, you're often willing to give "just a little bit more" to help it reach that higher level.

There is also something visionary here. You don't only create spaces that work—you imagine spaces that last. You can see legacy. You can imagine something that grows and deepens over time: an annual event, a long-standing community, a structure that serves people for decades. Your mind naturally stretches beyond the moment and into what this could become if it were built with care.

Card #2: Your Mars Card 8♠

Your Mars card, the 8 of Spades, is the fuel that keeps you building.

It's the energy of momentum. Of endurance. Of showing up again and again. You have an inner capacity to keep taking something to the next level—then the next—then the next. And this isn't driven by restlessness. It's driven by devotion. The 8 of Spades in Mars says, *keep going… keep refining the container… keep expanding what's possible… keep making space for what the world is becoming.*

This is one of the most quietly powerful parts of your chart. Because you are both someone who can create the "box"—the structure, the plan, the container—and someone who can think outside of it. You understand that the world is always changing, and that the spaces we build have to evolve in order to hold new ideas, new needs, new levels of truth. You can feel the evolution of communities. You can feel the evolution of culture. You can feel when the old container is too small for what wants to emerge. And instead of resisting change, you redesign the structure so that change can happen safely inside of it.

This is why so many 4 of Spades become trusted builders of community. Not because you control people, but because you know how to support growth. You know how to create continuity in a world that keeps shifting. You know how to keep people connected through transition.

Card #3: Your Neptune Card 5♥

Your Neptune card, the 5 of Hearts, brings in a very different kind of intensity: emotional intensity.

The 5 of Hearts is often at the forefront of emotional change. It is the part of you that sees how emotion impacts everything—mental health, relational stability, physical wellbeing, spiritual resilience. You can sense when people are overwhelmed. You can feel the weight they carry beneath their words. And you're often drawn to ask the question: *how can we catalyze a shift here? How can we help people feel differently—so they can live differently?*

But this sensitivity comes with a shadow that you will recognize if you've lived it. Sometimes your heart is so open that you don't know what to do with what you're absorbing. You can feel people's emotions around you. You can feel the intensity in yourself. And when that intensity gets too big, you may shut down—not because you don't care, but because caring feels like drowning.

This is where your chart asks for emotional capacity, not emotional collapse. The more you learn to keep expressing, keep making space, keep holding the conversation, the more your nervous system stretches. You become able to hold bigger emotions without being swallowed by them. And your 4-of-Spades gift becomes even more profound: you can create or work within structures that hold emotional intensity safely. You might not always need to build those structures yourself. You may thrive as part of a team—first responders, hospitals, classrooms, organizations—any environment where people are moving through intense experiences and need someone who can hold steady. But to do this well, you must learn how to regulate your nervous system so your empathy doesn't become overwhelm.

Card #4: Your Pluto Card 3♣

Your Pluto card, the 3 of Clubs, is the part of you that says: *do something with what you see and feel.*

Because if you don't, everything stays inside your body as intensity.

If your longing to help people stays unchanneled, it becomes agitation. It becomes emotional pressure. It can become the feeling of "I need to do something, but I don't know what."

The 3 of Clubs brings the mind in—not as a cold instrument, but as a balancing force. It helps you organize. Plan. Engineer. Design. It helps you take the emotional and spiritual insights you're carrying and translate them into something real: an event, a curriculum, a book, a program, a structure that holds growth. It's the part of you that can take a big, heartfelt vision and say, *okay... what are the steps? how do we build it? how do we make it work?*

And you may not love this part at first. Your chart is clear: leaning into the mind like this can feel uncomfortable. It can feel like it pulls you away from the heart. But in your chart, it does the opposite. It keeps your heart from being flooded. It keeps your sensitivity from turning into burnout. It gives your calling a channel. When you allow your mind to support your heart, you become more available—because you're not carrying everything internally. You're building something that can hold it.

Card #5: Your Cosmic Result Card 3♠

Your Cosmic Result, the 3 of Spades, is where it all merges.

Once you are able to bring your mind, your heart, and your calling into harmony, you naturally create from a higher perspective. You are able to make something that impacts people, not only because it's well built, but because it's emotionally intelligent. It's spiritually attuned. It's designed with human experience in mind.

This is why this chart is so powerful when it's seized. The 4 of Spades builds the container. The 8 of Spades keeps the container evolving. The 5 of Hearts fills it with emotional depth and catalytic compassion. The 3 of Clubs organizes that depth into something real. And the result is a kind of creative service that doesn't collapse under intensity—it transforms intensity into meaningful structure.

And when you live it this way, community becomes not just something you love... but something you are able to cultivate around you. The kind of community where love is tangible. Where people feel held. Where your life becomes an example of what it looks like to build spaces that change people for the better.

Integration — Your Healer's Code in Motion

The integration of this chart begins when you stop trying to carry emotional intensity with your heart alone.

Because your Neptune is powerful. Your empathy is strong. Your desire to help is real. And if you try to do it only through feeling—only through devotion—your system will eventually overload. You'll feel everything, and you won't know what to do with it. You'll sense the need for change and feel responsible for producing it. You'll want to hold space for everyone—and then quietly reach the edge of overwhelm.

Your chart does not ask you to close your heart.

It asks you to build a structure that can hold your heart open.

That's the key. The four is structure. The Pluto is mind. The Mars is endurance. You are meant to create containers that allow emotional transformation to happen safely—without requiring you to absorb everything personally. You are meant to let your mind organize what your heart can feel. You are meant to translate intensity into form.

And the subtle shift that changes everything is this: you begin to remember that holding space doesn't mean carrying people. It means creating conditions where something true can occur— while you remain regulated, present, and supported. It means knowing where your responsibility ends and someone else's process begins. It means learning how to hold steady when emotions rise, without shutting down or over-identifying.

So how do you know if you are living your chart?

You can feel it in your body first. When you are living your chart, your nervous system is not constantly overloaded. You may still be sensitive. You may still feel deeply. But you are not drowning in what you feel. There is a steadiness in you because you have a channel for your care. You have a structure for your compassion. You have a plan for your vision.

You can feel it in your relationships to community. When you are living your chart, you are surrounded by people—and it nourishes you instead of draining you. You are not resentfully holding everything together. You are not secretly wishing people would need less. You are building spaces where people can take responsibility for their own growth, and you are simply the one who holds the container with integrity.

And you can feel it in the way your gifts translate into something tangible. When you are living your chart, you are doing something with what you know. You are organizing. Designing. Building. Writing. Planning. Creating. The emotional intensity becomes movement. The higher vision becomes structure. The love you carry becomes a space others can enter and feel changed by.

That is the moment the 4 of Spades becomes what they were born to be: not just a loving presence, but a legacy-level space holder—someone who helps community evolve, not by force, but by creating the conditions where evolution can happen.

Affirmation of Alignment

I build structures that hold my heart open and my nervous system steady.

I am a space holder for change, and my gift becomes legacy.

5♠

Matt & Joy Kahn

Life Chart

		K♠	8♦	10♣			
A♠	3♦	5♣	10♣	Q♣	A♣	3♥	☿
2♥ JUPITER	HEALER'S CODE 9♠ MARS	9♣ VENUS	J♥ MERCURY	HEALER'S CODE 5♠ BIRTHCARD	7♦ MOON	7♥	♀
8♣ TRANS-FORMED SELF	J♠ COSMIC LESSON	HEALER'S CODE 2♦ COSMIC RESULT	HEALER'S CODE 4♣ PLUTO	HEALER'S CODE 6♥ NEPTUNE	K♦ URANUS	K♥ SATURN	♂
A♦	A♥	8♣	10♦	10♥	4♠	6♦	♃
5♦	7♣	9♥	3♠	3♣	5♥	Q♦	♄
J♦	K♣	2♣	7♠	9♦	J♣	Q♠	♅
Q♥	6♠	6♣	8♥	2♣	4♦	4♥	♆
♇	♅	♄	♃	♂	♀	☿	

JOKER

Card #1: Your Birth Card 5♠

If you are a 5 of Spades, life rarely asks you to live in only one lane. You are the kind of healer, coach, or leader who feels deeply responsible for people, and at the same time driven by ambition—not because you're "attached to success," but because something in you is genuinely motivated to build, achieve, and leave a mark. It can feel like you were born with two sacred callings that don't always seem to fit in the same room: *care for others* and *express your passion through the world*. And because both feel true, you can spend years trying to "balance" them, as if the only way forward is to divide yourself into parts.

But this chart isn't asking you to choose. It's asking you to integrate—to stop segmenting your purpose into separate identities and let it become one coherent life. When that clicks, you stop feeling like you're constantly managing two destinies, and you begin living from a deeper ease: *the same energy that helps you care is the energy that helps you succeed*. What changes then isn't your workload—it's your inner posture. You no longer need to "prove" you're devoted to people by carrying them, and you no longer need to "prove" you're committed to your path by pushing yourself past what's sustainable. You start building in a way that includes your heart instead of costing you your heart.

The 5 of Spades is also a card of lived transformation. You don't just understand change—you've *lived* through enough of it to become fluent. In early seasons, that fluency can come from vigilance: watching what's shifting, reading the room, tracking what might change next so you can protect yourself from being blindsided. Over time, that same sensitivity becomes a gift: you become someone who can feel when a turning point is real, when a pattern is ready to break, when an era is complete. But the deeper invitation is to stop treating transformation as something you must manage and start relating to it as something you can serve—in yourself first, and then in others.

Card #2: Your Mars Card 9♠

Your Mars card, the 9 of Spades, is the key that unlocks the version of your life that feels not just "good," but *extraordinary*. Because without this Mars energy, you can still do well—you can still help people, build a meaningful career, provide value, and be taken care of. But Mars isn't about "getting by." Mars is about fulfilling the deeper assignment your soul has been training for through all those years of pivoting and adapting.

The 9 of Spades teaches you something that can be surprisingly tender for you: the difference between a pivot and an ending. You are so skilled at making adjustments that you can keep something alive long after it's complete—relationships, roles, responsibilities, even versions of yourself. You can sense the shift, make the tweak, renegotiate the arrangement, and find a way to keep moving. And sometimes that's wisdom. But the 9 of Spades asks: *What if this isn't a pivot? What if this is an ending that needs to be honored?*

This is where you become a rare kind of leader. Not the leader who forces change. Not the leader who clings to comfort. But the leader who can stand at the edge of what's ending and say, with steadiness and compassion: "Let it end." When you embrace this in your own life—when you let certain things close cleanly instead of dragging them forward—you gain a new authority. You become someone who can sit with people in their most uncertain moments and help them tell the truth about what's happening. And that's your Mars power: presence at the threshold, clarity without cruelty, and courage that isn't performative—it's embodied.

Card #3: Your Neptune Card 6♥

Your Neptune card, the 6 of Hearts, gives you a beautiful and complex gift: the ability to see all sides. You understand where people are coming from almost instantly. You can feel context. You can sense why someone is doing what they're doing. Compassion comes naturally to you, and in many ways, it's part of why people trust you—because you don't reduce them to their behavior. You perceive the humanity underneath.

And yet, Neptune is where your compassion can become blurry. Because seeing all sides can quietly turn into over-extending grace—especially when your heart is involved. This is the place where you may give someone more understanding than is actually supportive. You may stay longer than you want to, carry more than is yours, tolerate dynamics that don't match your truth, simply because you can see why the other person is the way they are. The tenderness of your perception becomes the very thing that keeps you entangled.

The healing move here is subtle but powerful: compassion isn't the end of the process—it's the beginning of discernment. The 6 of Hearts invites you to ask, *with love and clarity*: Is this mine to be part of? Where is this actually leading? You don't have to stop understanding people. You simply have to include the bigger picture. And when you do, you become able to deliver truth with grace: *"Yes, I understand... and also, this is ending,"* or, *"Yes, I see you... and also, my relationship to this must change."* That's when Neptune stops draining you and starts guiding you.

Card #4: Your Pluto Card 4♣

Your Pluto card, the 4 of Clubs, is your breakthrough through structure—not the kind of structure that cages you, but the kind that protects what matters. When the 5 of Spades is ungrounded, it can live in a highly charged state: emotionally obligated, constantly responding, triggered into "helping," stretched thin by the pressure to care for everyone and also succeed at everything. The 4 of Clubs brings you back to the room. It asks you to step back and look at the *whole* situation, not just the emotional immediacy.

This is where you learn the sacred art of prioritization. Where will you commit your energy? Where will you commit your time? What deserves structure—and what is simply demanding your attention? The 4 of Clubs is the part of you that can say: *"Here is what's fundamentally important."* Not as a rigid rule, but as a stabilizing truth. When you lean into this Pluto energy, you stop being pulled around by what's urgent, and you begin building a foundation that can actually hold your gifts.

And when you become someone who can create structure around transformation—when you can communicate clearly, hold boundaries without shutting down, and create containers that support change—you stop trying to control transformation and start hosting it. You become the calm center people feel when their lives are in motion. And you feel that calm in yourself first—which might be the greatest wealth this chart can generate.

Card #5: Your Cosmic Result Card 2 ◆

Your Cosmic Result, the 2 of Diamonds, is the promise that your life does not have to be split down the middle. This is the energy of aligned partnership, healthy exchange, and supportive collaboration in the material world. It's the frequency where you no longer feel like you must choose between love and ambition, between care and career, between serving others and building your own life. Instead, you begin drawing in the right people, the right agreements, and the right opportunities—ones that don't require you to abandon yourself.

This is where prosperity becomes less about hustle and more about resonance. The more you honor endings as endings, the more you stop over-gracing dynamics that drain you, and the more you build clean structure around what you're here to do… the more the world responds with the kind of support that feels steady. Not dramatic. Not chaotic. Just real. The 2 of Diamonds is the feeling of being *met*—in business, in relationships, in energetic exchange—because you finally stopped trying to carry everything alone.

Integration — Your Healer's Code in Motion

The heart of your integration is this: you are not here to manage transformation—you are here to recognize it, honor it, and guide others through it without losing yourself inside of it. You are the one who can tell when something is simply shifting… and when it's time to let a chapter close. But the most important place you learn that is in your own life, where your compassion may have kept certain doors open long after your spirit was ready to walk away.

So how do you know if you are living your chart? You can feel it in the way you relate to endings. When you are living your chart, you don't keep renegotiating with what is complete. You stop calling exhaustion "loyalty." You stop calling over-functioning "love." You start letting things end cleanly, and you notice that the world doesn't collapse when you choose truth—it stabilizes. You also know you're living your chart when your ambition no longer feels like pressure, and your care for people no longer feels like a burden. Your life starts to feel like one integrated path, not two competing responsibilities.

And you know you're living your chart when your nervous system starts to calm in the presence of change. Not because change stopped happening, but because you stopped trying to control it. You became someone who can hold structure, speak clearly, honor what's ending, and choose partnership that supports your life instead of consuming it. That's the moment your power becomes sustainable—and your success becomes a byproduct of alignment, not a substitute for it.

Affirmation of Alignment

I honor what is ending, and I trust what is beginning.

I build my life in a way that supports both my heart and my purpose.

6♠

Matt & Joy Kahn

Life Chart

		K♠ (HEALER'S CODE) 8♦	10♣ (HEALER'S CODE)			
		JUPITER / MARS	VENUS			

A♠	3♦	5♣ (HEALER'S CODE)	10♦ (HEALER'S CODE)	Q♣ (HEALER'S CODE)	A♣	3♥	☿
TRANSFORMED SELF	COSMIC LESSON	COSMIC RESULT	PLUTO	NEPTUNE	URANUS	SATURN	
2♥	9♠	9♣	J♥	5♠	7♦	7♥	♀
8♣	J♠	2♦	4♣	6♥	K♦	K♥	♂
A♦	A♥	8♠	10♦	10♥	4♠	6♦	♃
5♦	7♣	9♥	3♠	3♣	5♥	Q♦	♄
J♦	K♣	2♣	7♠	9♦	J♣	Q♠	♅
Q♥ (MERCURY)	6♠ (HEALER'S CODE, BIRTHCARD)	6♣ (MOON)	8♥	2♠	4♦	4♥	♆
♆	♅	♄	♃	♂	♀	☿	

Card #1: Your Birth Card 6♠

If you are a 6 of Spades, your chart carries a kind of "on paper" strength that other people often admire from the outside. You tend to have the capacity to build a life that looks stable, capable, successful—sometimes even enviable. When you apply yourself, you can generate real results. You can create comfort. You can create prosperity. You can create a life that feels, at least externally, like it should be satisfying.

And yet, what's so important to name is that many 6 of Spades eventually realize they've paid for that stability with themselves. You can devote yourself to a path and become very good at it. You can hold a high level of responsibility and keep delivering. You can keep going longer than most people. But over time, the inner feeling that often accompanies that is: *I'm overworked. I'm carrying too much. I'm burned out.* Not because you are weak. Because you've been strong for too long without the right kind of support.

The 6 of Spades often lives with an internal pressure that says, "I have to be the one who stabilizes everything." In career. In family. In life. You may feel like you need to see the situation from the highest perspective, make the best decision, protect everyone around you, and outwork everyone to prove you deserve what you have. Your mind is rarely still. You are thinking, analyzing, processing, assessing, trying to find the best possible solution in every scenario. It can feel like your value lives in your ability to anticipate and manage reality.

And eventually, something has to give. Often the body is the first messenger. Because your body can only carry a certain amount of over-delivery before it starts to speak up in symptoms. Sometimes it is health. Sometimes it is family stress. Sometimes it is a life event that makes it unmistakably clear: *no amount of work will actually get you ahead in the way you believe it will.* The 6 of Spades is not here to be punished by life. You are here to be awakened out of a misunderstanding: the belief that you must earn peace through effort.

Card #2: Your Mars Card 8♦

Your Mars card, the 8 of Diamonds, is the momentum of the material world. It's part of why this chart can generate financial prosperity and real-world comfort—because your energy moves in a way that produces tangible results. You're often directly connected to revenue generation, or you feel responsible for supporting your livelihood and the livelihood of others. Work matters to you. Contribution matters. Progress matters.

But this is also where distortion can quietly form. Because when the 8 of Diamonds is running through Mars, it can begin to link value with output. The more I do, the more I'm worth. The more I work, the more I deserve. The more I carry, the more indispensable I become. And that mindset can become a trap—especially for someone as capable as you.

For the 6 of Spades, this can show up in a few very specific ways. You can give so much in your career that you become overqualified. You can become "too good" at what you do—so good that you become too expensive, too valuable, too relied upon, and suddenly the very competence that built your success starts to box you in. Or it shows up in the body: the pace becomes unsustainable, and symptoms begin to slow you down—fatigue, adrenal issues, burnout signals. Or it shows up financially in a way that feels maddening: you want more wealth, more stability, more expansion, but you can't compute how to get it without working more. And when your body can't do more, your belief system begins to collapse.

The invitation of the 8 is not to stop contributing. It's to redefine contribution. To learn that momentum can be intelligent. That progress can be strategic. That fulfillment comes from devotion to a path you love—not from doing everything yourself. Mars asks: keep moving toward your dream. But the deeper lesson is to stop equating "more" with "harder."

Card #3: Your Neptune Card Q♣

Your Neptune card, the Queen of Clubs, gives you an extraordinary gift: insight.

You can see into situations from a higher vantage point. You process information quickly. Your mind is sharp, and your intuition is active. You notice what other people don't notice. You can hold multiple variables at once and sense what's unfolding beneath the surface. You often know what needs to happen before anyone else is ready to admit it.

This is where the 6 of Spades can become both powerful and deeply frustrated. Because when you can see what needs to change, you can start to believe everyone else should see it too. You may find yourself saying some version of: "I'm telling you exactly what needs to change. I'm telling you the solution. Why aren't you listening?" And what you're running into is not a lack of stupidity, it's pace. It takes time for others to process what you process almost instantly.

This is why the Queen of Clubs can become one of your greatest assets in leadership, once you stop trying to drag people into clarity and instead learn to *bring them along*. You are designed to step back, assess what you're seeing, and then translate it in a way others can receive. When you do that, your insight stops isolating you and starts positioning you: you become the one who helps teams, families, and communities see what's true—and then move together.

Card #4: Your Pluto Card 10♠

Your Pluto card, the 10 of Spades, is the place your system may resist the most, because it asks you to do something that can feel almost unbearable to someone like you: do less.

The 10 of Spades is a card of witnessing. It says: step back. Breathe. Observe. Notice where transformation is already happening without you forcing it. Notice what is already unraveling and reorganizing in its own natural order.

For the 6 of Spades, this can feel like grief. Because you have likely been the one with your hands in everything. You have been the one pushing change into place. You have been the one carrying the ball to the finish line. And the 10 of Spades says: you are not here to carry the ball all the way. You are here to get it rolling.

This is a radical reorientation of your identity.

Because you have built a sense of self around being the implementer. The one who gets it done. The one who outworks everyone. The one who stabilizes everything. And the 10 of Spades asks you to let life show you something humbling and freeing: a lot of what you have been pushing never needed to be pushed. It needed a catalyst. It needed clarity. It needed a decisive nudge. And then it needed space to unfold through other people, through timing, through natural transformation.

The 10 of Spades does not make you passive. It makes you wise. It helps you distinguish between what requires your action and what requires your trust. It teaches you to witness change rather than muscle it into existence.

Card #5: Your Cosmic Result Card 5♣

Your Cosmic Result, the 5 of Clubs, is the liberation that comes when you stop confusing effort with destiny.

The 5 of Clubs is change that happens because truth has been spoken and seen. It is transformation that is catalyzed, not carried. It is the experience of watching the things that need to shift in your life actually shift—not because you did more, but because you stopped doing what was never yours to do.

This is a crucial distinction for you: you are not here to change everything. You are here to inform. To guide. To name what is true. To get the ball rolling. And then to allow others to carry it forward. The 6 of Spades often believes they must be the one implementing all the time. The 5 of Clubs is the correction: your role is catalytic. When you embrace that, your life changes quickly. Not because you push harder—but because you finally stop pushing against your own design.

Integration — Your Healer's Code in Motion

The integration of this chart is not about becoming less devoted.

It's about becoming devoted to the right thing.

Because your devotion has likely been poured into effort. Into responsibility. Into over-delivering as a form of safety. Into the idea that if you just work a little harder, solve it a little better, carry it a little longer, then everything will stabilize and you'll finally be able to rest.

But your chart is very clear: rest will not come from finishing everything. Rest will come from *redefining your role*.

You are here to see clearly.

You are here to initiate wisely.

You are here to guide transformation.

You are not here to carry transformation on your back.

This is where the Queen of Clubs becomes medicine. When you are aligned, your insight is not a weapon you use to force change. It is a lantern you hold up so others can see. You learn to translate what you know at the pace people can receive it. You learn to trust that clarity, delivered with patience, changes more than intensity ever could.

And this is where the 10 of Spades becomes freedom. You begin practicing the sacred act of stepping back. You let yourself watch what is already transforming. You let other people do their part. You let life meet you. And you notice—slowly, steadily—that the world does not collapse when you stop over-functioning. In fact, it often starts to reorganize into a healthier order.

So how do you know if you are living your chart?

You can feel it in your relationship to work. When you are living your chart, you still contribute —but you are no longer proving your worth through exhaustion. You are no longer equating value with over-delivery. You are no longer trying to earn prosperity by outworking your own nervous system.

You can feel it in your body. When you are living your chart, your body begins to soften. You may still be ambitious. You may still love progress. But you no longer live at a pace that quietly punishes you. Your health stops being the messenger of misalignment because you begin listening before it has to scream.

And you can feel it in the way change happens around you. When you are living your chart, you stop forcing. You start catalyzing. You speak what you see. You get the ball rolling. And then you let other people carry it. You witness transformation unfolding—sometimes faster than when you were pushing—because you finally stepped into the role you were designed for.

That is the moment the 6 of Spades becomes what it always wanted to be: not the one who holds everything… but the one who guides everything into a wiser order.

Affirmation of Alignment

I am a catalyst for transformation, not the carrier of everything.

I lead with clarity, and I allow change to unfold through shared hands.

7♠

Matt & Joy Kahn

Life Chart

JOKER

		TRANS-FORMED SELF	
K♠	8♦	10♣	

A♠	3♦	5♣	10♠	Q♣	A♣	3♥	☿
2♥	9♠	9♣	J♥	5♠	7♦	7♥	♀
8♣	J♠	2♦	4♣	6♥	K♦	K♥	♂
A♦	A♥	8♣	10♦	10♥	4♠	6♦	♃
5♦	7♣	9♥	3♠	3♣	5♥	Q♦	♄
HEALER'S CODE J♦ MARS	HEALER'S CODE K♣ VENUS	2♣ MERCURY	HEALER'S CODE 7♠ BIRTHCARD	9♦ MOON	J♣	Q♠	⛢
Q♥ COSMIC LESSON	HEALER'S CODE 6♠ COSMIC RESULT	HEALER'S CODE 6♣ PLUTO	HEALER'S CODE 8♥ NEPTUNE	2♣ URANUS	4♦ SATURN	4♥ JUPITER	♆
♆	⛢	♄	♃	♂	♀	☿	

Card #1: Your Birth Card 7♠

If you are a 7 of Spades, you were born with a doorway open inside you.

In your early years especially, you may have lived more in imagination than in the world around you. Not because you were avoiding life in a lazy way, but because your inner world was so alive it could feel more real than what was happening in front of you. You contemplated. You daydreamed. You wandered into possibility. You imagined a kinder world, a more beautiful world, a more enchanted world. There is something almost woodland-whimsical in this card—like the child who could walk through the forest and feel fairies in the air, not as fantasy, but as *the felt sense* that life is more than what we can explain.

And because that dream-world is so vivid, the physical world can feel... heavy. Loud. Conflicted. Demanding. You may have felt pulled toward nature early on because nature held something your nervous system could trust. Nature didn't argue. Nature didn't manipulate. Nature didn't require you to choose sides. Nature simply *was*. And in that "being," you could find your own anchor.

What's important to understand is that your dreaminess is not a flaw to correct. It is a gift to mature.

You are an incredible dreamer. You can see a transformed world that other people cannot yet see. You can imagine solutions, futures, harmonies, new possibilities. But the challenge of the 7 of Spades is that this vision can sometimes be used as a refuge—a way to keep life beautiful in the mind so you don't have to face the conflict you are trying to avoid. The 7 of Spades often wants to nurture the world into a higher vision so they can ignore what hurts, what is tense, what is broken, what needs confrontation. And this is where your chart begins to initiate you: you are not here to avoid the world. You are here to help it.

Card #2: Your Mars Card J♦

Your Mars card, the Jack of Diamonds, is one of the most quietly magnetic parts of this chart.

Because when you speak, people tend to believe you. There is a sincerity in your presence, a thoughtfulness, a dreamlike quality that makes others lean in. It can look, from the outside, like life is easier for you than it is. People may not see what you are avoiding, what you are managing internally, what you are trying to keep harmonious. They simply see the glow of your vision and the grace of your delivery.

This is influence.

Not forced influence. Not salesy influence. A natural influence that comes from your ability to articulate something that feels hopeful, meaningful, and true. And because it comes so naturally, you may not always recognize its power. You may underestimate the fact that your words change people's direction. You may think you're "just sharing," while someone across from you is having their life reoriented by what you said.

But Mars also asks for responsibility with your charisma. The invitation is not merely to be influential—it is to become conscious of *what* you are influencing. The Jack of Diamonds is playful, charming, persuasive. It can sell dreams. It can inspire visions. And your chart asks you to let your charm be anchored in learning, wisdom, and integrity—so your influence helps the world rather than simply enchanting it.

Card #3: Your Neptune Card 8♥

Your Neptune card, the 8 of Hearts, reveals the immensity of your love.

You have a big heart. A generous heart. A heart that can pour itself into a path, a person, a mission, a community. And when you love something, you can create momentum. You can feel, very early in life, the connection between devotion and results: *the more I love what I'm doing, the more life responds.*

This is one of your superpowers.

It's also one of your illusions.

Because there is a spell in the 8 of Hearts that can quietly form: *If I love something enough, it will love me back. If I pour my heart in, it will be rewarded. If I keep giving, it will become safe.* And sometimes that works—especially when your love is poured into the right path, the right mission, the right calling. But where people are involved, it can create confusion. You may give and give and give, only to realize someone was taking advantage. Or you may devote yourself to an experience and expect it to reward you, only to discover love cannot control outcomes.

This is where you learn one of the most important lessons of your chart: love is not a strategy for controlling reality. Love is a devotion to what is truly for you.

When you break free of that spell, your heart doesn't get smaller. It gets wiser. You learn about healthy attachments. You learn how to direct your devotion toward relationships and paths that can actually receive it. And you begin to love with clarity instead of longing.

Card #4: Your Pluto Card 6♣

Your Pluto card, the 6 of Clubs, is the place where your dreamy nature must become decisive.

Because your chart—your personality, your nervous system—wants harmony. It wants peace. It wants to keep things working. And you are so imaginative that you can see how almost anything *could* work. You can see a future where the relationship heals. You can see a future where the conflict resolves. You can see a future where the business turns around. You can see possibilities in every direction. And this is beautiful… until it becomes paralysis.

The 6 of Clubs asks you to look at the whole situation and make a practical decision. Not a reactive decision. A clear decision that serves your purpose.

And purpose here does not only mean your work as a healer, coach, or leader. It means the expression of your life. The expression of *you*. Because whenever a relationship, circumstance, or environment requires you to hold back your expression—whenever you are shrinking your purpose to maintain harmony—your chart is telling you something is begging for a new decision.

This is one of the most challenging aspects of being a 7 of Spades: you will often be the one who needs to end a situation. If you don't, you may wait until it is forced by circumstances, until the very end, until it collapses under its own weight. But Pluto wants you to become the catalyst. It wants you to embrace transformation as something you initiate, not something you endure.

When you learn to make decisions, your life begins to align with your vision. Your dreams stop staying in your head. They start becoming real.

Card #5: Your Cosmic Result Card 6♠

Your Cosmic Result is the 6 of Spades—the fulfillment of purpose through practical alignment.

This is where your higher vision is not merely imagined—it is lived. It is where your life becomes steady enough, structured enough, grounded enough, that your imagination can flow without turning into avoidance. The 6 of Spades is the ability to fulfill bigger dreams by being willing to make very practical decisions. It is the life where your dream-world and the physical world finally meet—and you no longer feel split between them.

When you live this chart, you stop trying to create harmony at all costs. You stop sacrificing truth for peace. You stop giving your heart away to prove devotion. Instead, you become someone who is both tender and grounded. Visionary and practical. Loving and discerning. And because you carry that integration, you become deeply helpful to others—especially those who feel lost in their own dreams, their own avoidance, their own confusion. You help them come home to the world without losing the beauty of their spirit.

Integration — Your Healer's Code in Motion

The integration of this chart begins when you stop treating your imagination like a place to hide and start treating it like a place to see.

Because you were never meant to "grow out of" your dreaminess. You were meant to mature it into vision.

You are not here to float above life, wishing it were different.

You are here to sense what is possible—and then bring your hands to the earth and build it.

This is why the world keeps calling you into the physical. It calls you into numbers, structure, tangible tasks, practical learning. Not to punish your sensitivity—thank goodness—but to ground it. Because when you are grounded, your imagination becomes a gift to everyone around you. It becomes creativity. It becomes strategy. It becomes a way of seeing that helps people move forward.

And this is where love becomes wise.

The 8 of Hearts teaches you that devotion creates momentum—but it does not control people. You learn to stop pouring your heart into what cannot receive it. You learn to stop loving as a way to make things safe. You learn to love what is truly for you, and to let your heart be guided by reality, not by longing.

And this is where decisiveness becomes liberation.

You begin to notice the places in your life where you are holding back your expression to maintain harmony. You begin to feel the subtle ache of shrinking. And instead of dreaming your way around it, you practice making a decision. A practical, clean decision. The kind of decision that serves your purpose and honors your life.

So how do you know if you are living your chart?

You can feel it in your relationship to conflict. When you are living your chart, you no longer avoid necessary tension. You don't seek drama, but you don't disappear from truth. You can stay present when something needs to be addressed. You can make a choice before life forces it.

You can feel it in your relationships. When you are living your chart, your heart is still enormous —but it is not confused. You give love where love can be received. You stop being mystified by who is taking advantage of your generosity because you learn to see attachment patterns clearly. Your devotion becomes a gift, not a vulnerability.

And you can feel it in your impact. When you are living your chart, you are no longer only a dreamer. You are a builder of dreams. Your charisma becomes conscious. Your vision becomes practical. Your decisions become the bridge between the world you imagine and the world you actually live in.

That is when the 7 of Spades becomes what they always were: a visionary here to help the world evolve—grounded enough to stay, brave enough to choose, and loving enough to lead.

Affirmation of Alignment

I ground my vision in practical truth, and I choose what honors my purpose.

My love is wise, and my decisions bring my dreams to life.

8♠ — Life Chart

Matt & Joy Kahn

K♠	8♦	10♣

A♠	3♦	5♣	10♠	Q♣	A♣	3♥	☿
2♥	9♠	9♣	J♥	5♠	7♦	7♥	♀
8♣	J♠	2♦	4♣	6♥	K♦	K♥	♂
A♦ VENUS	A♥ MERCURY	HEALER'S CODE 8♠ BIRTHCARD	10♦ MOON	10♥	4♠	6♦	♃
HEALER'S CODE 5♦ COSMIC RESULT	HEALER'S CODE 7♣ PLUTO	HEALER'S CODE 9♥ NEPTUNE	3♠ URANUS	3♣ SATURN	5♥ JUPITER	HEALER'S CODE Q♦ MARS	♄
J♦	K♣	2♣	7♠	9♦	J♣ TRANS-FORMED SELF	Q♠ COSMIC LESSON	♅
Q♥	6♠	6♣	8♥	2♠	4♦	4♥	♆
♆	♅	♄	♃	♂	♀	☿	

Card #1: Your Birth Card 8♠

If you are an 8 of Spades, you have likely lived much of your life balancing two forces inside you: what you feel you have to do, and what you genuinely want to do. You can feel obligation in the air—expectations from others, roles you've been given, pressures that seem to quietly follow you. And at the same time, there is a sincere inner drive to build a life that is yours, a life that reflects what you actually care about, not just what others assume you should carry.

There is also a peculiar kind of blessing that follows this card. Things can "work out" for you in ways that surprise people. Doors open. Support appears. Luck shows up at just the right moment. And yet, that same blessing can create its own burden—because when life seems to take care of you, people can unconsciously decide you are the one who can take care of *everyone*. They want something from you. They want you to help. They want you to hold. They want you to be the steady one. So your gift becomes a magnet, and your kindness becomes a responsibility you never formally agreed to.

You are also one of the hardest working cards when you are aligned. Not because you are trying to prove yourself, but because you have seen how success works. You've watched it happen again and again: when you keep taking action in the physical world, things change. When you keep showing up, momentum builds. When you commit to a direction, it tends to lead somewhere good. So you are willing to do the work. You are willing to self-reflect. You are willing to evolve. And that combination—action plus reflection—makes you powerful.

But what you truly crave is not just money, even though money often follows you. What you crave is fulfillment. You want to feel valued. You want to feel like your effort matters. You want to be part of something meaningful, something that actually helps people. You are deeply loving. Deeply kind. And because that love is real, you can sometimes forget that not everyone is doing the inner work the way you are. You can forget that your level of responsibility, integrity, and self-awareness is not universal. And that's where relationships become confusing.

You may recognize the pattern: unrequited love. Sudden endings. The feeling that you are not fully loved the way you want to be loved. Or the quieter, more private truth—*I don't love as deeply as I want to.* You can't quite find "the one." You find reasons to leave. And underneath it all is a yearning for something that feels ultimate, mature, mutual, true.

Card #2: Your Mars Card Q♦

Your Mars card, the Queen of Diamonds, is a key to your entire chart because it teaches you the true art of receiving.

The Queen of Diamonds says: let yourself be cared for. Let yourself be supported. Let yourself be held by life. And then—very important—don't be afraid to invest what you receive back into the world.

Because this is where the 8 of Spades often gets stuck. Money comes in, opportunities come in, support appears… and then you freeze. You want to "do the right thing." You want to be responsible. You don't want to waste what you've been given. So instead of allowing abundance to flow, you hold it tightly. Not out of greed—out of fear. Out of pressure. Out of the belief that if you let go, you might lose it, and then you'll have nothing to give.

But the Queen of Diamonds is a different lesson entirely. It is mature equity. Balanced give and receive. It asks you to enjoy what you are building so deeply that you stop trying to buy love with what you provide. It asks you to stop caring for and nurturing everyone physically as a way to prove devotion. It reminds you: you can be in relationships—romantic, professional, familial —where everyone shows up and does their work. You are not the only one responsible for carrying the load.

When Mars is aligned here, your actions become clean. You know when to give and when to hold. You know when to invest and when to rest. You stop leaking resources into people and situations that are not reciprocating. And you begin to embody a kind of prosperity that feels emotionally safe.

Card #3: Your Neptune Card 9♥

Your Neptune card, the 9 of Hearts, is the dream of the ultimate relationship.

This is the part of you that knows fulfillment in love is possible. Not fantasy love. Not performative love. But real, mature, mutual love that feels like home. And because Neptune is vision, this card lives as a yearning—sometimes an ache—that says, *it exists… and I won't settle until I find it.*

But Neptune also teaches through endings.

The 9 of Hearts in Neptune often requires emotional development through experience—through relationships that didn't match, through connections that taught you something, through endings that broke your heart open just enough to refine your discernment. You are not being punished. You are being shaped. Each time something ends, it is not just loss—it is education. It is your heart learning what it truly wants, and what it cannot compromise without diminishing itself.

Here is the tricky part: because you are so self-reflective, you can take responsibility for everything. If someone doesn't love you well, you may immediately turn inward and say, "No problem. I'll love myself. I'll do the work. I'll grow. I'll heal." And there is beauty in that. But over time, the inequity begins to register. You begin to feel that you are making accommodations that are not mutual. You begin to realize you have been using self-development as a way to tolerate dynamics that are not actually aligned.

Neptune is calling you into discernment not only about yourself, but about others. It asks you to notice: who is actually growing with you? Who is actually meeting you? Who shares your values, your goals, your level of emotional maturity? Because ultimate love is not found by doing all the work alone. It's found by choosing someone who is doing their work too.

Card #4: Your Pluto Card 7♣

Your Pluto card, the 7 of Clubs, is where your chart becomes decisive.

This is the mental clarity that allows you to assess a situation and make a choice without collapsing into guilt. It is the part of you that learns: *not everything is about my growth.* Sometimes it is about fit. Sometimes it is about alignment. Sometimes it is about who you travel with.

The 7 of Clubs helps you stop trying to keep everyone around you. It helps you recognize that being loving does not mean being endlessly accommodating. It helps you see that you can release relationships, roles, and dynamics that are not aligned without turning that release into a story about your failure. It is not failure. It is discernment.

This is where you learn to ask new questions. Not only, "Do I love them?" or "Do they love me?" but: *Do we have similar values? Do we have similar goals? Do we have similar belief systems? Does this relationship support my life, or does it quietly pull me away from myself?*

When you lean into this Pluto energy, you stop drifting in unspoken expectations. You stop making decisions based on longing. You begin making decisions based on truth. And that shift unlocks everything.

Card #5: Your Cosmic Result Card 5♦

Your Cosmic Result, the 5 of Diamonds, is a natural transformation in your material world—prosperity that continues to expand as you become clearer about what you will and will not carry.

Wealth is not something you will necessarily build through strategy alone. Your work in the world is love, care, creation. It is helping people focus on what matters and guiding them toward wholeness. And when you accept that—when you relax into the fact that money is often a side effect of your alignment—life supports you.

This is when your relationship with money changes. You stop proving your worth financially. You stop feeling like you have to buy love. You stop feeling like you must care for everyone physically in order to be loved. And as that distortion releases, the material world begins to reorganize around you. Opportunities appear. Resources flow. Prosperity increases—not as something you chase, but as something that naturally follows the frequency of wholeness you bring into the world.

Integration — Your Healer's Code in Motion

The integration of this chart begins with a very specific realization: you are not here to earn love by over-giving.

Because the 8 of Spades is loving. And the 8 of Spades is willing. And the 8 of Spades is capable. Which means it can be very easy to become the one who carries everyone—emotionally, practically, financially—without even realizing you've taken on that role. You may call it devotion. You may call it kindness. You may call it being "the strong one." But underneath it, there is often a subtle fear: *If I stop giving, will I still be loved?*

The Queen of Diamonds comes in like a correction. It teaches you that receiving is not selfish—it is balance. It reminds you that equity is part of love. That mature relationships do not require you to over-function. That your life is allowed to be enjoyed, not just managed.

The 9 of Hearts then deepens the work. It says: yes, ultimate love is possible—but you do not find it by tolerating inequity. You find it by allowing endings to educate you. You find it by letting your heart mature through experience. You find it by choosing people who match your level of intention, growth, and devotion.

And the 7 of Clubs becomes the turning point: you learn to decide. You learn that you don't have to keep everyone. You don't have to accept everything. You get to choose who you journey with. You get to choose what alignment actually looks like for you.

So how do you know if you are living your chart?

You can feel it in your relationships first. When you are living your chart, love feels mutual. You are no longer the one doing all the emotional labor. You are no longer quietly tolerating being under-met while telling yourself you "shouldn't need anything." You let yourself want what you want. And you let yourself choose relationships where that wanting is honored.

You can feel it in your relationship with money. When you are living your chart, money feels like support, not pressure. You stop gripping. You stop hoarding out of fear. You stop using resources as a way to secure love or safety. You allow flow. You allow investment. You allow yourself to be cared for—and you notice the universe meets you there.

And you can feel it in your inner state. When you are living your chart, you are still self-reflective, still devoted to growth—but you are no longer taking responsibility for everyone's emotional maturity. You stop making other people's inability to meet you a personal project. You become discerning. You become decisive. And life becomes lighter.

That is the moment the 8 of Spades becomes what it was always meant to be: a loving, hardworking, self-aware builder of wholeness—supported by life, clear in love, and finally free to receive as deeply as they give.

Affirmation of Alignment

I receive with grace and give with discernment.

I choose relationships and pathways that honor mutual love and true alignment.

9♠ — Life Chart

Top row: K♠ | 8♦ | 10♣

A♠	3♦	5♣	10♠	Q♣	A♣	3♥	☿
2♥ (MERCURY)	9♠ HEALER'S CODE (BIRTHCARD)	9♣ (MOON)	J♥	5♠	7♦	7♥	♀
8♣ HEALER'S CODE (PLUTO)	J♠ HEALER'S CODE (NEPTUNE)	2♦ (URANUS)	4♣ (SATURN)	6♥ (JUPITER)	K♣ HEALER'S CODE (MARS)	K♥ (VENUS)	♂
A♦	A♥	8♣	10♦	10♥ TRANSFORMED SELF	4♠ COSMIC LESSON	6♦ HEALER'S CODE COSMIC RESULT	♃
5♦	7♣	9♥	3♠	3♣	5♥	Q♦	♄
J♦	K♣	2♣	7♠	9♦	J♣	Q♠	♅
Q♥	6♠	6♣	8♥	2♣	4♦	4♥	♆
♆	♅	♄	♃	♂	♀	☿	

Card #1: Your Birth Card 9♠

If you are a 9 of Spades, you tend to find yourself standing at the edge of extremes.

People come into your life when they are at their breaking point. When the burden is heavy. When the addiction is loud. When the despair is real. When the spiritual crisis feels like it might undo them. You attract those who are at the very peak of challenge—or the very brink of breakthrough. And over time, you begin to understand something most people don't: those two moments are often the same.

There is something in your presence that does not flinch at intensity. You can sit in rooms where others feel overwhelmed. You can stay grounded when someone is unraveling. You can witness deep pain without judging it, and without collapsing into it. This is not accidental. It is a frequency. It is a capacity. You were designed to hold depth.

But in the beginning of your journey, you may not know how to hold that depth without taking it on. When someone is suffering, you may feel that it is your responsibility to rescue them. When someone is at their lowest, you may believe you must give more of yourself in order to make sure they survive it. You can confuse your ability to hold space with an obligation to carry someone else's weight. And that is where this chart begins to test you.

You are not here to drown with the people you help.

You are here to remain steady while they learn how to swim.

Card #2: Your Mars Card K♦

Your Mars card, the King of Diamonds, is the anchor that protects you from martyrdom.

This placement is not random. It is essential. Because your calling pulls you toward the divine— to hold space for transformation at a profound level. And without structure, that pull could easily consume your physical life.

The King of Diamonds in Mars says: build a foundation. Create a structure. Establish financial clarity. Make sure you are materially supported for the depth of the container you hold. You are not meant to hold space for everyone for free. You are not meant to sacrifice your financial stability because someone else's pain feels urgent. No one's suffering is so large that it requires you to collapse your own livelihood.

This is one of the most crucial lessons for the 9 of Spades healer. Because your instinct is generous. Your instinct is divine. Your instinct is to say, "Of course I will be here." And the King of Diamonds asks you to say, "Yes—and here is the container. Here is the structure. Here is the exchange."

When you honor this, something shifts. Your leadership becomes sustainable. Your service becomes respected. Your prosperity becomes aligned with your purpose instead of feeling separate from it.

Card #3: Your Neptune Card J♠

Your Neptune card, the Jack of Spades, is where illusion can quietly form.

You feel deeply connected to the divine. You feel called to something higher than the physical world. You can experience states of surrender, contemplation, meditation, and spiritual awareness that feel so expansive you would gladly trade material concerns for them. There is a part of you that would rather dissolve into the divine than deal with money, logistics, or worldly matters.

And this is beautiful—but it is also dangerous if misunderstood.

The Jack of Spades can blur boundaries between you and the divine. When someone is in deep despair and looks at you as though you are the light, it can be easy to feel like you must represent that light fully. To feel like you are the source. To feel like you must carry the divine presence for them. And that illusion can lead you to believe you are "above" money. Above practical needs. Above the exchange required to sustain your work.

But here is the grounding truth: you are not the source. You are a conduit. You receive strength just as your clients do. You receive guidance just as those you help do. You are not meant to be the divine embodiment for everyone else while neglecting your own humanity.

When Neptune becomes clear instead of confused, your spirituality becomes embodied. You allow yourself to be human. You allow yourself to receive. You allow your service to be sacred without being self-sacrificing.

Card #4: Your Pluto Card 8♣

Your Pluto card, the 8 of Clubs, is where grounding becomes transformation.

This card brings rationality. Mental clarity. Practical thought. It invites you to step back from spiritual overwhelm and ask, "What is realistic here? What is sustainable? What do I actually need?"

The 8 of Clubs helps you integrate your spiritual wisdom with your human needs. It reminds you that the mind is not the enemy of the spirit. Your intellect can support your calling. Your rational awareness can protect your nervous system. Your practical boundaries can preserve your longevity.

This is where you learn to evaluate your energy honestly. To recognize when you are overextending. To set fees that reflect the depth of your work. To build containers that hold you just as strongly as you hold others.

When you lean into this Pluto energy, you stop floating in spiritual ideals and start standing firmly in embodied leadership. You allow your mind to support your heart. And your work becomes stronger because of it.

Card #5: Your Cosmic Result Card 6 ◆

Your Cosmic Result, the 6 of Diamonds, is harmonious prosperity.

It is the balance of giving and receiving. It is the ability to still be generous without destabilizing yourself. It is the experience of being financially supported while doing work that feels sacred.

This result does not come from abandoning your calling. It comes from honoring your needs within your calling. When you bring attention to your material world—when you treat it as part of your spiritual practice rather than a distraction from it—life responds with balance.

You are able to give.

You are able to receive.

You are able to offer accessible support when aligned.

And you are able to maintain prosperity without guilt.

This is not greed. It is equilibrium.

Integration— Your Healer's Code in Motion

The integration of the 9 of Spades begins with a quiet but powerful shift:

You stop confusing compassion with self-sacrifice.

Your ability to sit with depth is a gift. Your ability to hold space at someone's lowest point is rare. But your chart is not asking you to merge with the pain you witness. It is asking you to remain sovereign inside it.

The King of Diamonds reminds you to build structure. The Jack of Spades reminds you not to confuse yourself with the divine. The 8 of Clubs grounds your spiritual intensity into rational clarity. And the 6 of Diamonds promises that when you honor all three, your life will balance.

So how do you know if you are living your chart?

You can feel it in your nervous system. When you are living your chart, you are not depleted by the depth you hold. You may feel compassion. You may feel intensity. But you are not drowning in it. There is space between you and the suffering.

You can feel it in your finances. When you are living your chart, you are not ashamed to charge. You are not resentful for giving. You are not confused about exchange. You understand that your container has value—and you honor it.

And you can feel it in your spirituality. When you are living your chart, your connection to the divine feels clean. You are not trying to be the source. You are simply participating in it. You receive as much as you give. And your leadership feels steady rather than sacrificial.

That is when the 9 of Spades becomes what it was always meant to be: a sovereign space holder —present at the edge of transformation, grounded in structure, and supported in the material world as fully as you support others in theirs.

Affirmation of Alignment

I hold space without sacrificing myself.

I honor my spiritual calling and my material needs in equal measure.

10♠

Matt & Joy Kahn

Life Chart

							Planet
		K♠	8♦	10♣			
A♠ (HEALER'S CODE) MARS	3♦ VENUS	5♣ MERCURY	10♠ (HEALER'S CODE) BIRTHCARD	Q♣ MOON	A♣	3♥	☿
2♥ COSMIC LESSON	9♠ (HEALER'S CODE) COSMIC RESULT	9♣ (HEALER'S CODE) PLUTO	J♥ (HEALER'S CODE) NEPTUNE	5♠ URANUS	7♦ SATURN	7♥ JUPITER	♀
8♣	J♠	2♦	4♣	6♥	K♦	K♥ TRANS-FORMED SELF	♂
A♦	A♥	8♠	10♦	10♥	4♠	6♦	♃
5♦	7♣	9♥	3♠	3♣	5♥	Q♦	♄
J♦	K♣	2♣	7♠	9♦	J♣	Q♠	♅
Q♥	6♠	6♣	8♥	2♠	4♦	4♥	♆
♆	♅	♄	♃	♂	♀	☿	

Card #1: Your Birth Card 10♠

If you are a 10 of Spades, you can feel consequence moving through the world in real time.

Not in a paranoid way. Not in a superstitious way. In a deeply sensitive, almost immediate way—like you can sense that the moment you put something into motion, life responds. Cause and effect doesn't feel abstract to you. It feels personal. It feels fast. It feels like the universe is always giving you feedback, sometimes before you even finish forming the thought.

This is why the 10 of Spades often carries what Joy called a frequency of karmic responsibility. You tend to feel an intense need to be ethical, integral, aligned with your values, and true—not just because it's "the right thing," but because you know what happens when you aren't. Your system respects higher ideals. You can sense that integrity is not merely moral—it is practical. It is how you navigate reality with less friction.

But living this way comes with a cost if you don't understand it. Because when consequence feels immediate, control becomes tempting.

You may try to control your mind so you don't "attract" something negative. You may try to control relationships so nothing destabilizes. You may try to control outcomes so you can stay safe. And because you are intelligent and self-aware, you can become one of the most monitored charts of all—the one who is constantly evaluating themselves, adjusting, improving, correcting, trying to stay pure, trying to stay right, trying to stay ahead of karma.

This is where the 10 of Spades can overwork inside their mind. You may think constantly. Review constantly. Manage constantly. You can become an expert in awareness—an expert in insight—while feeling strangely disconnected from the lived world. It can start to feel easier to be aware than to be embodied. Easier to observe than to act. Easier to "know" than to build. And for a healer, coach, or leader, that can create a quiet ache: *I can see what needs to change… but why does it feel so hard to implement it?*

Card #2: Your Mars Card A♠

Your Mars card, the Ace of Spades, is one of the keys that explains why taking action can feel so complicated for you.

The Ace of Spades knows that everything ends. It knows that every beginning contains an ending. It understands transformation as the nature of life itself. And because the 10 of Spades experiences consequence and completion so quickly, there can be a strange inner logic that forms: *Why start something if it's going to end? Why build something if it will change the moment it's built? Why put my hands into the world if everything moves so fast?*

This can make you hesitant. Not lazy. Not unmotivated. Hesitant.

Because action, for you, comes with immediacy. When you start something, you can often see the entire arc. You can sense what it will require. You can feel what it will become. And you can also feel the moment it will dissolve or need to evolve. That awareness can make effort feel futile—especially if you are tired from monitoring everything already.

But Mars is also where your passion wants to move. And the Ace of Spades is not inviting you to avoid transformation. It is inviting you to *lead it*. To take the wisdom you carry and participate in the very cycle you understand so deeply. The benefit of your chart is not in staying above life, watching it. The benefit is in leaning in and guiding transformation—in yourself, in others, in groups, in communities.

You don't have to build everything with your hands. You are not necessarily meant to be the one implementing every detail. But you are meant to be the one setting direction, catalyzing change, and taking an active leadership role in shaping what is next.

Card #3: Your Neptune Card J♥

our Neptune card, the Jack of Hearts, is where the heart tries to awaken you into motion.

Because the 10 of Spades can live so much in the mind—monitoring, assessing, controlling—that the heart becomes the medicine that gets you moving again. The Jack of Hearts brings a desire to help. To support. To serve. To open your heart to people and let your intelligence become relational, not just conceptual.

But Neptune can also blur this energy. Because the Jack of Hearts in Neptune can create more confusion than clarity for the 10 of Spades. Your heart can suddenly surge, and you can go from contemplation to "Mach 100" service. You may feel a savior impulse rise: *I have to help. I have to fix this. I'm the only one who can do it at this level.* And then you're in motion, over-giving, over-managing, over-responsible—until you burn out, and your mind returns to control.

This is not because you don't love people. It's because your heart is trying to motivate you into embodiment, but without structure it can become rescuing.

The deeper invitation is to let the Jack of Hearts open your heart without turning you into the sole caretaker of everyone's transformation. You are not here to save everyone. You are here to teach, guide, hold space, and help people learn to do what you can do—so you are not the only one doing it.

Card #4: Your Pluto Card 9♣

Your Pluto card, the 9 of Clubs, is the crucible where you learn to end things.

To make decisions.

To disappoint people when necessary.

To stop collecting people out of responsibility.

The 9 of Clubs is not only the ability to see where change needs to happen—it is the willingness to ensure that it does. It is the part of you that can say goodbye. The part of you that can end an agreement. The part of you that can release someone from your world without turning it into a moral crisis.

This is one of the most difficult lessons for the 10 of Spades, because your value has often been built around your ability to help. Around your capacity to guide, to rescue, to hold space. And the 9 of Clubs says: sometimes the most loving thing you can do is let someone go so they can develop. So they can build their own skills. So they can take responsibility for themselves.

This is not abandonment. It is empowerment.

And for you, it is liberation.

Because every person you keep out of guilt becomes another relationship you try to manage, another system you try to control, another mental workload added to the already-busy mind of the 10 of Spades. When you learn to end what is complete, your mind quiets. Your energy returns. Your leadership becomes more authentic.

Card #5: Your Cosmic Result Card 9♠

Your Cosmic Result is the 9 of Spades—and this is where everything you've been carrying begins to soften.

The 9 of Spades is transformation that happens naturally because space has been made for it. It's the moment you stop micromanaging change. You stop trying to ensure outcomes. You stop controlling the process. And instead, you become the one who holds space while transformation unfolds through the universe, through timing, through the natural intelligence of life itself.

This is not passivity. This is trust.

This is the moment you realize that you do not have to facilitate everything. You do not have to fulfill everything. You do not have to handhold everyone.

You can guide. You can teach. You can lead.

And then you can allow the universe to do the rest.

When you arrive here, your life becomes less mentally exhausting. Your ethics remain intact. Your values remain clear. But the control pattern dissolves, because you finally see that integrity is not something you enforce—it is something you embody.

Integration –Your Healer's Code in Motion

The integration of this chart begins when you stop mistaking consciousness for control.

Your awareness is real. Your sensitivity to consequence is real. Your desire to be ethical and virtuous is real. But when awareness turns into constant self-monitoring, you don't become more aligned—you become more tense. And tension is not the same as integrity.

This is where the Ace of Spades becomes medicine. You begin to accept that life is transformation. That every beginning contains an ending. That nothing you build will remain static. And instead of using that truth as a reason to hesitate, you let it become your permission to participate. If it's going to change anyway, you might as well create. You might as well lead. You might as well put your wisdom into motion.

This is also where the Jack of Hearts matures. You stop swinging between disassociation and savior energy. You stop going from "I'll just observe" to "I have to do everything." You learn a middle path: heartfelt leadership with boundaries. Service without rescuing. Love without martyrdom.

And then Pluto completes you. The 9 of Clubs teaches you to end what is complete. To release what is not aligned. To let people go. To stop collecting obligations. And every time you do that, your mind becomes quieter. Your energy becomes clearer. Your leadership becomes cleaner.

So how do you know if you are living your chart?

You can feel it in your inner world. When you are living your chart, your mind is not constantly scanning for what might go wrong. You still care about integrity—but it feels like a steady inner compass, not a frantic monitoring system. You feel calmer inside yourself.

You can feel it in your relationships. When you are living your chart, your heart is open, but you are not rescuing. You are guiding from a higher perspective. You are empowering others rather than carrying them. And you are willing to release those who are not meant to be in your orbit.

And you can feel it in the way transformation happens. When you are living your chart, you are no longer trying to ensure change through control. You create space. You set direction. You lead where you are called. And then you let the universe complete the work through timing, through consequence, through natural unfolding.

That is the quiet gift of the 10 of Spades: to become an ethical catalyst who no longer overworks in the mind—because you've learned to trust life to do what life does best.

Affirmation of Alignment

I lead with integrity without trying to control the outcome.

I create space for transformation, and I trust life to complete what I begin.

J♤

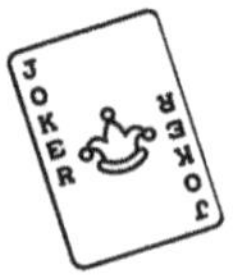

Matt & Joy Kahn

Life Chart

		K♤	8♢	10♧			
A♤	3♢	5♧	10♤	Q♧	A♧	3♡	☿
2♡	9♤	9♧	J♡	5♤	7♢	7♡	♀
8♧ MERCURY	HEALER'S CODE J♤ BIRTHCARD	2♢ MOON	4♧	6♡	K♢	K♡	♂
HEALER'S CODE A♢ PLUTO	HEALER'S CODE A♡ NEPTUNE	8♤ URANUS	10♢ SATURN	10♡ JUPITER	HEALER'S CODE 4♤ MARS	6♢ VENUS	♃
5♢	7♧	9♡	3♤	3♧ TRANS-FORMED SELF	5♡ COSMIC LESSON	HEALER'S CODE Q♢ COSMIC RESULT	♄
J♢	K♧	2♧	7♤	9♢	J♧	Q♤	♅
Q♡	6♤	6♧	8♡	2♤	4♢	4♡	♆
♆	♅	♄	♃	♂	♀	☿	

Card #1: Your Birth Card — J♠

If you are a Jack of Spades, you can feel two worlds tugging at you—almost like two different versions of you are trying to steer the same life.

One part of you wants the tangible things. You want stability. You want your needs met. You want to build a life that works in the physical world—money handled, responsibilities managed, a sense that your daily reality is solid enough to rest inside. You're not trying to be "above" the material world. You're trying to live in it without feeling constantly behind.

And then there is the other part of you—the part that cannot forget higher meaning. You feel purpose. You feel vision. You feel an almost magnetic pull toward wisdom that goes beyond surface reality. You want to understand what is actually happening underneath life: the forces of timing, the currents of transformation, the unseen intelligence that shapes why things unfold the way they do. You are wired for initiation.

This creates a very specific pattern early on. You want to understand deeper wisdom—but only enough to get the results you want. Not because you are lazy. Because you are practical. You may feel like there is too much to do, too many responsibilities, too much pressure to "get life together" to spend real time in devotion. So you try to shortcut the path. You try to learn just enough to change your outcomes without surrendering into the spaciousness true growth requires.

And when you live from that shortcut energy, life tends to feel harder. Your charisma can still draw people in, but you may feel like you're constantly managing outcomes. Like you're trying to control situations so things work. Like people don't want to pay you, or resources don't flow the way you expect. It can feel strangely frustrating: you have the magnetism, you have the ideas, you have the capacity—and yet the material world won't "lock in" the way you want it to until you stop trying to use it as proof that you're safe.

Card #2: Your Mars Card 4♠

Your Mars card, the 4 of Spades, is the moment your whole chart begins to make sense.

This is the part of you that learns how to create space. Not "time management" space. Not a spa-day kind of space. Sacred space—the kind of space where your nervous system can soften and your soul can actually hear itself. The 4 of Spades is the container that allows your transformation to happen without you forcing it.

This is why your breakthrough does not come through pushing harder. It comes through stepping back. It comes through creating spaciousness to connect to yourself. Spaciousness to connect to the Divine. Spaciousness to connect to life. And as you learn this for yourself, you naturally become someone who helps others learn it too—because you understand what happens when people are constantly in reaction, constantly in urgency, constantly in survival. You become a teacher of spaciousness.

The 4 of Spades also brings maturity to your charisma. It turns "drawing people in" into "holding people well." When you are aligned, you stop gathering people as a means to an end—recognition, money, validation, being loved—and you begin gathering people into something meaningful. Into an experience. Into a container. Into a space where transformation can actually occur.

Card #3: Your Neptune Card A♥

Your Neptune card, the Ace of Hearts, carries the longing for love in its purest form.

This is the part of you that loves beginnings. New love. New connection. New possibility. The Ace of Hearts brings sweetness, romance, excitement, the feeling that something is opening. And for you, this energy can be intoxicating. It can feel like proof that life is working again.

But Neptune is also illusion, and the illusion here is subtle: the belief that the beginning of love will sustain itself.

You may find yourself chasing that "first feeling" in relationships—wondering why it doesn't stay that way, why it fades, why real devotion feels heavier than the spark. You can become overly practical about fit, about how someone integrates into your life, about whether the relationship maintains a certain energetic payoff. And when it doesn't, you may move on—still longing for love, but not yet trained in the cultivation of it.

The Ace of Hearts in Neptune is not here to deny you love. It is here to initiate you into a deeper kind of love: the kind you build. The kind you nurture. The kind that becomes real only when you become real with yourself—when you anchor into your values, your ethics, your devotion. That's when the spark stops being something you chase and becomes something you cultivate.

Card #4: Your Pluto Card A♦

Your Pluto card, the Ace of Diamonds, brings the most grounding and liberating lesson of this chart: you must allow yourself to receive.

Not only love. Not only support. Money too.

Because when the Jack of Spades awakens spiritually, there can be a temptation to swing into an extreme: "I don't need money. I'll just serve. If I live my purpose, money will magically appear." And for you, that doesn't work—not consistently, not sustainably. Your chart asks for balance. Spirit and structure. Devotion and practicality.

The Ace of Diamonds says: be willing to bring in wealth. Take the material world seriously. Support yourself in your growth. And most importantly, learn to charge and learn to pay. If you want to carry deeper wisdom, you must be willing to invest in that wisdom—through mentorship, training, community, container. You must be willing to devote resources to your own initiation.

This Pluto placement matures your relationship to money. It stops money from being a frantic goal and turns it into a sacred energy of exchange. You begin to understand: when you value your growth, life values you back. When you honor the container, the container holds you.

Card #5: Your Cosmic Result Card Q ◆

Your Cosmic Result, the Queen of Diamonds, is the feeling of harmonious flow.

Money moving through your life in a way that feels like ease. Receiving without guilt. Giving without depletion. Charging without shame. Paying without fear. Love without urgency. Devotion without pressure.

This is not the Queen of Diamonds as "luxury for luxury's sake." This is the Queen of Diamonds as embodiment—the ability to live in the physical world with grace. To enjoy what you have built. To feel supported while you support. To let prosperity become a natural side effect of devotion to what matters most.

And because you are a Jack, you don't just experience this for yourself. You teach it. You model it. You become the kind of leader whose life demonstrates that spiritual depth and material harmony are not enemies—they are partners.

Integration – Your Healer's Code in Motion

The integration of this chart begins when you stop trying to rush your own initiation.

Because the part of you that feels pressed to "get life together" will always try to convince you that spaciousness is a luxury you can't afford. But in your design, spaciousness is not a luxury. It is the gateway.

The 4 of Spades asks you to step back often enough that you can actually hear yourself. It asks you to stop gathering people to meet your needs and start gathering people into a container that serves something higher. It asks you to create the kind of structure that can hold love, wisdom, and transformation without turning your life into constant management.

The Ace of Hearts asks you to mature love. To stop chasing the spark and start cultivating what is real. To let love be something you devote to, not something you sample. And the Ace of Diamonds asks you to stop treating money as either a savior or a distraction. Money becomes exchange. Support. Structure. A way you honor what matters.

So how do you know if you are living your chart?

You can feel it in your pace. When you are living your chart, you are not scrambling for results. You are creating space for development. You are less reactive. Less entitled. Less frantic. And life begins to feel more responsive because you are no longer trying to force it.

You can feel it in your relationships. When you are living your chart, you are not addicted to beginnings. You are learning devotion. You are choosing love that is worth cultivating. You are letting the sweetness of the Ace become a doorway into maturity rather than a reason to run when things deepen.

And you can feel it in your relationship to money. When you are living your chart, you are not afraid to charge and you are not afraid to pay. You honor the value of wisdom. You invest in your own growth. And you allow receiving to become part of your spiritual practice.

That is when the Queen of Diamonds arrives—not as something you chase, but as something you become aligned enough to hold.

Affirmation of Alignment

I create spaciousness for my initiation and honor devotion in both love and money.

I receive with ease, give with integrity, and allow harmony to flow through my life.

Q♠

JOKER

Matt & Joy Kahn

Life Chart

		K♠	8♦	10♣			
A♠	3♦	5♣	10♠	Q♣	A♣	3♥	☿
2♥	9♠	9♣	J♥	5♠	7♦	7♥	♀
8♣	J♠	2♦	4♣	6♥	K♦	K♥	♂
A♦	A♥	8♠	10♦	10♥	4♠	6♦	♃
5♦ MOON	7♣	9♥	3♠	3♣	5♥	Q♦	♄
J♦ URANUS	K♣ SATURN	2♣ HEALER'S CODE JUPITER	7♠ HEALER'S CODE MARS	9♦ VENUS	J♣ MERCURY	Q♠ HEALER'S CODE BIRTHCARD	♅
Q♥	6♠	6♣ TRANS-FORMED SELF	8♥ COSMIC LESSON	2♠ HEALER'S CODE COSMIC RESULT	4♦ HEALER'S CODE PLUTO	4♥ HEALER'S CODE NEPTUNE	♆
♇	♅	♄	♃	♂	♀	☿	

Card #1: Your Birth Card Q♠

If you are a Queen of Spades, you have a direct line to wisdom that often surprises even you. You can see what is happening underneath what is happening. You can sense the hidden pattern, the real motive, the deeper truth, the inevitable consequence. Sometimes you understand things you have no logical reason to understand. It simply arrives—clear, immediate, undeniable—like an inner knowing that doesn't require permission.

And yet, one of the most defining experiences of this card is how quickly you can doubt yourself. The very brilliance that moves through you can make you question your own sanity, your own credibility, your own right to speak. You may feel the impulse to prove what you know, justify what you know, explain it perfectly, gather feedback that confirms you are not making it up. You may quietly monitor how others respond, hoping to see recognition in their eyes that matches the depth of what you are seeing.

This can create a loop that is exhausting in its subtlety. Wisdom comes through. Doubt rises. You attempt to prove. You attempt to convince. You attempt to gather evidence. And because the world often cannot meet you at the level of your perception, you can end up feeling like you are living inside a private reality—rich, true, and vivid—yet constantly questioned by the part of you that wants external validation before you take action.

As a healer, coach, or leader, this can show up as a strange hesitation. You may be the one who sees what no one else sees, and yet be the last one to speak. Not because you lack courage, but because you're still trying to find the perfect way to say it. You're trying to make it land. You're trying to make it undeniable. You're trying to make sure nobody can dismiss you. And the irony is that the more you try to prove your knowing, the more you postpone the very work you were born to do: share it.

Card #2: Your Mars Card 7♠

Your Mars card, the 7 of Spades, intensifies this inner world. Your passion is internal. Your drive is internal. Your movement is internal. You don't burn with loud ambition—you burn with refinement. You want to understand what you know at a higher level. You want to see the truth from an even higher perspective. You want to keep clarifying until your knowing becomes something you can articulate with precision.

This is a gift, and it is also the test. Because the 7 of Spades can keep you in the laboratory forever—studying, refining, thinking, upgrading, questioning, deepening. It can make it feel like you should not share yet, because the insight could still be improved. The teaching could still be cleaner. The words could still be more accurate.

But the purpose of your Mars is not to make you "know more." The purpose is to initiate you into your teaching role. This card asks you to own the fact that the wisdom moving through you is not only for you. It is meant to become a pathway others can walk. You are not here to convince people that your knowing is real. You are here to share it in a way that invites exploration. When you shift from proving to offering, something in you relaxes. Your insight becomes usable. Your passion becomes productive.

And that shift—subtle as it is—is one of the most important thresholds in this entire chart.

Card #3: Your Neptune Card 4♥

Your Neptune card, the 4 of Hearts, pulls you toward community.

It would be easy for you to live inside your inner world and never truly need other people. Your inner life can be that rich. Your connection to what you sense can be that satisfying. Your capacity to process, transform, and alchemize within yourself can make external relationship feel optional.

And yet, the 4 of Hearts is a call you cannot ignore forever. It invites you into commitment. Into relationship. Into group. Into the emotional reality of being human with humans. It asks you to let your wisdom drop out of your mind and into your heart and body through real connection— through conversations, community, shared experiences, collaboration, and belonging.

There is also an illusion here that can feel spiritual: the belief that if you can think something and feel it internally, that is enough. That internal understanding equals fulfillment. But the truth of your chart is that community is not the finish line—it is the beginning. Your wisdom is meant to be lived with people, not held in isolation. You are meant to experience emotional commitment, not just spiritual insight.

When Neptune is aligned, you stop using your inner world as a refuge. You let it become a resource you bring into relationship.

Card #4: Your Pluto Card 4♦

Your Pluto card, the 4 of Diamonds, is where your chart becomes unmistakably practical.

This is the place you may resist the most—not because you are lazy, but because you are so capable of living in the realm of knowing that physical action can feel crude. Slow. Messy. Unrefined. It can feel like the physical world doesn't move fast enough to match your perception.

But Pluto asks you to build.

Not just think.

Not just sense.

Build.

The 4 of Diamonds says: take what you know and create something tangible with it. A structure. A business. A book. A practice. A method. A program. A container people can enter and experience. Because what you see is not meant to be a private experience. It is meant to shape the world.

This card asks you to get in the trenches. To get your hands dirty. To physically engage in life. To be outside. To be embodied. To take action in the physical world so your wisdom doesn't stay trapped in thought.

And yes—sometimes this means letting someone else stop being the one who "does the doing" for you. It can be tempting to want others to execute while you remain the visionary. But your chart is clear: you must participate. Your wisdom needs your hands. Your awareness needs your body. Your insight needs structure.

Card #5: Your Cosmic Result Card 2♠

Your Cosmic Result, the 2 of Spades, is the promise that there are people who can meet you.

There are partners who understand depth. There are collaborators who can hold complexity. There are relationships that do not require you to shrink your knowing or translate yourself into something simpler so you can be loved.

This is important, because when you are young—or when you are unintegrated—you can believe you are alone. You can believe that no one sees what you see. And while it may be true that most people cannot meet you at that level, your chart is not a sentence of isolation. It is an invitation to refinement. It is an invitation to build the life that attracts your people.

The 2 of Spades is also the gift of discernment in partnership. You learn who is aligned. You learn when to commit. You learn how to co-create. And you learn that being deeply wise does not mean being alone—it means being selective.

Integration – Your Healer's Code in Motion

The integration of this chart begins when you stop trying to make your wisdom believable and start making it *livable*.

Because the part of you that doubts is not actually doubting the truth. It's doubting whether you're allowed to trust yourself without consensus. It's the old pattern of needing the room to agree before you move. And that pattern will keep you stuck in your head, endlessly refining, endlessly proving, endlessly preparing—while your life waits for you to step into the world.

This is where Mars becomes medicine. The 7 of Spades does not ask you to perfect your truth— it asks you to own it as a teaching. You let it be shared. You let it be explored. You stop convincing and start offering. You accept that your wisdom will never be universally understood, and you release the need for it to be.

Then Neptune opens the heart. The 4 of Hearts asks you to commit to being with people. Not only as a teacher, but as a human. It asks you to let relationship become part of your curriculum. It asks you to let community turn your insight into embodiment. This is where your wisdom becomes warm. It becomes relatable. It becomes something people can feel, not just something they can admire.

And Pluto makes it real. The 4 of Diamonds asks you to build. To create something physical that carries your insight into the world. To let your hands meet your knowing. To step into the trenches of life so your wisdom doesn't stay theoretical.

So how do you know if you are living your chart?

You can feel it in your relationship to your own knowing. When you are living your chart, you trust what you see. You still refine, but you no longer delay your life waiting for certainty. You act from wisdom without needing everyone to approve it.

You can feel it in your relationship to people. When you are living your chart, you stop isolating inside your inner world. You create real connection. You commit to community. You share your ideas in ways that invite others in rather than keeping them at a distance.

And you can feel it in the physical world. When you are living your chart, something exists because you acted. Something is built. Something is structured. Something tangible is holding your wisdom. And through that structure, the right partners begin to appear—people who can meet you, co-create with you, and walk beside you without requiring you to shrink.

That is the Queen of Spades in alignment: not just someone who knows, but someone who builds, connects, and teaches—without needing proof that what they know is real.

Affirmation of Alignment

I trust my inner wisdom and bring it into the world through structure, community, and action.

I no longer prove what I know — I live it.

K♠

Matt & Joy Kahn

Life Chart

	HEALER'S CODE		
	K♠ BIRTHCARD	8♦ MOON	10♣

HEALER'S CODE				HEALER'S CODE			☿
A♠ NEPTUNE	3♦ URANUS	5♣ SATURN	10♣ JUPITER	Q♣ MARS	A♣ VENUS	3♡ MERCURY	
2♡	9♠	9♣	J♡ TRANS-FORMED SELF	5♠ COSMIC LESSON	7♦ COSMIC RESULT (HEALER'S CODE)	7♡ PLUTO (HEALER'S CODE)	♀
8♣	J♠	2♦	4♣	6♡	K♦	K♡	♂
A♦	A♡	8♠	10♦	10♡	4♠	6♦	♃
5♦	7♣	9♡	3♠	3♣	5♡	Q♦	♄
J♦	K♣	2♣	7♠	9♦	J♣	Q♠	⛢
Q♡	6♠	6♣	8♡	2♣	4♦	4♡	♆
♆	⛢	♄	♃	♂	♀	☿	

Card #1: Your Birth Card K♠

If you are a King of Spades, you are not here to think like everyone else.

Your mind doesn't simply collect information. It *sees*. It finds vantage points other people don't even consider. You can look at a situation and sense the hidden architecture beneath it—the pattern underneath the pattern, the direction underneath the chaos, the inevitable consequence that no one else is naming yet. And because you can see that far, you can feel like you're living slightly outside the room, slightly above the conversation, slightly ahead of the timeline everyone else is tracking.

This is part of why this card can become reclusive. Not always physically, but energetically. When your awareness is that active, it can feel easier to stay inside your mind than to participate in the messiness of human exchange. It can feel easier to observe than to engage. And when you're not careful, you can start to drift into a kind of isolation that looks like "independence," but actually feels like disconnection.

What makes this even more complex is that you aren't cold inside. You may look distant, but you often deeply want connection. You want celebration. You want to feel included. You want the joy of being with people in a way that's simple. But when your mind is on all the time, your presence can feel split. And when others sense that split, they may interpret you as unreachable. Which can trigger another layer: the ego's desire to be acknowledged. To be seen as wise. To be recognized for how much you perceive and how much you contribute.

So the King of Spades carries a very specific life lesson: you are not meant to hide your wisdom, and you are not meant to demand recognition for it. You are meant to become a thought leader in the spaces that truly matter to you—not the leader of the world, not the president, not the one at the top of some arbitrary ladder, but the one who knows exactly where your wisdom can make the greatest difference, and is willing to place yourself there.

Card #2: Your Mars Card Q♣

Your Mars card, the Queen of Clubs, is how your passion moves into the world.

This is the gift of learning quickly and translating what you learn even faster. You can take in new information, process it, and then articulate it in a way that makes people feel oriented. You can simplify vast ideas without watering them down. You can make the complex feel usable. And this is part of what makes you so valuable in leadership—people don't just need insight, they need insight they can actually apply.

In some lives, this looks like teaching. In others, speaking. In others, writing. In others, leading teams and shaping strategy. But the throughline is the same: you are meant to communicate.

And because it comes naturally, you may underestimate it. You may think, "Anyone could explain it like this." They can't. What's effortless for you is a rare intelligence: the ability to hold a high altitude view while still speaking in human language. When you embrace this Mars card, you stop waiting for the "perfect moment" to contribute and begin sharing what you see in real time. Your wisdom becomes useful because it becomes available.

Card #3: Your Neptune Card A♠

Your Neptune card, the Ace of Spades, is your relationship to transformation.

You are not afraid of endings the way many people are. You tend to accept change. You may even respect it. You understand that everything evolves, everything shifts, everything eventually ends. And over time, you can develop real wisdom about this—an ability to see the blessing in completion, the liberation in closure, the intelligence inside an ending.

But Neptune is where even wisdom can become an illusion.

Because when you know everything changes, it can start to feel like nothing is worth investing in. Why begin anything if it will end? Why pour your attention into a project if it will transform beyond recognition? Why commit your heart if life will eventually demand surrender? And if you're not careful, this subtle philosophy can feed the reclusive side of your card. It can make withdrawal feel rational. It can make detachment feel wise.

The deeper invitation here is not to deny impermanence. It is to let impermanence make the journey meaningful. When you stop fixating on the end, you begin living the richness of what is happening now. You begin building because building is part of being alive. You begin creating because creation is how your wisdom becomes embodied. You begin investing because the point isn't to avoid endings—the point is to let life be worth living in between them.

Card #4: Your Pluto Card 7♥

Your Pluto card, the 7 of Hearts, is the place your mind cannot solve.

This is the part of your chart that asks your heart to lead alongside your intellect. Not instead of it. Alongside it.

The 7 of Hearts is love in its refined form. It is discernment. It is emotional wisdom. It is the recognition that love is not a feeling you get swept into—it is something you embody through integrity, consistency, and truth.

And for someone whose mind is as powerful as yours, this is the crucible. Because the mind wants certainty. The mind wants proof. The mind wants to be right. The heart asks for something different: presence. Vulnerability. Devotion. The willingness to be moved by love even when it doesn't "make sense."

This Pluto placement invites you to stop leading from analysis alone. To let love inform your decisions. To let relationship matter. To allow the human experience to soften you rather than distract you. And this is not sentimental—it is strategic in the most sacred way. Because when your mind and heart become allies, your wisdom becomes not only brilliant, but trustworthy. People feel you. They don't just admire you.

Card #5: Your Cosmic Result Card 7 ◆

Your Cosmic Result, the 7 of Diamonds, is the wealth that becomes possible when the journey feels worth it.

Not just money as numbers. Wealth as richness. Wealth as blessing. Wealth as the willingness to receive the good that life offers instead of staying slightly apart from it.

This is important, because the King of Spades can absolutely become materially prosperous. In fact, you can be one of the wealthiest charts when you allow yourself to stay engaged with life instead of withdrawing from it. But the key is emotional engagement. The key is allowing love to make the journey meaningful. When love is present—when your heart is part of your leadership —prosperity stops feeling like a hollow achievement and becomes a natural extension of alignment.

The 7 of Diamonds also refines your relationship to value. You stop seeking acknowledgment for your wisdom and start allowing your wisdom to create value that speaks for itself. You become less concerned with who notices you and more devoted to what you're here to build. And that devotion has a way of being rewarded—not because you chase reward, but because you finally allow yourself to receive it.

Integration – Your Healer's Code in Motion

The integration of this chart begins when you stop using your awareness as a reason to stand apart from life.

Your ability to see endings is real. Your acceptance of change is real. But when that wisdom becomes a reason to disengage—when it becomes a reason to avoid investing, avoid committing, avoid beginning—your gift turns into isolation. You begin to lose the very joy you secretly want.

This is where the Queen of Clubs becomes medicine. You begin to share what you see. You let your mind become a bridge instead of a private universe. You allow your wisdom to be spoken in ways that help others orient. And as you do, your leadership becomes less abstract. More human. More present.

This is where the Ace of Spades becomes engaged. Instead of fixating on the end, you begin participating in the middle. You allow yourself to start things anyway. You build anyway. You commit anyway. Not because you deny impermanence, but because you accept that impermanence is what makes the journey sacred.

And this is where Pluto completes you. The 7 of Hearts invites you to let love lead with the mind. To allow emotional wisdom to shape your decisions. To stop treating the heart as a distraction and start treating it as a compass. Love doesn't make you less intelligent. It makes your intelligence trustworthy.

So how do you know if you are living your chart?

You can feel it in your relationship with people. When you are living your chart, you are less reclusive inside your mind. You still need solitude, but you are no longer hiding. You allow connection. You allow celebration. You let yourself be seen without demanding recognition.

You can feel it in your relationship to beginnings. When you are living your chart, you start things with less hesitation. You invest your attention without needing guarantees. You allow the journey to matter, even knowing it will evolve.

And you can feel it in your leadership. When you are living your chart, your wisdom is not just impressive—it is lived. Your heart is present in your decisions. Your communication is clear. And the value you create is undeniable because it is rooted in both truth and love.

That is when the King of Spades becomes what they were always meant to be: not a recluse guarding wisdom, but a wise leader whose life is rich enough to receive the very blessings their mind once kept at a distance.

Affirmation of Alignment

I let love guide my wisdom, and I invest in the journey without fear of the ending.

My leadership is clear, human, and richly supported.

JOKER

JOKER

Matt & Joy Kahn — *Life Chart*

	HEALER'S CODE **K♠** BIRTHCARD	**8♦** MOON	**10♣**

HEALER'S CODE **A♠** NEPTUNE	**3♦** URANUS	**5♣** SATURN	**10♠** JUPITER	HEALER'S CODE **Q♣** MARS	**A♣** VENUS	**3♥** MERCURY	☿
2♥	**9♠**	**9♣**	**J♥** TRANS-FORMED SELF	**5♠** COSMIC LESSON	HEALER'S CODE **7♦** COSMIC RESULT	HEALER'S CODE **7♥** PLUTO	♀
8♣	**J♠**	**2♦**	**4♣**	**6♥**	**K♦**	**K♥**	♂
A♦ MERCURY	HEALER'S CODE **A♥** BIRTHCARD	**8♠** MOON	**10♦**	**10♥**	**4♠**	**6♦**	♃
HEALER'S CODE **5♦** PLUTO	HEALER'S CODE **7♣** NEPTUNE	**9♥** URANUS	**3♠** SATURN	**3♣** JUPITER	HEALER'S CODE **5♥** MARS	**Q♦** VENUS	♄
J♦	**K♣**	**2♣**	**7♠**	**9♦** TRANS-FORMED SELF	**J♣** COSMIC LESSON	HEALER'S CODE **Q♠** COSMIC RESULT	♅
Q♥	**6♠**	**6♣**	**8♥**	**2♠**	**4♦**	**4♥**	♆
♆	♅	♄	♃	♂	♀	☿	

Your Birth Card: The Joker

To be born as the Joker means you enter this lifetime without a narrow lane.

Most Birth Cards carry a clear developmental arc. There is a recognizable tone to their personality, a consistent rhythm to their growth, and predictable themes that shape their path early. The Joker enters differently. Instead of a single dominant current, you arrive with range.

From an early age, you may have noticed that you could move in multiple directions with equal competence. You could lead or support. You could build systems or disrupt them. You could nurture people or challenge them. You could reinvent yourself entirely and still feel authentic.

This range is not confusion. It is capacity.

But without conscious direction, capacity can feel destabilizing.

You may have struggled when asked to define yourself. You may have shifted roles, identities, or environments more than once. You may have felt frustrated by expectations to "pick one thing" while sensing that narrowing prematurely would cut off parts of you that are real and viable.

The Joker carries the frequency of Zero — not as emptiness, but as unassigned potential. Your design does not force a fixed identity. It requires conscious choice.

That distinction matters.

If you do not choose intentionally, life will choose through circumstance. You may drift between opportunities, pivot just as momentum builds, or resist structure because it feels limiting. Beneath that pattern is often a subtle concern: If I commit to one path, I lose access to the others.

In reality, the opposite is true.

When you choose, your influence stabilizes. When you commit, your impact compounds. When you align intentionally — even for a defined season — your power becomes directional rather than scattered.

The Joker's strength is not endless openness. It is sovereign selection.

Developmental Currents of the Joker

Over time, most Jokers experience distinct phases of expression. These are not random shifts. They are developmental refinements.

There are seasons when you will lead primarily through connection.

In this expression, you initiate emotional honesty. You create space for conversations others avoid. You soften rigid systems without collapsing their structure. As a healer or coach, this may show up as relational depth and intuitive attunement. As a leader, it may show up as the ability to humanize complex environments.

The refinement here is boundary maturity. Compassion must become sustainable. Influence must replace rescuing. You are not here to carry others emotionally; you are here to activate their capacity.

There are other seasons when you will lead through clarity and authority.

In this expression, you value truth over approval. You stabilize uncertainty. You introduce structure where there is drift. You make decisions that others hesitate to make. As a practitioner, this may look like direct intervention. As a leader, it may look like decisive reorganization.

The refinement here is integrity under pressure. You must tolerate being misunderstood. You must trust your discernment without hardening emotionally. Authority must be clean — not defensive.

Eventually, many Jokers mature into integration.

To support your highest potential and expression of your purpose, you can choose to follow the growth pattern of the King of Spades or the Ace of Hearts. (*You can read more about either of these charts in the previous sections.*)

This is where emotional intelligence and structural authority coexist. You no longer oscillate between over-giving and over-leading. You understand when to open space and when to direct movement. You can nurture without rescuing. You can lead without isolating.

This integrated phase requires development across emotional, mental, and spiritual domains. It asks for internal stability so that your range becomes an asset rather than a liability.

Integration — Your Healer's Code in Motion

When we step back and look at the Joker's chart as a whole, one pattern becomes clear:

You were not designed for limitation.

You were designed for intentional authorship.

Your growth edge is not talent. It is commitment.

In distortion, the Joker can appear scattered. Projects remain unfinished. Roles shift frequently. Identity feels fluid but not anchored. Flexibility becomes avoidance. Freedom becomes diffusion.

Over time, this creates exhaustion — not because you lack ability, but because energy without direction disperses.

In alignment, something stabilizes.

You begin choosing your lane consciously. You understand that selecting a focus does not erase your range — it strengthens it. You allow structure to support you instead of interpreting it as confinement. You recognize that discipline is not the opposite of freedom; it is the container that makes freedom productive.

For healers, coaches, and conscious leaders, this becomes your medicine.

You are uniquely equipped to guide reinvention because you have lived it. You can support clients who feel undefined or in transition because you understand how identity evolves through choice. You model that sovereignty is not rebellion — it is responsibility.

Your leadership becomes catalytic when you stop sampling life and start shaping it.

So How Do You Know If You Are Living Your Chart?

Notice whether you are drifting or directing.

Notice whether your flexibility feels empowered or scattered.

Notice whether you resist commitment because it feels restrictive — or whether you understand that alignment concentrates your influence.

Notice whether you are over-identifying with being "limitless" while avoiding the discipline that would focus your capacity.

Notice whether your current path energizes you — or whether you are spread thin across too many roles.

The Joker matures when possibility becomes purpose.

You are not here to remain undefined.

You are here to consciously decide what the world receives from you — and to deliver it fully.

Affirmation of Alignment

I choose my path with clarity and follow through with strength.

My range is an asset, and my commitment gives it impact.

ABOUT JOY AND MATT

Joy and Matt Kahn are transformational teachers, authors, and speakers devoted to helping people awaken to their purpose and highest potential. Through their books, courses, and global programs, they guide individuals to develop intuition, emotional resilience, and aligned leadership. Their work is anchored in the belief that each person is here for a reason — and their invitation to *Become the Healer You Were Born to Be* reflects their commitment to empowering healers, coaches, and conscious leaders to understand their unique gifts and make meaningful contributions to the world. Together, they are devoted to fostering a movement of purpose-driven living rooted in compassion, clarity, and service.

You can follow their work through the following channels:

- Website: MattandJoy.org
- YouTube: @joyandmattkahn
- Facebook: https://www.facebook.com/mattandjoykahn

YOUR NEXT STEP INTO THE HEALER'S CODE

If you're reading this book it's because you know you're here to heal, lead, or guide at a deeper level.

Reading The Healer's Code cracks the shell.

The Healer's Code Incubator is where you step into the fire and let it change you.

What the Incubator Is

A 4-week live immersion for coaches, healers, and leaders who are ready to:

- Clear the core pattern that keeps you doubting, hiding, or undercharging for your gifts
- Expand your nervous system capacity to be more seen, better paid, and deeply resourced
- Shape or refine an offer that carries your real medicine into the world, not your mask
- Format: Weekly live sessions, guided practices, and integration support between calls
- Designed for: Serious readers of this book who are done circling the same patterns alone

If You're Feeling the Pull, Here's What to Do

- Go to www.mattandjoy.org/incubator
- Join the next Healer's Code Incubator cohort
- Check your email for your welcome, dates, and preparation steps

You can also scan the QR code below to go directly to the Incubator page.

Scan me

We keep each cohort intentionally intimate.

If your body knows this work is for you, trust that knowing and take your place in the circle.